# Building Cloud Value

## A Best Practice Guide, 2016

Mary Allen, Michael O'Neil, and contributing members of the
Toronto Cloud Business Coalition (TCBC)

# Dedications

Dedicated to the memory of William J. O'Neil, 1930-2015

My father was a gentle soul, intensely interested in understanding and celebrating the achievements of everyone around him, especially family members. He was the king of small kindnesses, and the sum of a lifetime of warm words and deeds defined his limitless generosity of spirit.

He wouldn't have understood much of what's in this book, but he would have been proud of me and Mary for writing it. I can only aspire to being as good a man and father for our kids as he was for me.

-Michael O'Neil

This book is also dedicated to Michael O'Neil, who is father to another child – the Toronto Cloud Business Coalition.

Michael demonstrates a unique ability to infect others around him with the same enthusiasm he can muster for new projects, and the creativity needed to translate good ideas into productive enterprise. These qualities, combined with a wealth of experience reflecting, analyzing and communicating on change in the technology industry, have helped him to engage in ongoing invention, including the TCBC.

*Building Cloud Value* is the product of input contributed by multiple experts from across the Canadian cloud landscape, and we are grateful for their part in helping us prove out the advantages of crowdsourcing collective wisdom. As Michael has said many times in building support for this initiative, "All of us are smarter than any one of us on our own."

-Mary Allen

# Contents

*Chapter 1.*

# Cloud Business Models, Metrics and Imperatives

Essential guidance on how best to engage non-IT senior executives in scoping, planning and delivering cloud initiatives

*Contributing community experts: AJ Byers (JEDTech Group), Sylvia Bauer (CenturyLink), Tracey Hutchison (Cisco), Brandon Kolybaba (Cloud A), Matt Ambrose (PwC), Brian Ochab (Unity Connected Solutions)*

*Initial publication date: November 2015*

# Cloud Business Models, Metrics and Imperatives

## Definition and context

Two of the most important trends around cloud (and technology in general) are the increasing strategic importance of technology, and the increasing importance of business (rather than IT) leaders in determining technology strategy. These trends are tightly coupled: today's business executives are intimately aware of the role that technology plays in all manner of corporate and personal activities, and they have a much better understanding of what technology might be able to deliver than did previous generations of non-IT specialists.

Broad awareness of the potential of technology has changed the dynamic in IT-related communications targeted at the non-IT executive. This is no longer an exercise in basic education: with a powerful grasp of business objectives and a reasonable understanding of technology, the C-level executive may be better positioned to understand the strategic potential of technology than the CIO responsible for IT management. But there is still need to provide business-relevant technology insight to executives. Most business leaders understand technology as a potential means of responding to points of pressure within their operations. Most do not fully grasp the opportunity for using connected systems to build new capabilities and competitive advantage.

The process of addressing this issue starts with defining a desired outcome: bridging operational siloes between different business activities and between IT and business activities through the establishment of cloud business models, metrics and imperatives that align cloud-based IT options with strategic objectives. This can be depicted (as it is in Figure 1-1) in terms of the tension arising from business issues and the options enabled by cloud.

One issue that is difficult to reflect in a graphic like Figure 1-1 is the tension between pressure for rapid outcomes vs. the need for sound execution of new initiatives. Any of the issues shown on the periphery of Figure 1-1 might demand rapid turnaround to meet a specific corporate objective. However, cloud-powered acceleration of new system introductions can create problems in turn: it is important for cloud-based systems to support business outcomes as consistently and securely as on-premises systems do. There is inherent in this additional tension a need for the business to transition to new methods of deploying systems. With cloud-based solutions, the business has less execution control, and a much wider span of requirement for management of business process issues, including integration and security. This argues for development/acquisition of skills that differ (at least somewhat) from those that the enterprise previously needed from its IT department.

*Figure 1-1. The role of cloud business models, metrics and imperatives in addressing executive-level business concerns*

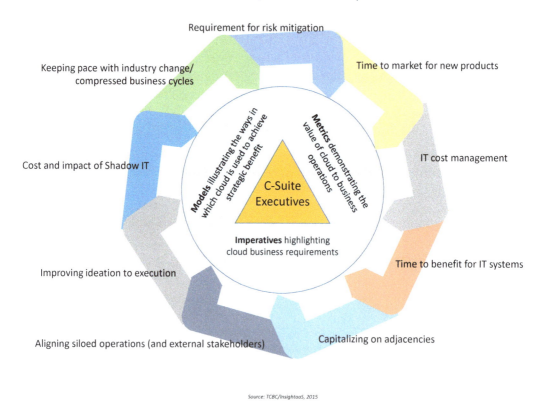

Addressing sources of business pressure with cloud business models, metrics and imperatives

Source: TCBC/InsightaaS, 2015

Figure 1-1 illustrates the role that cloud business models, metrics and imperatives should play in helping senior executives to understand and capitalize on the potential of cloud. In this context, cloud is not simply – or even primarily – a technology option. It represents a means of enacting measurable operating models that respond to key management imperatives.

## Reference sources

Additional references that readers can use to better understand the key issues defining advanced cloud applications and adoption and enablement issues include:

- Julie Bort. The feud between Oracle and Oregon over Obamacare has gotten even uglier. Business Insider, February 2015. This article provides a powerful example of how quickly and explosively issues with cloud-based systems can escalate beyond IT and into the press (and the courts).
- Michael O'Neil. The Death of Core Competency: A management guide to cloud computing and the zero-friction future. InsightaaS Press, 2014. This management text sketches out the perils of a business-as-usual management strategy in the cloud era, and positions cloud as a means of enabling "omnicompetency."
- Martin Reeves, Ming Zeng and Amin Venjara. The Self-Tuning Enterprise. HBR, June 2015. The article discusses the importance of moving from top-down to enterprise-wide decision making, and sets out five keys for reinventing the enterprise.

## Business objectives and benefits

The phrases aligned around the perimeter of Figure 1-1 illustrate a number of the challenges faced by business executives. Drilling down into each provides an indication of why an effective strategic response is critical for business success; adding perspectives on cloud business models, metrics and imperatives that might usefully be applied within this strategy underscores the importance of positioning cloud as an essential management option.

- Risk mitigation is a phrase that has several different cloud-related implications. The negative side is clear: expanding the data perimeter to include remote storage and processing can strain traditional approaches to security and audit/compliance monitoring. There is a positive aspect as well: embracing cloud enhances technological currency, reducing the risk that strategically important IT systems and infrastructure will become obsolete. There is a third aspect of risk mitigation, a notion of business risk that courses through several of the other categories, and which is captured in the phrase attributed to Klaus Schwab of the World Economic Forum: "In the new world, it is not the big fish which eats the small fish, it's the fast fish which eats the slow fish." Firms that fail to effectively adopt cloud are at clear risk of joining the "slow fish" category.

  o *Cloud connections:* Companies that are effective in mitigating operating risks around cloud will be better positioned to embrace cloud-based infrastructure and applications, reducing the risk of technological or market obsolescence.

- Time to market for new products. In many markets, the time required to develop new products exceeds their market life, and responses to competitive offerings are expected to be nearly instantaneous. Take the example of a product manufacturer who is unable to align orders and inventory in real time, or a services provider that is unable to respond to another firm's pricing action. In both cases, a lack of agility impedes competitiveness.

  o *Cloud connections:* Cloud's primary business function is as an agility platform. Cloud is inherently agile as an IT service delivery platform, and this in turn enables the deployment and scale-up of core business solutions and of analytics services that enhance understanding of IT and business issues.

- IT cost management. In many organizations, IT costs represent approximately 5% of revenue, and demand for IT services – new applications, storage and networking – increase constantly.

  o *Cloud connections:* Cloud is typically less expensive than conventional technology as a compute and storage resource. It is often much less expensive as a platform for business continuity/disaster recovery. And cloud-based applications can be anywhere from 33%-75% less expensive than server-based equivalents. Additionally, since cloud providers are paid on usage (rather than on an initial transaction), they have a clear incentive to drive the adoption and use of their products, thereby better aligning cost and utility.

- Time to benefit for IT systems. Often hidden in the depths of IT budgets and operations, time to benefit is a critical IT success factor. If IT is a strategic asset, its ability to pay back quickly has strategic benefit; only systems that are in production help the business to be more agile and competitive. Additionally, IT funds tied up in work-in-progress (WIP – systems that are not yet delivering benefit) act as a drain on resources needed to keep pace with market opportunities and competitors.

- o *Cloud connections:* Cloud provides an "always on" option for deploying new systems. To repeat an oft-cited example, it is generally thought that ordering, setting up and deploying a server can take six weeks or more. The same capability can be sourced through the cloud in a matter of minutes.
- Capitalizing on adjacencies. In traditional software systems, monolithic core applications are modified to address related tasks or market opportunities through the addition of new upgrades or modules. This is a costly and time-consuming approach. Agile businesses succeed by connecting processes in new ways, and by moving rapidly to exploit demand in new market segments.
  - o *Cloud connections:* A well-structured approach to cloud allows for tools and applications to be connected via APIs (application programming interfaces). Businesses that rely on the cloud can use cloud tools to expand process or market options. At the same time, innovation within the cloud itself produces new applications that can lead to opportunities not previously identified by business staff.
- Aligning siloed operations (and external shareholders). Most businesses operate in distinct 'silos', with limited numbers of well-defined interaction points connecting otherwise-discrete operations. Channels connecting the organization to its customers, prospects and suppliers are similarly narrow and rigid. In some cases, this design serves the needs of the business, but in others, it acts as a constraint to innovation. Aligning siloed operations into a unified organization, and involving customers, prospects and/or suppliers in richer dialogue where it is needed to unlock new opportunities, can provide significant competitive advantage to the business.
  - o *Cloud connections:* Cloud systems can morph quickly to connect different parts of the enterprise and/or to enable customer/prospect communications. Additionally (and importantly), collaboration is a core attribute of cloud applications, as is analytics. With these capabilities embedded, executives can identify and address disconnects in internal and external communications.
- Improving ideation to execution. Many organizations have a significant gap in their ability to develop new ideas and then move them into test and production.

In theory, use of IT infrastructure can accelerate this cycle, but business leaders generally rely on testing, experience, and iteration, and IT resources often become a choke point in this process.

- *Cloud connections:* It is common for traditional enterprise software projects take years to complete, which ensures that the user-driven specification will be obsolete before delivery, and rules out any form of iteration. Agile development methodologies compress the delivery cycle to weeks or even days, but these approaches rely on (or at least, benefit tremendously from) access to cloud resources. Cloud-based organizations gain the ability to try different approaches to a common problem, to test and change new ideas, and to collaborate with internal or external experts via the cloud.

- Cost and impact of Shadow IT. It is estimated that SMBs in the US will spend $25 billion on shadow IT in 2015. "Estimated" is an important qualifier, though – while shadow IT is acknowledged as a widespread phenomenon, it is difficult to measure with any precision. What *is* understood, though, is that shadow IT has several different costs to the business. It has a financial cost; it has a cost in the form of poorly managed and poorly secured systems that are generally outside of IT audit and control processes; and it has a productivity cost because it creates poorly-integrated data repositories that do not contribute to the enterprise's understanding of its own business.

  - *Cloud connections:* Cloud is often a *platform* for shadow IT, as business professionals can avoid delays attributable to IT by procuring access to applications and infrastructure via the cloud. However, a robust enterprise cloud strategy can help consolidate these activities by providing a managed, corporately sanctioned avenue for cloud use. This gives management more control over IT expenditures, and benefits the entire business by providing for higher levels of security, auditability and data access/integration.

- Keeping pace with industry change and compressed business cycles. Technology both enables progress within traditional industries and threatens their existence; both issues need to be on the radar of senior executives. Technology can enable traditional businesses to evolve with (or ahead of) direct competitors in their industries, particularly in situations where data itself can be packaged and analyzed to provide differentiation for core products or net-new revenue streams. At the same time, the phenomenon of "Uberfication," in which technology-based companies disrupt existing industries, is spreading to many sectors of the economy. It is thought that – despite having no actual properties – Airbnb will book more rooms in 2015 than any of the world's largest hotel chains; Alibaba, which is profiled in the HBR article referenced above, is one of the world's largest retailers, but owns no inventory.

> o *Cloud connections:* Cloud-based storage and analytics systems offer unique advantages in both data collection and presentation. Cloud's "fail fast" capabilities allow businesses to test new approaches with limited exposure: successful initiatives can be scaled up, unsuccessful ones can be wound down with little or no lingering cost exposure.

## Reference sources

Additional references that readers can use to better best practices in cloud business models, metrics and imperatives for non-IT executives include:

- Anurag Agrawal. SMB Shadow IT, BDM spending amount to nearly $100 billion in the US alone. Techaisle Research, 2014. This post provides a rare data-driven perspective on shadow IT.
- Gene Kim, Kevin Behr and George Spafford. The Phoenix Project. IT Revolution Press, 2013. This fictitious account of how technology saves a manufacturing firm focuses on the importance of DevOps – but the key turning point occurs when the team turns to cloud.
- General Stanley McChrystal. Team of Teams. Penguin Publishing Group, 2015. This book by the general responsible for the US Joint Special Operations Task Force in Iraq describes how McChrystal "remade the Task Force…into something new: a network that combined extremely transparent communication with decentralized decision-making authority." The book is now being praised for management insights that can be applied in many different fields.
- Stacey Schneider. How VMware Reduced Provisioning Time by 80% by Using vFabric Application Director and More. VMware, 2012. This blog includes a table with apples-to-apples comparisons of hybrid cloud vs. virtualized on-premise infrastructure for time to deployment, cost, and other issues.
- PGi halves the time-to-market for new products with cloud infrastructure solutions from CA Technologies. CA Technologies, 2011. It's generally thought

that cloud is a platform for agility and that savings are on the order of 50%; this document provides a case study to that effect.

## Best practices in delivering cloud business models, metrics and imperatives to executives

Figure 1-1 and the subsequent discussion of business objectives and benefits illustrate the key starting points for a cloud solution discussion with senior management. It's essential to anchor the management dialogue in the business considerations that are most compelling to the executive in the context of his/her business imperatives, and to describe outcomes in financial terms. The items circling the outside of the diagram describe issues pertaining to customer service, finances, time-to-market and business strategy. It's not necessary to start the cloud conversation by covering *all* of these issues; but the relevance of the cloud discussion to the senior executive starts with a realistic assessment of where and how the cloud solution ultimately delivers business advantage. In each case, the executive will understand the implications of action (or inaction) in revenue or cost terms, and they will want to understand the cost of a cloud solution in the same context.

This is a substantial challenge for buyers and sellers alike, as both are undergoing significant (and simultaneous) changes. Sellers need to match offerings to needs in ways that are more complicated than the "this type of software requires that hardware configuration" models that were used in the past. Meanwhile, the needs themselves are changing, as corporate technology itself fragments into two distinct camps: a core function subject to structured (and potentially, restrictive) professional oversight and the more business-driven approaches used outside the IT department, and which are often (but certainly not always) delivered via shadow IT.

### Models

Against this backdrop, rule #1 in developing models that can be used by C-level executives to grasp the rationale for cloud deployment is, "rely on <u>clear financial calculations</u> that are <u>responsive to executive objectives</u> and <u>supported by real-world examples</u>." All three of the underlined phrases are important.

- As a first consideration, the benefits need to be aligned with the executive objectives. Take the example of an application that expands sales performance by 30%. Some executives will see that as a means of increasing revenue by 30%, while others will interpret the same data as meaning that they can reduce their sales force by 30%. Which outcome is more important to the executive reviewing a proposed cloud initiative, and what evidence can be provided to support the claim that the solution will achieve this goal? Aligning the financial model with the executive objective is a complicated but necessary step in building a cloud model for a C-level audience. It is also the key to positioning the model: the starting point is the objective, not the technology or its rationale.

- o There are objectives that align very well with cloud. For example, a business focused on cost containment may well appreciate a CAPEX-based approach that emphasizes predictable expense, or a business that is focused on improving cycle times might appreciate the speed to market provided by cloud-based systems. There are two key issues implied here, though: that the executive objectives are clearly (and correctly) defined, and that cloud is well aligned with these objectives. If cloud is not a good fit with corporate priorities, there's little point in creating a model demonstrating its benefits for C-level executives. If cloud does address business concerns, it's important to demonstrate the ways in which embracing cloud will positive affect operations.

- Secondly, clear financial calculations are always important to building a model that C-level executives will accept. These models generally include both hard and soft costs and benefits; the hard costs and benefits generally form the basis for analysis, but soft cost issues should be highlighted within the model, too. On the hard dollar side of the ledger, it's important to capture and present all relevant costs for both current and potential solutions, as omitting relevant factors makes it appear that the recommendation is incomplete and faulty. Soft-dollar issues should, wherever possible, reflect the concerns shown in the Figure. For example, if a cloud-based solution decreases risk by providing for continuous operation in the event of an emergency but increases risk by demanding scarce skills, both issues should be described in business terms and then calibrated in terms of estimated cost/benefit value.

- o Productivity is always important in this context, but is very hard to quantify directly. Claims that a new system will allow a smaller number of workers to achieve a higher level of throughput – as with the sales example above – can be assessed in different ways. In general, it's best to use conservative assumptions, so that discussion focuses on the model and the solution rather than on the potential variance in the associated claims.

- Thirdly, the evidence used to support benefit estimates need to be fact-based and credible. If a SaaS application (like the one in the example above) is positioned as increasing performance in a specific function by 30%, or an IaaS resource is positioned as being 30% less expensive than conventional alternatives, detailed cost comparisons based on actual (and hopefully, referenceable) customer experiences should be provided to support the claim.
  - o In general, analyst reports from sources like Gartner Group or 451 Research are viewed as credible, as are articles sourced from IT or business magazines. Materials sourced to vendors are not viewed as credible in many situations.

## Metrics

As is the case with models, metrics begin with executive objectives. Where is the business focused? If it is on growth, then the metrics need to align with growth – so in the example above, they need to reference the ability to drive a 30% increase in revenue without new sales headcount. If the focus is on cost control or cash management, the metrics would focus on reducing headcount without having a negative impact on sales. In both cases, the metrics themselves could include issues like time to conversion or value per contract – measures aligned with the executive objective.

Beneath the business outcomes calculations, there is a second set of metrics concerning the cost of delivering the systems needed to support the business benefits. These calculations require the staff member(s) making the recommendation to delve into differences between CAPEX-based acquisition of technology as a product and OPEX-based acquisition of technology as a service. The difference between the two acquisition models can and should be quantified – e.g., traditional technology would require a CAPEX budget of $'x', staff resources of 'y' weeks, and a total time to benefit of 'z' months (plus an OPEX allowance for ongoing maintenance and licensing), while a cloud based solution requires up-front OPEX investment of $'x', staff resources of 'y', and time to benefit of 'z' (plus a monthly fee for operations). Executives need to understand how/whether cloud is a superior option to traditional infrastructure for a specific application, and why some solutions are only feasible in a cloud model. IT-expert staff add value to the business discussion by quantifying these differences and providing financial metrics that can be tracked to support future initiatives.

A concluding analysis section should tie the first two items together. What is the real benefit (ROI, time to benefit, IRR) associated with the solution, and how does this vary with a cloud-based vs. traditional infrastructure-based solution? This calculation pulls together the different components of cost and benefit in a way that is meaningful to executives.

Feedback from the working group on metrics includes the observation that relatively simple measures, such as ROI, cash payback and payback time are adequate in this context; "the biggest issue," one member stated, "is what you include in the math." As an example, he outlined a scenario in which a business was able to remove all of its servers. This would mean, of course, that there is no need for the staff that currently manages the servers. But does it follow that the staff cost is entirely gone? Or is this headcount simply transferred, both (in a positive light) to address issues that are in need of action, or (less positively) because managers are very reticent to give up existing headcount? Accounting for the impact of staffing changes, the group observed, is an issue with which cloud planners struggle.

Quantifying the impact of risk or downtime reduction is another tricky area from a metrics perspective. One approach that has worked in the past is to discount from a common benchmark. For example, a cloud plan might include something along the lines of, "Gartner says the financial impact of reduced downtime is $x; if, being conservative, we assume that in our context, it is only 10% of that figure, we're able to identify ($x/10) in benefit from an approach that substantially reduces or eliminates the threat of downtime."

A third issue raised by the group – one which can also be problematic for staff quantifying the benefits of a cloud solution for non-IT executives – is the fact that the most efficient platform for a solution may vary depending on utilization rate. For example, Cisco has found that it is less expensive to run an in-house server operating at over 40% utilization than it is to acquire equivalent capacity in the cloud. It's unusual for servers to operate at this level (studies have found that server utilization rates of 5%-10% are common), and there may be other reasons to use cloud-based rather than in-house resources. But it's important for executives to have the best possible understanding of the costs and benefits associated with all alternatives as input to strategic decisions.

## Imperatives

In contrast to measurements and metrics, imperatives provide a broader canvass for depicting the benefits of cloud solutions. Certainly, there are imperatives that align strongly with metrics and measurements: drive growth, control costs, manage cash flow, and improve profitability. But there are other imperatives that resonate with senior executives and that support the case for cloud solutions. Examples vary by the specific context of the discussion, but might include one or more of:

- *Brand and reputation.* Market perception is an important factor in corporate success, and an important reflection of executive effectiveness. Cloud can be positioned as a contributor to brand and reputation protection/enhancement in several ways: as a means of providing for operational continuity (and so, not disappointing customers and suppliers), as a means of delivering solutions that are consistent with market best practices (presenting the firm as being current with market trends/opportunities), as a means of providing up-to-date capabilities (giving employees – inside and outside of IT – the sense that they work for an agile employer).
- *Security.* The discussion around security – both the ways that cloud alters the definition of what needs to be protected, and how, and the ways in which cloud can contribute to an improved security stance – are part of the brand and reputation discussion, but security has taken on such an overwhelming importance that it needs to be dealt with discretely. Executives are (or should be) becoming more concerned about the safety of corporate data, and many firms lack both the technology and processes to demonstrate that they are being as conscientious as possible in protecting that data. By its nature, cloud expands the potential threat perimeter, but it also opens avenues to managed services and other options that can reduce risk. Cloud strategies need to include specific reference to security (and governance, risk and compliance) to ensure that all parties within an organization understand the security strategy, and can support it operationally and explain it to relevant stakeholders.
- *Productivity.* In many enterprises, increases in productivity are the most direct route to improvements in financial performance. All executives recognize the benefit of productivity gains, and most believe that IT is an important means of pursuing this outcome. It may be that including productivity in "the math" begs more questions than it answers, but specifying the ways that cloud-based

solutions yield productivity improvements is important to building a complete view of cloud's benefits, especially with respect to SaaS solutions.

- o One of the reasons why quantifying productivity improvements can be problematic is that they are often linked to business process change. For example, implementing a new mobility or sales automation system might improve sales department productivity, but only if the sales process itself can be altered to capitalize on the new system capabilities. The application needs to follow business process optimization; if it does not, it will probably have a more limited impact than might be expected. The key, working group members agree, is to re-engineer a business process and then deliver support for the improved process via the internet – to deliver "cloud enabled" solutions, rather than focusing strictly on the "cloud" as a standalone imperative.
- *Speed and agility.* Financial models that attempt to quantify the impact of a company's speed in reacting to changes in market requirements or opportunities are complex, and firm financial claims based upon them may be met with some skepticism. However, beyond specific calculations, executives understand that speed and agility are important to success. Being able to couple evidence that cloud improves agility with hard-dollar metrics and measurements enhances the overall business case for a C-level audience.
    - o The differences between CAPEX and OPEX-based acquisition of technology capabilities, and the associated, oft-cited notion of "fail fast," fits under this heading. While (as per Metrics, above), the difference between the two acquisition models should be quantified, there is additional agility benefit contained in the capacity to ramp up new systems more quickly, and to abandon systems that do not have substantial business impact without needing to write off capital investments.
    - o At a higher level, the tools needed by a business change as the business itself evolves. Cloud provides an excellent platform for the adoption and integration of new capabilities, but organizations need to establish a plan for accelerating change and improving agility within their operations to take best advantage of the platform and its features.
- *Human impact.* Describing the benefits associated with new cloud technology or the savings that can be gained through improved productivity helps support the

cloud business case, but it can leave some important human issues unanswered. If productivity increases (as in several of the examples above), making it possible to perform work at an acceptable level with fewer resources, what are the options associated with the now-unneeded people? Are they to be deployed to meet unmet needs elsewhere in the organization, or let go to free up cash or headcount in other areas? And on another tangent, what will the impact be of expecting staff to take on new, changed or expanded roles? Will this improve morale by exposing staff members to new opportunities, or will it strain the culture and create skills-based gaps necessitating staff training or replacement? In some cases, the human impact may be a primary driver (we need to reduce headcount or improve retention by providing a more interesting work environment), but even where it is not, there are human factors associated with new systems that should be considered by business management.

## Examples

Examples that can be cited when looking at the issue of positioning cloud for non-IT executives include:

- *Salesforce* is an example of a supplier whose connection with customers is heavily based on speed and agility: the product was positioned to a senior business executive (VP sales) as a means of obtaining business-relevant features that would have a positive impact on sales performance (a metrics/measurement issue) and obtaining these features faster than IT could deliver them (a speed and agility issue). As a supplier, Salesforce was very crisp in its messaging and approach. The company worked closely with its target customers, focused on two to three issues (like those around the outside of Figure 1-1) it could address, and delivered a clear value proposition.
- *GE* is a firm that is used as a model of a traditional manufacturer that has grasped the need to evolve into not only new businesses but new IT-enabled operating models. GE chair and CEO Jeff Immelt has been famously quoted as saying "If you went to bed last night as an industrial company, you're going to wake up today as a software and analytics company.[1]" This embrace of IT as a core component of business strategy is estimated (by GE, as reported in Fortune

---

[1] Thor Olavsrud. "GE Says Industrial Internet Is Here." CIO Magazine, 2014. Heather Clancy. "How GE generates $1 billion from data." Fortune, 2014.

Magazine) to be worth over $1 billion annually already, and to provide an important window on a $1 trillion market for the company's core products.

- *Netflix* is often viewed as one of the pioneers of cloud computing. The company leveraged Amazon Web Services infrastructure to revolutionize video, building a multi-billion dollar enterprise by delivering billions of hours of content to customers located around the world. Along the way, Netflix also decided to capitalize on another important IT trend: the company has open sourced many of the management tools it has developed, meaning that Netflix benefits from the input of developers who are outside of the company's IT department.

- *Uber* and *Airbnb* provide two more contemporary examples of how a cloud-based service can disrupt major industries. Uber has revolutionized the taxi industry: a five-year-old start-up, it is expected to hit total bookings of roughly $10 billion in 2015, and has a market valuation of over $40 billion.[2] Airbnb offers a parallel example: founded in 2008, Airbnb is expected to book over 60,000 room nights in 2015 (with a total booking value of more than $6 billion), making it a leader in the $500 billion global hotel market. Airbnb is currently valued at $20 billion. Uber and Airbnb demonstrate the type of innovation that cloud unleashes. One article noted that Uber has become "a massive hit...because technology has emerged that freed Uber from having to be an expert on absolutely everything in its app. Mapping services, location services, optimization services (to pick the closest driver), payment services and rating and feedback services are among the behind-the-scenes technologies that Uber has harnessed. The company didn't have to invent them – instead, it just accesses them through the cloud."[3] Airbnb (like Netflix, an Amazon case study account) is also beholden to cloud: because the company doesn't need to manage infrastructure, it can dedicate its entire engineering team to solving "problems unique to Airbnb."[4]

- *Amazon* itself provides an example of how cloud can expand business horizons. The world's largest online retailer, in June Amazon's market capitalization surpassed Wal-Mart's, making it (by value) the largest retailer of any type. But

---

[2] Alyson Shontell. "Uber is Generating A Staggering Amount Of Revenue." Business Insider, 2014.
[3] Kyle Alspach. "Why Uber – and whatever is coming next – is really about the rise of the APIs." Boston Globe, 2014
[4] Matt Weinberger. "How Airbnb Used Amazon Web Services to Conquer the Rental Market." CIO Magazine, June 2014

referring to Amazon strictly as a retailer is misleading. Amazon's AWS (Amazon Web Services) operation recently reported 1Q15 revenue of more than $1.5 billion, and margins of nearly 17%.

- *Technology companies* such as Microsoft are using the cloud to establish more direct relationships with customers. Past generations of Microsoft software, such as Office, have been sold by and delivered through intermediaries. With cloud-based systems like Office 365, Microsoft can establish direct links to customers, expanding the company's ability to renew and upsell. This approach may not be ideal for customers requiring the support services that intermediaries provide (and certainly isn't preferred by the intermediaries themselves!), but it does provide Microsoft with business options that it did not previously have available.

- *Traditional industries* are using cloud to expand their product lines and relevance. The automobile industry is an excellent example, using cloud-based services like mapping to enhance the features that they sell to customers. The automotive industry is looking to expand these "connected vehicle" services – for example, by providing feedback on relative driving efficiency and preventative maintenance alerts to drivers. The importance of cloud-based services will expand further with the introduction of autonomous (driverless) cars, which will capitalize on cloud-based systems for scheduling, payments, mapping and other core services. This pattern of using cloud-based interaction and data options to enhance current offerings and support the introduction of new products is likely to be replicated in many industries.

## A point of caution

Cloud service providers and IT department buyers are apt to describe cloud in technical terms. While this works at a technology level, it isn't helpful in constructing the models, metrics and imperatives needed by corporate (non-IT) executives. Executives and IT staff understand language in different ways: for example, when IT professionals use the word "agile," they are often referring to a software development methodology, while C-level executives use "agile" to describe an organization that is able to seize on new opportunities to increase revenue. Similarly, IT executives talk about "mapping business processes to IT systems," while business management views IT as an enabling layer; if they consider "mapping" at all (and with cloud, they should), business executives would start with the business process and look at how IT can be mapped against their requirements, rather than vice-versa. These are just examples drawn from a much broader discourse, but they illustrate how language can obscure communications between technology-oriented and business-oriented managers. There is a place and requirement for technical language and explanations, but that place isn't here, where we are looking at how to position cloud for the non-IT executive. Discussions involving non-IT business leaders need to stay consistent with business discourse and expectations.

*Figure 1-2. Positioning cloud solutions for C-level executives*

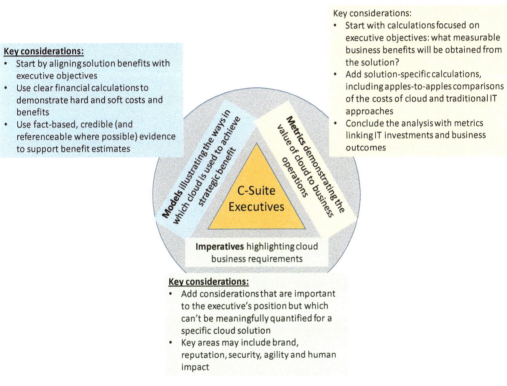

Key considerations:
- Start by aligning solution benefits with executive objectives
- Use clear financial calculations to demonstrate hard and soft costs and benefits
- Use fact-based, credible (and referenceable where possible) evidence to support benefit estimates

Key considerations:
- Start with calculations focused on executive objectives: what measurable business benefits will be obtained from the solution?
- Add solution-specific calculations, including apples-to-apples comparisons of the costs of cloud and traditional IT approaches
- Conclude the analysis with metrics linking IT investments and business outcomes

**Models** illustrating the ways in which cloud is used to achieve strategic benefit

**Metrics** demonstrating the value of cloud to business operations

**C-Suite Executives**

**Imperatives** highlighting cloud business requirements

Key considerations:
- Add considerations that are important to the executive's position but which can't be meaningfully quantified for a specific cloud solution
- Key areas may include brand, reputation, security, agility and human impact

*Source: TCBC/InsightaaS, 2016*

## Reference sources

Additional references that readers can use to better understand the best practices in cloud business models, metrics and imperatives for non-IT executives include:

- AWS Case Study: Netflix. This video discusses the importance of AWS technology to Netflix's business success.
- Denise Deveau. "The great communications divide." InsightaaS, 2015). This article discusses impacts and ways of addressing communications gaps between development teams and the business units they support.

## Metrics and milestones

Although cloud is a complex subject, the working group has found that straightforward financial metrics such as ROI or cash payback are sufficient to demonstrate the benefit of cloud investments to senior managers. A more complicated issue can be 'what is included in the math?' For example, an IaaS proposal might indicate that the activities of individual members of the IT team are no longer needed. Does this lead directly to cost savings associated with letting these individuals go? If the individuals are reassigned to other tasks, how is the value of the new activity reflected in the calculations – are the salaries fully assigned to a new activity, or is there a transition period in which the salaries and associated overhead expenses are still part of the IT infrastructure cost? Is the benefit of the new activity included as a benefit of the cloud initiative? There is no universal answer for these questions – but it is universally true that the assumptions need to be endorsed by the executives in order for the cost calculations to be accepted.

Risk elements can be similarly difficult to quantify. What is the actual cost of downtime in your environment, and what is the real impact of cloud in diminishing the threat of downtime? As is discussed under the "Brand and Reputation" header in the Best Practices section of this document, it is probably best to use this kind of element as an addition to, rather than core component of, the financial calculations used to support the cloud business case.

The working group identified several issues that should be considered when structuring quantitative and qualitative guidance for non-IT senior executives, including:

- *Understand payback periods and their importance:* A solution with a payback period of less than twelve months is easy to justify to a C-level executive. A project with payback of 12-24 months still often represents a very good initiative from a corporate perspective. There's no firm guidance for cloud initiatives with payback periods in excess of 24 months; the extent to which this is expected/acceptable varies by industry. Generally, SaaS suppliers can meet the 12 or 24-month time frames, while IaaS suppliers may struggle to provide clear payback within that period.

- *Understand industry norms for evaluation:* Variability by industry is a factor in the previous point, but needs to be called out as a specific issue. Different industries have different ways of assessing the desirability of an initiative. In some contexts, the magnitude of payback on a project (measured as a percentage of its cost) is a critical consideration, while in others, it's sufficient to meet a specific set of payback hurdle rates and timeframes. In OPEX-intensive services industries, OPEX-defined contracts are well aligned with management perspectives on cost and cash flow; in CAPEX-intensive industries (such as manufacturing), an OPEX-heavy approach may be at odds with prevailing management practice.
- *There's no magic ROI benchmark:* It would be convenient to specify an ROI clip point that would define initiatives that will obtain executive management support, but unfortunately, this isn't possible: as one working group member said, "every CFO is different, even within a single industry."
- *"The math" only really matters in context:* To build on a point made above, individuals used to dealing with senior non-IT executives have found that in a majority of cases, demonstrating an understanding of the business context and focusing on key areas is more important than the payback rates themselves.

## Reference sources

References that readers can use to better understand the measurements and metrics used by non-IT senior executives to assess cloud business models, metrics and imperatives for non-IT executives include:

- Dave Collings. "Cloud and the SMB manufacturer." InsightaaS, 2016. This piece, written by an experienced IT manager, highlights some of the difficulties involved in applying cloud in an SMB manufacturing context. The impediments would not apply evenly in another context (such as a services enterprise located in a city core), but the piece does a good job of illustrating the importance of cloud issues in different business context.

- David Linthicum. "3 secrets to creating a business case for cloud computing." Infoworld, 2012. This article highlights issues that are neither particularly "secret" nor especially unique. But they align with key topics from the working group sessions, and may be useful for positioning recommendations to "define the cost of what's not working" (from a business rather than IT perspective), to "move beyond the buzzwords to the heart of the business problems," and to "understand that the business case needs to be specific and tied to an overall plan."

- William M. Sinnett. Building the business case for cloud computing. FERF, 2012. This whitepaper was sponsored by a vendor of cloud-delivered financial software, and (unsurprisingly) focuses on the benefits of cloud-delivered financial software, but it is an interesting read regardless of this provenance. Using results from four interviews with CFOs (plus sponsor input, of course), the whitepaper provides relevant and digestible information on motivations for choosing a cloud solution, the tangible benefits of cloud, and how cloud can transform the finance function, plus brief profiles of the four firms interviewed for the report.

*Chapter 2.*

# Planning for the Cloud/Cloud Strategy: Enterprise

Essential guidance on how best to develop plans and strategies to guide cloud adoption and use within large enterprise environments

*Contributing community experts: Shawn Rosemarin (VMware), Roy Hart (Seneca College), Joe Belinsky (Moneris), Jeff Cohen (KFC and Pizza Hut Canada), Sangam Manikkayamiyer (Symantec), Stefano Tiranardi (Symantec), Chris Vernon (Symantec), Wil Stassen (Cushman & Wakefield), Matt Starkie (Microsoft)*

*Initial publication date: December 2015*

# Planning for the Cloud/Cloud Strategy: Enterprise

## Definition and context

There is a sense of urgency around cloud adoption that the TCBC Enterprise Cloud Planning working group believes can lead some to "shoot first, ask questions later." Growing awareness of the competitive advantage that cloud computing has delivered and the opportunities it can help generate has created impatience in many organizations – and within individual business units – to take advantage of cloud without due consideration for adoption criteria that address the needs of the business as a whole. A commonly held view associates cloud with 'agility' and 'rapid time to value' and a common expectation, fueled often by vendor positioning on cloud technologies, is that adoption similarly should be simple' and 'instant'. But cloud deployment is not limited to decisions around technology in isolation, rather it is the working group's contention that a key requirement for successful implementation is for the user organization to "get its house in order before leaping to cloud." This entails planning across multiple cloud-powered activities, whether these involve decision-making related to procurement of SaaS applications, or sourcing the infrastructure needed to deliver an application or service to internal and external customers. Optimal planning focuses on supporting the transitions that will be experienced by people, and in business processes and technology that accompany migration to cloud.

The TCBC Enterprise Cloud Planning working group believes that transformational change management is a foundational principle that frames proper planning for cloud adoption and use. This exercise has multiple components, but in the cloud context consists of four primary requirements:

- Managing the end-user experience, which is likely to change when a cloud based solution is deployed;
- Managing roles and responsibilities, which are likely to change when operations are moved to a cloud provider;
- Business workflow and process change needed to accommodate the addition or subtraction of application features that may accompany migration; and
- IT change and release management, including processes to enable the security of IT environments, and the business of IT (Who pays for what and how?).

Cloud spells transition for IT, but it can also entail loss of control over both the user experience and the technologies that support business and IT processes – dynamics that can and should be considered in cloud adoption planning.

At a technology level, it is also possible to apply a systematic approach to cloud planning which focuses on identifying what problem needs to solved at each logical layer. In the case of applications, cloud deployment aimed at providing a better way to deliver applications and services operates in the following ways:

- At the device layer, delivering application capability across any device;
- At the control plane layer, optimizing the operations and automation of application workloads and showing/charging back for them appropriately; and
- At the infrastructure abstraction layer, driving maximum utilization across all hardware assets whether service is delivered from within the data centre or via the public cloud.

As a broad approach to cloud strategy, this systematic line of attack has much merit, and is one that the working group would urge end user organizations to consider as a means to comprehensive cloud planning. The goal of the working group, however, is not to address planning considerations at each layer of the stack or in all change management scenarios, but rather to adapt this principle of problem solving in specific areas that have been identified as key issues hindering cloud adoption in the Canadian marketplace.

Aligned with the need to address change requirements in transition planning for people, processes and technology, the working group has identified the following issues as most important with respect to the development of best practices:

1. **Roles and Responsibilities**

   - How does cloud impact roles within the organizational structure and hierarchy and how are these roles evaluated?
   - How can existing IT organizations transition away from traditional infrastructure maintenance to new, higher-level service delivery functions such as enterprise architecture and cloud brokerage?

- What is the best way to encourage interaction and drive alignment between IT, Finance and the Line-of-Business to ensure cloud decisions are evaluated in the best interest of the company?
- What is the best way to develop a shared set of values and accountability between development and operations teams to drive greater collaboration and ownership across the application lifecycle?

2. **Skills Training and Upgrade**

- Cloud adoption and management demands many new skills sets. At a foundational level, enterprise architecture now spans beyond the walls of the data centre and therefore requires diverse experience and training to fill this "knowledge gap." Specifically, tomorrow's enterprise architects will need to well versed across on-premise and public cloud architectures in order to determine the best place for a given service to reside.
- The end-user experience will likely change with cloud adoption. How can the organization better predict the potential for staff members to need education and training on the new features, processes, interfaces associated with cloud migration? What is the best mechanism for delivering this essential skills upgrade to ensure minimal productivity hit at launch?

3. **Organizational Controls and Governance**

- Since cloud may entail some loss of control over data management, what must be in place to ensure sensitive data is protected? Is it possible to plan and contract for data governance within service provider cloud environments?
- Which existing processes and policies will translate to a cloud world and which will not? How can an organization optimize workflows and simplify approvals to ensure that the new cloud based service delivers against its agility goals?
- Data stewardship is a critical undertaking in any IT environment; however, cloud has catalyzed this discussion since data is highly

mobile in cloud scenarios, and since cloud entails some devolution of control over data to the third-party service provider. What does the user need to understand in terms of data residency requirements from a legal perspective, and what policies need to be in place to provide transparency on where the data has travelled, what it touches (in a multi-tenant environment), and who has access rights?

- What techniques can be developed to re-evaluate standard organizational workflow and approvals as the organization transitions to cloud? How does the organization assess whether or not approvals and process flows need to remain the same, or change within a cloud context? If these change, does the user organization build functions to accommodate transition or hand these off to a third-party and what are the criteria for making this decision?

### 4. Assessing Cloud Readiness

- What factors should user organizations take into account when deciding if the business and culture are ready for cloud, and if cloud is the best option for the business?
- Which applications are best delivered via SaaS, which are better delivered via public cloud based infrastructure services, and which are best delivered via on-premise private clouds, and what determines this?
- How can advanced infrastructure capabilities such as blueprints, cloud automation and orchestration in internal private cloud or public cloud environments improve application service delivery and agility?

### 5. Cloud Connections

- How does the organization enable seamless mobility between clouds for test/development and disaster recovery scenarios? What architectural considerations must be enabled to support mobility between clouds?

- How can the organization ensure that cloud services interoperate with on-premise or other third-party cloud services in order to provide seamless application delivery?
- What standards must we set upon our Application Programming Interfaces (API) to ensure simple and efficient communication between services?
- How can a standard set of cloud automation blueprints optimize service delivery across heterogeneous clouds?

6.  **Exit Strategies**

- How difficult, costly or complex is the process of "unrolling" cloud deployments if business circumstances change?
- How seamlessly can an organization move its application workloads between private and public cloud platforms?
- How can organizations identify and avoid vendor lock in with cloud providers, and what contingency plans should be in place around portability of data, services and "logic"?
- How important a consideration is an exit strategy in the decision to move to the cloud, and what is an appropriate planning horizon? Is the time frame in planning for cloud exit equivalent to planning for ERP – i.e. a twenty-to-thirty-year decision?

Figure 2-1. Planning for the enterprise cloud: managing layers of change and control

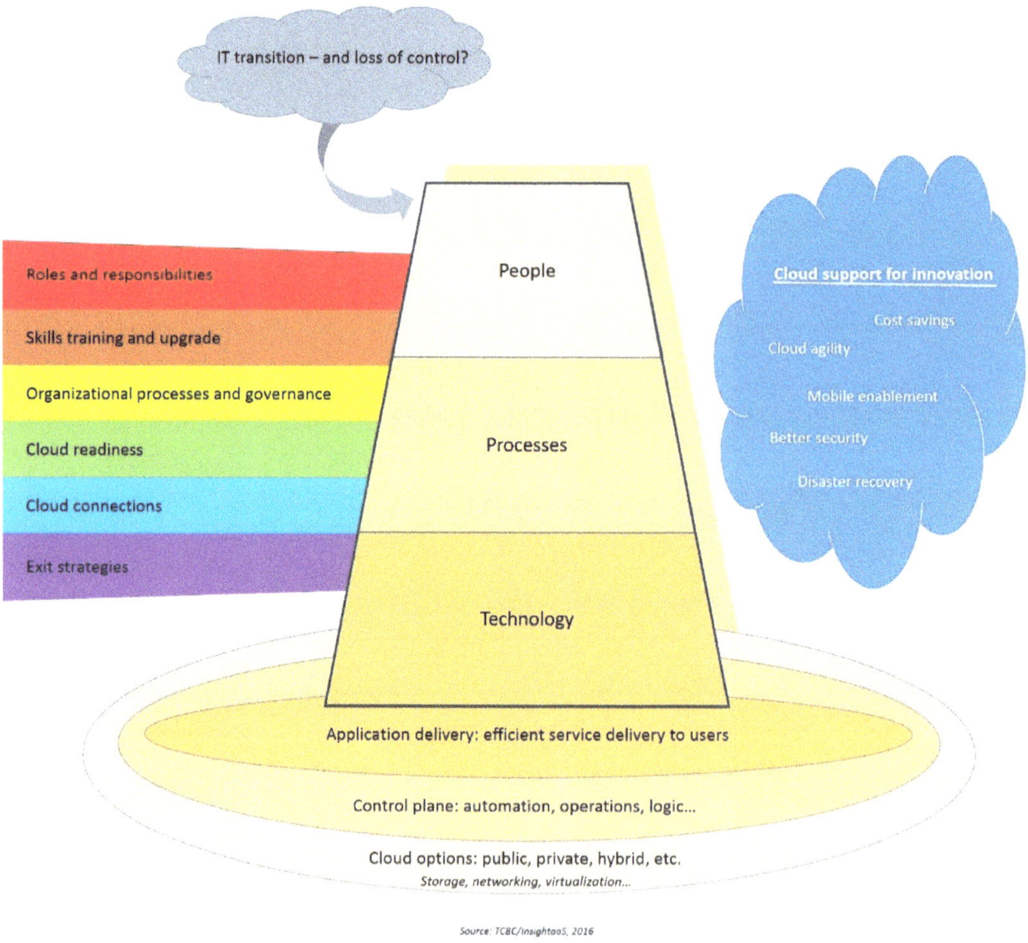

IT transition – and loss of control?

Roles and responsibilities

Skills training and upgrade

Organizational processes and governance

Cloud readiness

Cloud connections

Exit strategies

People

Processes

Technology

Cloud support for innovation

Cost savings

Cloud agility

Mobile enablement

Better security

Disaster recovery

Application delivery: efficient service delivery to users

Control plane: automation, operations, logic...

Cloud options: public, private, hybrid, etc.
*Storage, networking, virtualization...*

Source: TCBC/InsightaaS, 2016

## Business objectives

At its inception, cloud was viewed primarily as a means to cutting costs in IT service delivery. However, with greater experience of cloud, organizations are beginning to sketch out a much larger value proposition for the technology. While some cost savings may be available, the ability of cloud computing to support innovation within the organization is now viewed as the key business benefit. Without this support for innovation, the cost curve in and of itself is not nearly compelling enough to be the single or largest driver of cloud adoption. In fact, the Enterprise Cloud Planning working group has identified five primary adoption drivers that are aligned with an organization's business objectives.

## Cost savings

The sharing of resources has enabled higher utilization rates for infrastructure in multitenant cloud. Combined with other technology efficiencies, this sharing produces cost savings that may be passed on from the provider to the consumer. Other sources of savings for the user organization include outsourcing of IT support and maintenance. New payment models may also appeal to the end user organization: a shift to OPEX for on-demand resources from CAPEX investment in IT equipment may reduce overprovisioning and large up-front costs, and SaaS subscription-based spending may better accommodate some user budgets.

## Cloud agility

Cloud technologies enable business agility on a number of levels. While SaaS applications may deliver a better user experience and greater reliability to enhance worker productivity, 'try and buy' options for cloud solutions increase the likelihood that organization procures the most appropriate technologies. Similarly, use of cloud infrastructure can improve development cycles by reducing the time required for stand-up of minimally viable products from months or weeks to hours, and by enabling fast testing of new products for commercial viability. The result is shortened time-to-market and more rapid capture of demand, as well as the ability to test the limits of demand for existing products in new geographic or other markets. Through instant access to infrastructure resources and on-demand consumption, IaaS offers opportunity for easier product/market experimentation, as well as potential for creating new, agile operating models for cloud native businesses.

## Mobile enablement

Serving as the central repository for corporate data and applications, cloud technologies are powering the emergence of a new mobile workforce that can access content anywhere, anytime. Productivity benefits derived from workplace flexibility are augmented by cloud's ability to support collaboration between workers in remote locations, and communication between businesses and their customers, supply chain partners and other stakeholders.

### Better security

IT security is an ongoing challenge for many organizations, and the issue continues to become more pressing with evolution of the threat landscape, and business practices such as BYOD that introduce additional risk. A successful defence requires the knowledge and expertise of the cloud service provider, which is often in a better position to engage and maintain needed security expertise. In addition, the cloud provider is likely to have invested in the acquisition of security certifications that require skills and ongoing investment that may be out of reach of the end user organization.

### Disaster recovery

Business continuity is an increasingly prevalent use case for cloud technologies. The cost and complexity associated with maintaining mirror data centre facilities in locations that are far enough apart to avoid simultaneous outage from physical disaster, yet close enough to support the low latency requirements of modern applications are driving increasing numbers of organizations to outsource DR to lower cost, third-party cloud storage specialists.

The working group's view is that a good starting point for cloud planning is to identify the pain point(s) that cloud is expected to address, and ensure that deployment will address a sufficient number (two or more) of these adoption drivers. Combined, these cloud-based capabilities work to support business innovation, helping organizations to sustain their momentum in the market. Successful implementation is less about "cool technology" than about alignment of cloud with business objectives: an ability that is increasingly critical for the organization in ultra-competitive markets, and understanding of which IT leaders are increasingly expected to demonstrate. The role of IT has changed. It no longer functions simply as a buyer of IT equipment; increased scrutiny and tighter budgets mean IT must now must explain to the CFO what business problem a project addresses before gaining approval. IT is a value organization in any business, but must be able to outline the business value in technology implementations in order to remain relevant.

Planning can be instrumental in this process. Inadequate planning, on the other hand, results in ad hoc adoption that fails to capitalize on the synergies available through cloud orchestration, as well as growth of 'shadow IT' and its associated security and compliance risks. While the IT organization has traditionally been responsible for governing and operating all IT services, cloud adoption ease – of SaaS applications, for example – has produced a shadow IT phenomenon in which cloud resources are sourced by various individuals or business departments outside the purview of IT. Staff who may not have proper authorization or training in contractual obligations sign on to cloud services, and through misuse of corporate identity may bind the employer organization to terms in an agreement which are not well understood or that incur unacceptable risk/liability, as failure to properly plan around the legal liability for data can leave organizations open to considerable exposure.

The challenge is to ensure the IT organization governs all workloads or services, whether or not it operates them, a goal that may be realized through planning, processes and policies that holds IT accountable for governance of services, regardless of where these are operating. Many organizations are now maturing processes that can identify areas where shadow IT might be occurring and working to enable a transition plan that will introduce greater accountability; however, most likely remain unaware of just how much cloud they are actually consuming. The working group agrees that "shadow IT is not necessarily a bad thing but it needs to be managed."

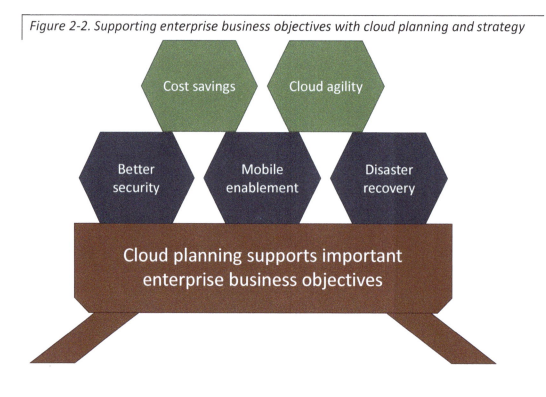

Figure 2-2. Supporting enterprise business objectives with cloud planning and strategy

*Source: TCBC/InsightaaS, 2015*

## Best practice and processes in enterprise cloud planning

### Roles and Responsibilities

The discourse over cloud's impact on staffing within the adopting organization has been ambiguous. While the IT community's first response to cloud automation was fear for the displacement of traditional IT workers, this concern has been mitigated through the articulation of new roles and responsibilities that would allow IT staff to grow and develop expertise beyond "keeping the lights on" – beyond the performance of routine maintenance tasks in the data centre that could be automated through cloud. A good deal of attention was also devoted to the "cloud broker," a service function that would be responsible for the dynamic procurement and management of services potentially spanning private-public and hybrid cloud. But how has this shift played out in real life, and what needs to be in place from a people perspective to achieve effective cloud transformation?

At a basic level, the impact of cloud varies from organization to organization, and depends on the impetus for change within. In 'top down' scenarios where the driver of cloud adoption is the CXO who creates cloud by principle, the IT department is likely to embrace the operational efficiencies that can be achieved in certain areas – service desk, for example. In cases where the Line-of-Business manager drives cloud adoption, focus is on agility for the rapid delivery of business value, with little regard for the cloud provider's underlying functionality, or the IT department's capability to support it in the longer term. The optimal scenario is for these two worlds to meet: for the business unit manager to source cloud within the security and governance parameters established by IT, and for IT departments to aim not only for the efficiency gains that virtualization of IT infrastructure can bring, but also for the adoption of solutions with the characteristics that are unique to cloud – on-demand, self-service and pay-per-use.

To effect this culture shift, it is the working group's belief that cloud implementation, in both private and public contexts, demands first a new way of thinking about service delivery on the part of IT. The delivery of efficient IT services is no longer about "cost savings," it's about saying yes to more innovation and driving "revenue gains." "Embrace change; it is coming" as one group member put it, through more open collaboration and interaction at top levels between IT and the business units to better align operational planning with longer term business needs, and through better coordination of operational and development activities. To accelerate the pace of change, the working group recommends adoption of the agile "DevOps" approach in which development and operations teams break down walls and deliver seamless services with a single shared goal – to help foster innovation.

If operations in traditional legacy environments can be characterized by what the working group describes as an "assembly line, batch mentality," adoption of public cloud services calls for thinking in real time about integration points between corporate applications and data and external systems, also referred to as a "service based architecture." While integrations are required in traditional, monolithic IT environments, they tend to be hard written into the applications within millions of lines of code and dependant on their original architecture. Service based architectures, in which micro services deliver on the premise of interoperability without dependency, are different in that each individual service is designed to be flexible in its integration with other services. Traditional IT organizations need to move "up the stack" to focus more on the way that services are architected, built and maintained across the enterprise and less on the underlying infrastructure or platforms that they sit upon. But managing multiple integration points involves different skill sets, different management practices and more timely response: in twenty years' time, the working group expects the IT organization look different than it does today – and feature an expanded role for integration specialists, and cloud brokers tasked with adapting the organizations unique business and IT needs to available services.

At an organizational level, another area that cloud will shape is data sovereignty and data lifecycle management. Understanding where data resides and what permissions exist, can be more complicated questions in a cloud environment, a consideration that is likely to entail an expanded role for the CISO in ensuring appropriate data governance is in place, as well as new requirements in the development of information architectures. Today, for example, in the vast majority of SaaS solutions the SaaS provider retains all data. In future, it may be that SaaS will allow for multi-site architectures where data sits "on-premise," Or perhaps cloud organizations will begin to expand into the business of data lifecycle management, contracting for the delivery of data retention, compliance and security requirements.

This kind of proposition can be very complex, as cloud adoption in the case of highly regulated industries in particular demonstrates. In banking, a common practice involves the deployment of public cloud for a certain service, followed by the creation of a backup environment for this in on-premise infrastructure. This data replication and the local run of applications is designed to satisfy auditors of compliance with data retention and archiving policies in the (frequent) event full risk and accountability is not guaranteed by the public cloud service provider. "In the haste to embrace the cloud, you need to measure twice and cut once," one working group member noted, applying creative architectural solutions that consider the entire lifecycle of the data to ensure that data processes and protection remain intact, without the layering on of additional overhead to accommodate company policies.

In the cloud era where architecture is out of the sand box and nebulous, a key role that is evolving is the enterprise architect who has world experience, who can visualize service delivery across multiple clouds and business functions, and who can apply simplicity of design to information management. In the working group's view, the creation and support for what the analyst firm Gartner calls the "Vanguard Architect" is of critical importance in cloud adoption as the level of insight that these have will be a huge factor in determining the appropriateness of the architecture that will be built to support IT service delivery. At the same time, the working group believes that the "Vanguard Architect" should not be a role singled out from others but rather a philosophy for all architects to embrace.

## Skills Training and Upgrade

Cloud demands new skills at many levels of the organization. While the leadership team must learn to envision cloud potential and develop strategies for driving the transformational change that cloud can bring, business unit managers must familiarize themselves with cloud capabilities to adjust product/market cycles to the pace of IT service delivery that cloud delivers. For their part in ensuring successful implementation, information managers must develop understanding of cloud's potential impact on data location and governance. Though infrastructure staff may believe that information resides within the boundaries of a specific region, it is the information/privacy officer who has responsibility for understanding the risks associated with cloud deployment and for initiating information management processes that mitigate this risk. He/she must learn how to ensure that data within a service provider environment is not replicated to another country, or if it is, what privacy/access legislation would apply, how to classify data in terms of sensitivity and potential risk and whether other cloud storage arrangements, including data retention cycles and disclosure provisions, might compromise data privacy. In cases where this knowledge base is not available internally, the information or decision support specialist must know where to access it – and whether this information is best accessed in contractual discussions with the cloud vendor or through discussion with a third party consultant. In addition, the business of cloud demands knowledge of the legal ramifications of data migration to an external provider: who is responsible (the cloud service provider or the customer) for the impact of data breech, and how might cloud outsourcing contracts affect insurance policies/premiums that the adopting organization has in place to manage data risk.

In many ways, the enterprise architect straddles the worlds of business and IT operations, acting as a bridge that links awareness of the business and information needs of the organization with their execution through IT services. As such, the enterprise architect must develop new levels of understanding about the flow of information and business logic beyond the walls of the enterprise to cloud repositories for storage and processing, creating appropriate access points for business along the way.

At the technical level, the working group points to a number of new areas that will demand skills upgrade to support migration to cloud: cloud ops, for example, which is designed to enable cloud automation, operations and financial transparency across clouds. In addition, network architects and administrators must learn how to build out a "virtual network" that allows workloads to easily span Layer 2/3 between clouds.

At a practical level, the notion that one professional would possess all required networking skills is unrealistic. The working group believes that teams with business analysis skills, with technology skills from a networking perspective, and technology skills from a security perspective will all be needed to perform the cloud appropriate audits, to implement security controls at the right exit point and the right entry point into the network, and in conjunction with business owners, to manage access to applications and data that reside in the cloud. To ensure coordination of tasks and that the right skill sets are in place, the group notes that new levels of collaboration between technologists, network and security administrators and the business units are critical to successful cloud implementation.

Skills upgrade may also be required at the end user level. While application training in the case of SaaS adoption vs. deployment of a new software on-premise in traditional IT environments may be similar regardless of the infrastructure it sits on, this is not the case in all instances. For example, proprietary applications by their very nature are designed to address the unique needs of the organization from a business process or workflow perspective: with popular SaaS applications, on the other hand, application capabilities are typically developed to meet the need for standard delivery of functionality across the broadest possible base of customers. With SaaS, clients are encouraged to minimize customization to accelerate deployment and minimize expensive implementation services and post-sales support. Successful cloud adoption – including extensive uptake of the cloud-based service – depend on educating business unit managers of the limits of customization with popular CRM or sales management apps, and on adjusting workflow and providing end user training on the new technology to build familiarity with the new interface and on new processes.

## Organizational Controls and Governance

Broadly defined, 'governance' is the combination of processes and workflow implemented by corporate boards to inform, direct, manage, secure and monitor the activities of the organization as is works toward the achievement of its goals. Often associated with fiscal transparency and fairness, in the cloud context, governance may be understood as guidance for building processes in support of the organization's migration objectives, while addressing potential risk issues associated with transition to the new IT paradigm that cloud represents. Its companion – 'control' – is defined as the actions taken by management, the board or other parties to manage risk and to increase the likelihood that the established goals will be achieved. With cloud implementation, these objectives may include cost savings, greater business agility, faster time-to-market for products and services, or simply access to new IT functionality, outcomes that are more likely to be realized with effective planning, sufficient action and control.

The enterprise planning working group suggests that the technical approaches to control governance in cloud deployment vary with the organization, and depend on company goals, on how much governance can be put in place to manage the risk associated with cloud migration. In addition, control statements can be implemented using different technologies. In the case of highly confidential financial information, such as the enterprise's profit and loss statements or balance sheets, for example, a control statement would say that this information should not move out of the enterprise before earnings are announced, and several different technologies could be deployed to ensure adherence. These might include web or email filtering mechanisms or data loss filtering when information is transferred to the cloud, or the encryption of financial data and its storage in a secure repository that only the auditors can access. A high-level control statement would say that anything which has been labelled as confidential needs to be handled in a certain way, and IT would work with security personnel to identify the right technology to secure the data when it needs to leave the organization – as when data moves to a cloud repository.

While transferring data governance matters to the cloud service provider would be appealing due to simplicity of the solution, ultimately, responsibility as well as legal liability for data resides with the customer organization, which also has corporate interest in ensuring levels of process – for auditability, for example, which some standardized provider infrastructure offerings may not be ready to deliver. In assessing governance and control matters that are important to cloud migration, the working group suggests enterprise planners consider the following issues:

*Data stewardship*

With the dissolution of central records bodies back in the 1980s, discipline around information management and retention schedules was lost in most organizations. The last thirty years have been characterized by undisciplined information collection across most enterprises, and reliance on search capabilities, rather than organization of data, for information retrieval. Issues with data retention have been compounded by the proliferation of places that data can now be stored – including traditional, on-premise databases, branch or central office locations, hosted and cloud repositories – making the timely and effective retrieval and disposal of information for legal or regulatory purposes highly problematic.

In addressing this issue, it is incumbent on the enterprise to know where data resides, how to find information within the data, and what information will be deleted by when. Retention schedules are highly complicated, and vary depending on the nature of the data. In healthcare, for example, data associated with a patient must be kept for the life of that individual, but as a transitory record, an email between hospital administrators may not need to be saved longer than two years, even though it may contain information that is of critical importance to the institution. Engineering and other information on a building must be retained as long as the structure stands – potentially hundreds of years.

In most organizations, responsibility for the protection of key information has been delegated to the Chief Information and Security Officer (CISO), who works with the CIO to ensure that private information is protected and governed appropriately. CISO and the Chief Privacy Officer are relatively new roles within the corporation that typically hail from administrative offices that used to have responsibility for policy on physical records; however, these often assume a conservative stance in regard to information management policy due to data loss challenges. For example, in the case of a data breach, organizations are typically compelled to report that all data has been compromised – a practice that can overestimate risk but satisfy requirements for transparency. The working group suggests that data stewardship that includes a schedule around retention/deletion of data will help ensure that data is not stored longer than it need be, or longer than the organization is required to produce it from a legal perspective, is an important step to data governance in the cloud. Securing disparate storage repositories with policy-based security will also ensure that damage from a potential breach is minimized.

*Identity management and encryption*

Enforcement of data protection policy can only be accomplished with a focus on policy-based identity management and encryption. Data may be secured, for example, by identifying an individual or organizational role and granting permissions to access specific data sets based on that identity, and by limiting access to those individuals only who have appropriate credentials. Industry best practice is now to follow the path of "least privilege" giving employees only access to what they absolutely need and re-qualifying access to sensitive data on an ongoing basis. Encryption of data at rest and in transit to and from the cloud repository that does not affect application performance is another key technology designed to fulfill data protection requirements. These technologies, when combined with general security precautions, provide an approach that is different in kind from an earlier "Castle and Moat" model where firewalls would be built around servers to deliver protection. In a cloud world, the organization does not own the servers, the servers move, as do the buildings that house them, and VPNs to manage data traffic over the Internet do not scale directly with the multipoint transmission of corporate data.

Successful security management depends in many ways on balancing IT interest in security with the business end users' need for an experience of security technology that does not unduly interfere with work activities. Single sign-on identity management solutions implemented with single or dual factor authentication schemas are a recent approach to the challenge of reducing complexity for the user while maintaining protection for corporate data that is touted to work well in multi-cloud or hybrid environments. The working group advises caution in use of this technology, though, as it relies on the use of one master key to provide user access to many different processes. While the user need not remember more than one set of credentials, if the key or credentials are compromised, hackers gain access to all cloud applications. In order to address these concerns, the addition of a second factor of authentication is recommended to mitigate such risk.  A Single Sign-On (SSO) platform with integrated strong authentication, access control and user management will provide a better experience for users, control for administrators and security for the organization.

A more balanced strategy involves decision-making around which applications may be single sign-on enabled, and which may need an additional layer of inspection.  As example, the working group points to the approach taken by the banks' anti-fraud and anti-money laundering groups, which dictates the placement of additional fraud prevention engines to run on top of the transaction data. Even though bank may offer single sign-on, personal online banking trackers can flag more than 10 account transfers within a specified time using the fraud engine, and outlier behaviours will trigger a call to action – a follow up automated text/phone call that improves security and with it, the customer experience.

### Workflow transitions

As organizations transition to cloud, change in workflow processes and approvals operates on three levels: at a strategic, organizational level, and at the application and infrastructure layers. Any evaluation of techniques should start from the perspective of business and regulatory risk, considering how and where use of cloud affects relevant workflows. Where cloud is introduced as a component of a process that carries business or regulatory risk, the enterprise will need to take three steps. The first, which is important to compliance, is to identify where and how external processing and storage of data affects how core systems of record may be accessed or altered. The second step is to evaluate supplier SLAs, identify where and how they do or do not correspond to business and/or regulatory requirements, and work to aligning the SLA with corporate practice and regulatory guidelines. This process can take several forms: some cloud vendors will adjust SLAs to accommodate a client and others will not. If a supplier will not, then the organization must decide whether they will alter their business practice and expectations or seek another supplier. The third step involves creating a "plan B" to address business risk in the event the cloud service becomes unavailable.

A good starting point for identifying and managing process change resulting from cloud application deployment is to first consider which existing internal processes will be disrupted by the move to cloud. This decision is based on a variety of factors, such as tolerance to security risk and other corporate drivers, or even corporate cultural norms that admit the use of public cloud services or that insist that data be kept under lock and key on-premise. In still other cases, business drivers, such as data residency or uptime requirements, will have primary influence over the identification of applications that can be adapted to cloud delivery models.

For example, unlike the deployment of packaged applications in traditional IT environments, use of SaaS applications may not allow for the levels of customization that the organization is used to, or that is possible with enterprise development of proprietary software designed to serve specific business needs. In these situations, transition to SaaS may entail alignment or change of business process to match application functionality or capabilities, a process that is best addressed in advance of deployment through "business blueprinting" – mapping out a business function from end-to-end to see all elements of workflow. In procurement of SaaS-based applications, the user organization should take into account the costs business change management might entail, as well as the SaaS application's ability to withstand industrial usage, balancing these factors against the cost and convenience of using cloud-based applications. Ultimately, the rule of thumb here is to avoid any customization unless it is absolutely necessary. Although organizational change is hard in the long-term, the upfront effort of customizing a solution to suit your business coupled with the ongoing costs of supporting it can have a dramatic impact on project success and delivering a positive ROI.

In the IT department, the key shift is from task-oriented processes to vendor management. For example, removing responsibility for maintenance activities such as patch management, which may be automated in a cloud context, will simplify process for IT operators; however, responsibilities must be parsed out, delegated either to in house staff or to the cloud provider. In many ways, the biggest challenge, and one that spans infrastructure and applications, is the alignment of technology system change with process change. Areas that can be overlooked in migration to cloud infrastructure, but which require detailed process documentation include: management of CMDB (change management database), change control, ticketing systems, approval processes (for access to cloud apps and data), data classification to determine sensitivity and storage in different cloud modes, and in implementations featuring cloud self-service, deciding who has access and what are their permissions. To ensure successful cloud migration, enterprises are advised to support implementation with plans that does not neglect process change.

### Assessing Cloud Readiness

An organization's readiness to adopt cloud varies with the application and with the state of existing capabilities. In cases where the on-premise solution is not reliable or not meeting the needs of the business user, and a cloud solution is available that has greater potential to meet current and future needs at an equivalent or lower cost, the organization's decision for cloud is a straightforward proposition. Email is a good example: many organizations have opted for SaaS delivery of a reliable, relatively low cost productivity solution that offers an additional adoption incentive, namely the replacement of constraints on storage in existing infrastructure with flexible storage resources for the end user and a lower TCO for the business.

In other cases, cloud deployment is driven by the end user, who may be looking for additional features that are not currently available via on-premise systems. Rogue use of popular file sharing applications, for example, would suggest that the user culture is ready for cloud adoption, even if the IT department continues to have concerns over loss of control of upgrade schedules, feature sets or the look and feel of the SaaS application. As one member of the working group put it, in assessing cloud readiness from a cultural perspective, it is important to consider the "low hanging fruit in terms of the services that you operate that are not up to current standards," and address these first to build buy-in from the end user community and the business as a whole. Another good indicator of readiness for cloud is the presence of 'workarounds' that users create, such as replication to ensure remote access to applications and data – emailing GBs of data for work outside the office – which may result in additional risk associated with loss of control over where data is stored. As a means of managing this activity, moving to more accessible cloud-based platforms and applications would offer significant benefit as it could simultaneously meet users' productivity requirements and reduce data-related security and audit threats for the organization as a whole.

Cloud readiness may also be evaluated from a risk perspective, where an understanding of business requirements is critical. Key questions the organization may ask to assess risk tolerance include: is the application targeted at a B2B or B2C relationship? What kind of adherence to security practices, policies and standards are required? And what risk tolerance can be entertained for migration of that specific application to the cloud? Answers to these questions may indicate whether on-premise, cloud or hybrid approaches are better options for particular applications.

Beyond this focus on data security needs for specific applications, policy may also play a role. In some organizations, for example, a 'cloud first' policy established at executive levels and based on the balance of generalized risk evaluation and cloud benefit may serve to encourage greater momentum towards cloud delivery.

*Figure 2-3. Key issues in enterprise cloud planning best practices*

## Roles and responsibilities

Shift in service delivery approach
Data sovereignty and data lifecycle management

## Skills training and upgrade

Data management skills and expertise in enterprise architecture
Technical skills: e.g., cloud ops, network architecture and administration
User skills: ability to align workflow with cloud applications

## Organizational controls and governance

Development and consistent handling of control statements
Data stewardship
Identity management and encryption
Workflow transitions: strategic, organisation, and application/workload

## Assessing cloud readiness

Aging or unreliable infrastructure vs. capable cloud alternatives
Requirement for agility, time-to-benefit, cost benefits, and/or scale
User readiness (as seen in use of 'rogue' SaaS apps)
Risk profile and corporate policy

## Cloud connections

Data portability
System interoperability and APIs
Network communications, security, access identification management

## Exit strategies

Vendor-agnostic deployment environments
Data and application architecture

*Source: TCBC/InsightaaS, 2015*

Moving down the stack, the application's ability to run on cloud infrastructure is another critical factor in assessing cloud readiness. Many legacy applications that were developed using older coding languages are not capable of running without interruption in distributed operating environments that (likely) include virtualized storage and virtualized networking, or of withstanding load balancing in dynamic environments characterized by continuous virtual machine migration. In these situations, the adopting organization may consider a couple of options – rebuild the application using more modern programming languages (Python, Java, etc.), continue to fix problems as they occur, or replace the application. When proprietary applications are differentiated for vertical markets or specific use cases and otherwise unavailable, rebuilding with new software may be indicated. If the application is at end of lifecycle, the replacement option may be the most appropriate; however, in this situation, the working group advises taking time before migration to properly prepare and cleanse data in advance of transition to cloud.

This focus on the application is also a critical input to an organization's readiness to deploy in public provider resources. Ideally, the enterprise should be able to point to existing business process workflow, and have the same process mapped onto the cloud service as well. Cloud readiness for application migration in the public infrastructure context entails ensuring that the business process flow can also be extended to the cloud environment.

The cloud readiness equation also involves weighing the cost and agility benefits that may substantiate the business case for cloud adoption. Evaluating the relative cost of cloud vs. on-premise deployment is a complex equation that includes estimates for capital expense, staff time and licensing; and the terms fluctuate depending on the number of servers involved, on the server utilization in existing, traditional infrastructure, and by the type of workload or application. The challenge in building IT-centric cost models has led many organizations to focus on specific areas of cost that may be optimized through cloud deployment. As example, the working group cites the case of one large Canadian organization that was finding it difficult to attract new staff talent due to older applications, older infrastructure and the lack of user access to applications. In addition to an IT infrastructure assessment, ROI for this organization included the potential to address operational cost issues associated with talent acquisition.

Much of the discourse around cost control associated with advanced cloud capabilities has focused on the potential to reduce staff engaged in infrastructure maintenance task – "keeping the lights on" – and their reassignment to higher-level activities. This proposition assumes the easy transition of workers. The training and experience of IT professionals would indicate otherwise: a network administrator, for example, will have very different skills than a developer. That said, automation of tasks in everyday operations, such as provisioning servers or terminating unused instances through advanced configuration tools, load sharing across compute, storage and network resources, and dynamic management of the rollout of complex systems at the software layer, can reduce the potential for human error in manual management of these tasks.

While automation of processes such as the provisioning of resources for new employees may be available in more traditional infrastructure, automation is a core competence in cloud-based, software-defined infrastructure that can rapidly decrease the time needed for resource provisioning and consequently increase organizational agility. At the same time, advanced capabilities that are now built into private cloud or service provider public infrastructure may improve an organization's cloud readiness by addressing many of the skill gaps identified as a barrier to an organization's ability to realize cloud benefits. Blueprinting or intelligent architecture solutions can enable a rapid and massive scale-up of cloud resources that cannot be accomplished manually. Cloud orchestration provides the workflow required to optimize this scale of infrastructure, and at the application layer, orchestration works to integrate siloed resources (including multiple clouds in hybrid scenarios) needed for the organization to take full advantage of the insight offered through the interaction of cloud data and apps. Armed with advanced management tools, which may operate across on-premise, private, hybrid and public cloud environments, organizations may improve cloud readiness and speed time to deployment.

## Cloud Connections

The need to manage across silos of information assets is a familiar challenge in organizations with traditional IT infrastructure. Evolving out of enterprise acquisition of new corporate entities with their own systems, operation of individual business units or branch locations with unique IT resource needs and procurement budgets, or the pre-cloud tendency to assign applications and data to specific server resources, information silos are an impediment to business collaboration. In the cloud era, this tendency towards information silos can be exacerbated by the relatively greater ease of adopting cloud resources, and the ad hoc deployment of SaaS apps and cloud infrastructure by business unit managers who are increasingly influential in ever more distributed IT purchase decision making.

But there are techniques that can help address issues with cloud silos. Application Program Interfaces (APIs) are a set of routines, protocols and tools for building applications that provide building blocks for the programmer to use, and specify how software should communicate with operating systems or other control programs. In a cloud context, APIs can support the orchestration of disparate clouds or cloud applications to optimize business operation integration. APIs may also function at a process level, facilitating the user organization's communication with external clouds ease functions such as cloud onboarding. For example, migration to cloud may entail redesign of access to the cloud application, which takes into account risk components such as how access is created, revoked and integrated into user resource provisioning and application lifecycle management. Unless the IT organization has already carried out integration into processes defined by proprietary cloud platforms, an API architecture must be developed that can handle security, sign on and communication between clouds.

In theory, when APIs are leveraged across platforms and applications, adopting organizations can more quickly integrate with cloud provider systems and create integration between clouds. Open APIs accelerate this process, as long as proper documentation on use of the API has been generated from within the open community.

There can be other obstacles to API-based linkages as well. Vendors sometimes deliver connectors that meet the needs of only a small subset of the user community, or that do not address the need for extraction of data – which may compromise data feeds and customized reporting. As a member of the working group explained, "When you first start peeling back the layers to think about how you will integrate, even for organizations that have undertaken automation initiatives, what you can send to the cloud and what you can get back may not be at the level of detail or the quality that would make integration with orchestration platforms useful." In the access management example noted above, though this may be difficult from a cost or development perspective, the group advises enterprises to "aim high" in their use of APIs for cloud connection: a secured, authenticated link into the API should be established, and the business should maintain the same level of control that is used in manual provisioning of end user access, including the ability to create direct access for many accounts very quickly as well as bidirectional flow of configuration data at a granular level. Though many early stage clouds were built for the unidirectional flow of information – assuming customers would move to vendor platforms but never away – bidirectional data flow enhances usability.

Wherever possible, the working group advises enterprises adopting cloud to look to leverage open, well-documented APIs in their application architectures and to be cognizant of potential issues in leveraging proprietary APIs. A well-integrated API can ease development tasks for the organization, and will also help create a good and transparent user experience for customers of the adopting organization. This is especially important in areas such as epayments, where a bounce back to different sites in transaction processing may compromise the trust an organization is trying to build in ecommerce. The working group notes, however, that transparency to the user does not mean that security and risk aspects of API integration on the back end are neglected. There should be keen focus on identity and access management components, a task that may be further complicated by remote or mobile access to cloud applications and business need for a simplified user experience.

A strategy around single sign on identity management that addresses use of federated IDs or other tools is critical, especially in the situations where solutions are comprised of multiple, integrated cloud systems and applications. Another critical input to ensuring seamless application delivery in a multi-cloud environment (or indeed in use of single clouds) is "BYOK" – "Bring Your Own Key" approaches – in which the user organization maintains the encryption key to its own data, protecting it against the eventuality that one or more provider clouds will be breached. Offered by third party providers as a cloud service, BYOK capabilities may offer the user of integrated cloud applications a simpler approach to securing multiple applications and associated data.

A technique developed by public cloud providers to ease deployment of infrastructure is cloud 'blueprints', otherwise known as 'recipes' or 'templates'. Essentially, the blueprint is an automated script that enables automated, repeatable creation of a set of infrastructure components, including an operating system, application and configuration. Designed to support rapid scale provisioning, blueprints may introduce complexity when the goal is service delivery across heterogeneous clouds, as each blueprint is aligned with a particular vendor platform, and requires familiarity with different native tool sets. Today, a blueprint that is created for a specific cloud is tightly coupled to that cloud: providers use proprietary hypervisors, different distributions of operating systems and applications that are unique to their cloud. For the customer looking to deploy multiple clouds, this conveys a requirement for adaptation to each platform, including learning each native blueprint and the use of separate tool sets. A generic blueprint system that would allow the user to create a common tool set that could be used across multiple clouds would represent a logical middle step for management of multiple cloud blueprints.

Cloud connections operate at three layers:

- At the base is networking, where moving applications in traditional environments has required reassignment of IP addresses that were tied to physical infrastructure in the networking fabric. By extending switch fabric and routing through software defined networking across multiple environments and clouds, ubiquity of communications is achieved in the IP schema.
- At the next level up is security, where firewall rules and access control lists operate differently from cloud site to cloud site. At this level, a key question is, "is it possible to extend layer 4-7 feature sets, virtualizing capabilities like firewalls and load balancing (as in NFV) so they are not proprietary to a particular cloud service provider premise, but rather ubiquitous across sites?"
- A final layer involves access identification management – BYOK encryption, for example.

To ensure cloud interoperability and the seamless movement of workloads, communication and cabling links must be established across these three areas.

### Exit Strategies: understanding how to check out of a cloud environment

Clearly, moving *to* the cloud requires a great deal of planning. However, this planning exercise needs also to consider how to move *from* a specific cloud environment if necessary.

At a high level, the working group advises that enterprises should first consider the architectural decisions that need to be made in order to deploy an application as a service. While there are relatively few difficulties in moving infrastructure components such as the virtual machines from cloud to cloud, the situation is different with applications.

The fastest way to develop an app on public cloud infrastructure is to leverage the provider's platform-dependent micro services; however, in return for accelerated time to value, the user is unable to move the application to another provider's cloud service without breaking and rebuilding the application. While it may be possible to develop an application on what one member of the working group called a "cloud independent platform" to enable shift of the entire application infrastructure to multiple clouds, development may well take longer without the rich deployment feature sets available with proprietary micro services within cloud dependent platforms.

The working group advises enterprises planning deployment of applications on cloud to consider, "how much time, effort and money is it going to cost me to move this application in the event that I have to change clouds?" and what accelerated time-to-market advantage the organization would achieve by tightly coupling the application with the service provider cloud. Netflix, for example, has been three to four years ahead of competitors in terms of bringing steaming content services to market as it has taken full advantage of AWS services, but the company is now unable to port its service to another provider without significant expense.

What is the best way to the balance of the efficiency benefits gained in writing natively to the cloud provider platform – architecting the solution to take full advantage of unique platform features – against the flexibility won by writing to an agnostic platform? Ultimately, cloud mobility will entail assessment of three decision criteria: what architecture 'gets me there the quickest' (likely to be proprietary to a specific cloud); what architecture provides maximum flexibility to move between clouds; and is more rapid time-to-market worth the cost of vendor lock-in? When an application or service has been built for the cloud and is heavily dependent on provider functionality, rollback of the application may be prohibited by complexity or cost. It may be necessary, for example, for organizations looking to re-host an application to rebuild functionality that may only be available as an out-of-the-box feature with a specific provider platform.

In decisions around cloud application mobility, login visibility into cloud provider systems is another important consideration. In the case of a provider breach, for example, it is critical that the user organization have granular login information on the consumption of cloud services in order to develop the required replication, and also to respond to stakeholder questions about levels of organizational risk arising from the provider breach. A provider's ability to deliver this transparency through features built into the application and infrastructure, and confirmed in contractual agreements, should be a key consideration in the evaluation different provider services. This need for transparency may also impact the user's ability to migrate applications from one provider to another: even if the enterprise has granular information from its primary provider, it must have access to comparable data in comparable data formats to allow porting of the application to a next, or additional provider.

Good exit strategies must be grounded in a good backup plan, where either the application or physical environment is in place to roll back cloud services to in-house resources or another provider environment. As the source of migration, the internal user organization may be challenged to establish appropriate staging, testing and migration processes; however, as each component of the application is built, the user should consider if it is possible to roll back the application and data from a specific cloud environment, and how this might be accomplished. This is especially difficult with born-in-the-cloud services – such as the one highlighted in the Netflix example – where rollback represents migration to a net-new environment – essentially, starting over from scratch.

The complexity of the service to be moved in many ways determines the complexity of the migration. Simple applications may be easier to move than more intricate applications, and modern applications may be easier to rebuild than their traditional, legacy counterparts. Going forward, the working group looks forward to an increasing community of third party integration service companies who will build "babble fish" capabilities to enable the rapid and automated re-architecting of modern applications. This approach would offer greater tie-in to new infrastructure than does today's app migration, and would contribute to application optimization through ongoing introduction of new value-added features. Managed cloud services like these would allow customers to take better advantage of continuous innovation occurring in the provider community.

Ultimately, planning for cloud exit – insurance in the eventuality that cloud applications will need to migrate – returns to considerations of data architecture. Many applications have been built organically and have their own data; however, very few organizations have established common understandings around where data is, who pushes it, who is the steward, where is the data pushed from, where does it reside, and what is being done to secure it. In the working group's view, data architecture considerations are prerequisite to cloud strategy as a whole. A lack of data architecture planning may impact the potential for cloud integration/portability and may also imperil an enterprise's regulatory or governance imperatives. While data governance concerns are common to traditional IT environments, cloud may exacerbate these issues as the application of data governance or policies may be overlooked, neglected or applied after the fact in cloud migration scenarios.

To ensure that data governance is encompassed in cloud planning, the working group encourages enterprises to "think about the exit before you think about the entrance." It is likely that an organization will eventually encounter a situation requiring migration; it is incumbent on the cloud planner to ensure that this does not impose insurmountable challenges to data protection and operational viability.

In the final analysis, exit strategies should involve input from multiple C-level executives. The development of exit strategies should be owned by the CTO, and overseen by the CFO, who addresses risk management by assessing contractual agreements, whether the application can be run without the cloud service, and what might be the impact on the business in the event that the enterprise needs to migrate away for a specific supplier. This evaluation can and should be informed by the CIO and CRO (risk officer), who can offer input on data governance and migration in and out of cloud.

## Reference sources
Reference sources helpful in illustrating cloud planning best practices include:

- The Institute of Internal Auditors. Governance, Risk & Control.
- National Institute of Standards and Technology. NIST Cloud Computing Standards Roadmap. US Department of Commerce. Special Publication 500-291.
- Michael O'Neil. The Death of Core Competency: A management guide to cloud computing and the zero-friction future. InsightaaS Press, 2014.
  The book is structured in four sections that combine to provide management insight into where and how cloud is important to business strategy as well as guidance on how to align cloud investments and activities to obtain the maximum benefit from cloud strategies. The book is available as a paperback from Amazon, for Kindle in the US, in Canada, in India, and in all other ebook formats.
- OpenStack Documentation.

*Chapter 3.*

# Planning for the Cloud/Cloud Strategy: SMB

Essential guidance on developing cloud adoption, expansion and use strategies relevant to small and mid-sized businesses

*Contributing community experts: Alex Sirota (NewPath Consulting), Brandon Kolybaba (Cloud A), Jeff Lamboy (GoDaddy), Mathew Gancarz (de Souza Institute), Dave Collings (Do IT Lean), Matt Ambrose (PwC), Sangam Manikkayamiyer (Symantec)*

*Initial publication date: March 2016*

# Planning for the Cloud/Cloud Strategy: SMB

## Definition and context

The TCBC Planning for the cloud/cloud strategy: SMB working group is focused on a complex set of issues: what is it that SMBs need to consider, as they adopt hosted and cloud solutions to address different needs within their businesses?

Definition in this context, as is illustrated by Figure 3-2, spans several related considerations. The first concerns the target population: what is an "SMB" from a cloud adoption process? The TCBC working group believes that SMB perspectives and requirements are shaped by two issues – business size and technical vs. non-technical buyers.

As a starting point, the group divided SMBs into three categories: microbusinesses of 1-19 employees, small businesses of 20-99 employees, and mid-sized businesses of 100-499 employees.

The second issue is to define the types of cloud buyers in each category, to identify who should be involved in the cloud planning/strategy process. In all three categories, the key non-technical buyer is the senior business manager. This group is looking to embrace cloud-based systems to add new functionality to business processes, and/or to simplify and reduce the cost of IT. Hosted solutions offer a compelling value proposition to this group, but over time, integration gaps between disparate systems can eat into the benefit that each individual solution provides.

We do not believe that there are technical buyers in microbusinesses, except for those that are in the business of IT – tech start-ups, often looking to develop SaaS applications. In small and (especially) medium businesses, there will be a technical buyer, generally, the development lead. These buyers are looking for cost efficient, scalable development platforms. They are often challenged by the absence of effective business processes within SMBs – they deploy new applications but have issues with managing the spread of those applications, and as a result, the accompanying requirements for integration and support.

Figure 3-1. SMB cloud buyer segments

| Organization Size | Technical Buyer | Non-Technical Buyer |
|---|---|---|
| 1-19 | Only tech start-ups | Senior business management |
| 20-99 | Development lead | Senior business management |
| 100-499 | Development lead | Senior business management |

## Definitional framework

Once the core SMB constituency is identified, it's possible to develop a framework to define the key dimensions that apply to SMB cloud planning and strategy.

The working group started by identifying the differences between three IT delivery options available to SMBs. The first, traditional infrastructure, is built on-site from hardware and software components. It is often managed internally (in some cases, with assistance from a third-party supplier who performs on-site maintenance), and provides local access and support for users. This type of infrastructure is in place in many small businesses and virtually all mid-sized businesses today. It has the advantage of providing (in some cases, more by osmosis than design) a consolidated source for infrastructure and applications. However, this is not an agile approach to IT. New workloads require capital investments, and therefore, generally demand extensive planning tied to a 3-5 year use case. They also require internal or contracted IT resources for set-up, deployment and support.

Buyers working with providers for hosted solutions (such as web sites) or applications have a different set of options, opportunities and constraints. It is generally much easier to add a service than to buy, integrate and deploy a component-based system. Hosted solutions are most often purchased on a "pay as you go" model, with firm commitments generally limited to a year or less, and with no capital outlay. They are provided as services, so there is less (or no) need for internal or contracted IT resources to deliver set-up, deployment and support. They are designed for remote access, and as a result, are often better suited to supporting mobile users than are systems based on traditional infrastructure. And at their core, hosted services represent a 'partnership' between the developer and the client: the supplier offers a solution to a defined issue, the buyer looks for this solution to address that issue within his/her business.

There are several potential drawbacks to the hosted solution model. Hosted solutions are as a rule well aligned with defined problems, but they are not generally very flexible:

buyers need to select a solution that meets their needs, or understand that they may need to modify their expectations in accordance with the constraints of the solution. Also, while each solution is managed by the provider, the integration between these systems, and between each system and the internal processes it is used to support, is the responsibility of the buyer. These issues aren't insurmountable, but they need to be considered when developing a cloud strategy and planning for its implementation.

Cloud infrastructure represents another IT option. Like hosted solutions, cloud infrastructure is delivered on-demand to SMB buyers; also like hosted solutions, cloud infrastructure is an operating rather than capital expense, and support of the offering is provided by the supplier.

However, there are some important differences between hosted solutions and cloud infrastructure. One is the opportunity for customization. While hosted solutions tend to be rigidly defined, cloud infrastructure providers frequently offer the ability to configure offerings to meet specific requirements. This may take the form of opting to use dedicated or shared (virtual private cloud) resources, and will generally also include options for processor, storage and memory capabilities and configurations, and sometimes, for specific software options (operating system, database, etc.). This flexibility allows cloud infrastructure customers to align the offering with their needs, and enables cloud infrastructure providers to align pricing with usage.

The most important difference between cloud infrastructure and hosted solutions is the extent of IT services required from the buyer. While a hosting provider takes responsibility for the infrastructure and the application, the cloud infrastructure provider only manages the core platform – the application is the responsibility of the client. As a result, cloud infrastructure is generally sold to, and used by, technical buyers who are capable of capitalizing on its agility and cost advantages. This group benefits especially from the ability to rapidly launch, scale up/down, and decommission virtual infrastructure. As is noted in Figure 3-2, this group also has a requirement to manage the sourcing and integration of the different applications developed or hosted on cloud infrastructure, and may well need to understand how to integrate (and secure, etc.) workloads and data sets that extend across traditional and cloud environments.

Situated between the definitions of traditional infrastructure and hosted solutions – and not included in Figure 3-2 – is colocation, in which a company places its own assets in a third party facility. This approach adds third-party facility management (and in some cases, third party asset support) to the traditional infrastructure approach. Although it is possible to host private cloud on assets housed within a colocation facility, this option is not included within the focus of the SMB cloud strategy working group.

Figure 3-2 combines the essential elements of SMB cloud planning/strategy.

*Figure 3-2. Planning for the cloud/cloud strategy for SMB: key issues*

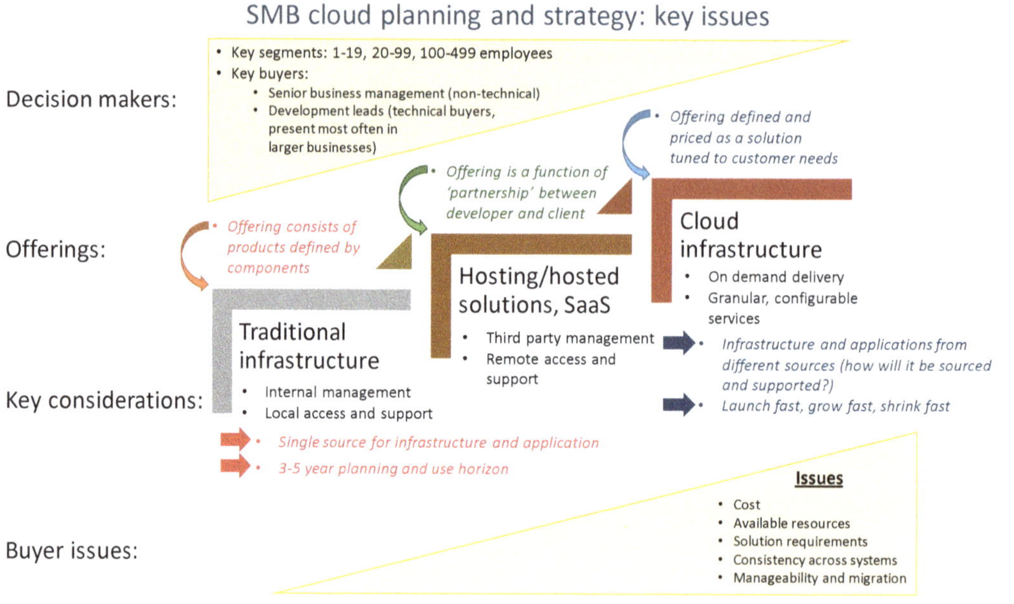

## SMB cloud planning and strategy: key issues

**Decision makers:**
- Key segments: 1-19, 20-99, 100-499 employees
- Key buyers:
  - Senior business management (non-technical)
  - Development leads (technical buyers, present most often in larger businesses)

*Offering is a function of 'partnership' between developer and client*

*Offering defined and priced as a solution tuned to customer needs*

**Offerings:**
*Offering consists of products defined by components*

**Cloud infrastructure**
- On demand delivery
- Granular, configurable services

**Hosting/hosted solutions, SaaS**
- Third party management
- Remote access and support

**Traditional infrastructure**

**Key considerations:**
- Internal management
- Local access and support

*Infrastructure and applications from different sources (how will it be sourced and supported?)*
*Launch fast, grow fast, shrink fast*

*Single source for infrastructure and application*
*3-5 year planning and use horizon*

**Issues**
- Cost
- Available resources
- Solution requirements
- Consistency across systems
- Manageability and migration

**Buyer issues:**

Source: TCBC/InsightaaS, 2016

## Key planning/strategy issues

What are the key issues that SMB cloud planning/strategy needs to consider, as firms look across this framework to identify the portfolio of products/services that best meets their business needs? The working group identified five key issues that are intrinsic to development of SMB cloud strategy:

- Cost: Cost is always an issue in business decisions, and especially so within SMBs. With cloud, though, cost takes on some additional meanings. Cost isn't only a reduction in overall expenditures on IT. Cost can relate to the missed revenue that will result from an inability to address new market demands. Cost could be a function of needing to recover from a catastrophic event (such as data loss) within the business. Cost can be related to a perception that competitors are pulling away, or simply a realization that business as usual is no longer enough – that traditional approaches are no longer effective. Cost can also be defined in terms of CAPEX vs. OPEX; in some environments (such as services firms), CAPEX avoidance and 'pay as you go' scale up is an important cost issue, while in others (for example, many manufacturing and energy environments), CAPEX allocated to physical products in lockstep with full order books or high oil prices is preferable to recurring costs that are not aligned boom and bust cycles. Cost, across these many dimensions, is an essential factor in building a cloud strategy.

- Available resources: For the most part, microbusinesses lack technical resources; in these situations, cloud offers a means of adding IT capacity without also adding internal or contracted headcount. In small and mid-sized businesses, cloud expands the impact of scarce IT resources. However, cloud is not a resource-free endeavour. Cloud requires an ability to connect new solutions to business user requirements, and to each other. Planning for support of cloud systems, especially as they increase in number and scope, is an important aspect of SMB cloud strategy development.
- Solution requirements: As is noted above, the options that are available to SMBs – especially, the hosted solutions that are the primary option for non-technical buyers – are relatively rigid: they will accommodate a predefined set of requirements and uses, but often can't be easily modified beyond these predefined parameters. It's essential for SMBs to understand the requirements associated with a solution, in terms of functionality and integration (both process and technical integration) in the development of a cloud plan.
- Consistency across systems is not an issue at the outset of cloud, but it becomes on as cloud scales across users and workloads. This is an especially important issue from an infrastructure perspective: have you identified an approach that will create an agile platform for future development and integration?
- Manageability and migration: the systems that enhance the productivity of non-technical users rely on data – often, on data that is resident in one form or another within the SMB today. SMBs are often (unpleasantly) surprised by the effort and cost involved in migrating data to new systems. SMBs that adopt

multiple cloud-based solutions may be further 'surprised' by the complexity of managing across multiple environments. A roadmap connecting the needs of the business with its cloud (and traditional) technology options and requirements is essential to minimizing surprise and maximizing manageability.

Figure 3-3 provides a representation of these key input factors to SMB cloud planning.

*Figure 3-3. Key input factors in SMB cloud planning and strategy*

Source: TCBC/InsightaaS, 2016

## Business objectives

Before venturing into the 'how' of cloud, SMBs need to answer a fundamental question: *why* would they embrace cloud-based resources? What drives the need to understand and invest in cloud services? The key planning/strategy issues description in the previous section identifies five factors (cost, available resources, solution requirements, consistency across systems, and manageability and migration) that shape the direction of SMB cloud initiatives. But what prompts the demand that makes these factors relevant to an SMB executive? Here are three sources of pressure that affect the SMB community, and ways in which cloud addresses these constraints.

## The desire to exert control over an uncertain business environment

SMB executives are sometimes seen as "small fish" in a pond that is also home to much larger creatures. They know, or have at least a sense, that they are subject to tides and actions that are understood only when they are felt: when business lags, when orders grow sparse, when supplier costs increase, when the competitive environment changes.

Cloud offers direct relief for several of these issues. In a very real sense, cloud delivers a degree of certainty and control over cost/performance and time. Cloud infrastructure and applications can be deployed rapidly, shrinking the time between decision and benefit. And cloud's costing system associates payments with use – meaning that the small business executive doesn't have to launch a new initiative by making a commitment of scarce capital to new systems and software, and then hoping for downstream results that are equal to or greater than the cost of operation plus the amortization expense over the depreciation period.

It's possible to make a further argument here: that the analytics that are embedded in cloud systems, and the analytics applications that are available via cloud and used to evaluate cloud-based data help further reduce business uncertainty. For SMB executives who understand how to work with data, this is true. It's likely the case that most SMB executives are not especially well versed in using data analytics to inform business decisions, so cloud-delivered analytics is probably more of a future than current means of managing business volatility. In the future, though, analytics will indeed prove to be another cloud-delivered benefit that helps SMB executives to exert greater control over their environment by increasing the transparency and predictability of their operations. SMBs that build systems that embed analytics capabilities can 'grow as they learn'; those that do not will be forced either to make future changes or to complete without the benefit of data-driven business insight.

There's a third point to be made in this context as well: that when it comes to electronic sales and marketing, cloud is both "the medium *and* the message." Cloud based systems (such as marketing automation and CRM) often connect seamlessly with online marketing channels, which can in turn be connected with cloud-resident content management systems integrated into hosted websites. SMBs rely on cloud-based systems to support both marketing and transactions, providing extended visibility into sales funnels and revenue.

## The need to manage technology as a business asset

Most SMB executives understand that technology plays a central role in their management processes. Many would also understand the notion that payback on any asset increases as you approach full utilization, and that economies of scale tend to benefit larger rather than smaller organizations.

Executives who understand IT enough to dig into their corporate infrastructure (or who work with third parties able to provide a window into use) will know that they can't realistically target optimal IT resource utilization. A small business has trouble consuming all of the capacity of new gear, meaning that they often pay for resources they aren't using. Those that do get to full utilization often have a different problem: systems that lack adequate storage, memory and compute capacity frequently crash, and SMBs aren't geared towards rapid deployment of new servers, storage and networking equipment. Even if they were, the SMB would know that it is paying some form of e-size premium: an SMB will never get to the purchase volumes needed to warrant large scale discounts.

Here again, cloud provides some intriguing options. An SMB using cloud works with a provider capable of sustaining high utilization levels, which reduces the per-cycle cost of the underlying assets. And a cloud provider is able to purchase new gear in greater volumes than an SMB – qualifying it for greater scale-based discounts – and is attuned towards more rapid, 'just in time' deployment of new systems. By centralizing workloads from multiple SMBs, cloud makes economies of scale attributes to firms that could not attain these benefits individually.

## The opportunity to expand the scope of skills

Every very small business, and even many larger SMBs, would concede that they are constrained by the staff they can engage. In all ways, this is a money issue, but it is manifested in several ways: SMBs lacking the funds to hire as many people as they would like, lacking the funds and business scope to hire and fully engage specialists with important domain knowledge, and/or lacking the funds to employ or develop more skilled staff across their current organizations.

The operations supporting cloud and cloud-based systems helps to reduce some of the frictions that impede SMBs from addressing these staff issues. Because cloud is delivered 'as a service', important functions are handled by the supplier, so that the

SMB doesn't have to dedicate employee budgets to IT staff with specialized skills that support core systems but don't meaningfully differentiate the company. Cloud applications generally embed operational expertise sourced from industry leaders, so the SMB is able to quickly adopt processes that have been vetted in other organizations. In addition, cloud-based systems have established fractional work as the norm in many sectors in the economy: with the collaboration capabilities that are implicit in advanced cloud applications (and with cloud-based collaboration systems), SMBs are able to integrate remote, part-time but specialized resources into their business processes.

*Figure 3-4. Sources of SMB cloud benefits*

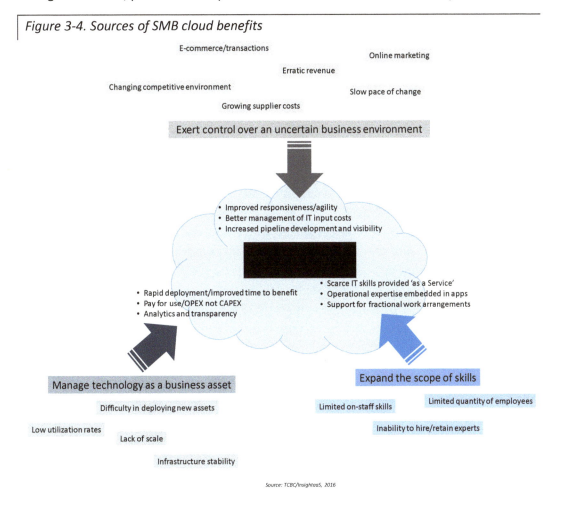

Source: TCBC/InsightaaS, 2016

## Best practices in SMB planning for the cloud/cloud strategy

It is especially difficult to draw a 'box' around strategy issues within SMBs: the connection between strategy and action is so direct in small businesses that a discussion of strategy and planning often migrates quickly into a discussion of tactics and execution. For firms that do want to work through the cloud planning process before jumping headlong into cloud (or even 'dipping a toe in' without understanding where the longer path might lead), the TCBC working group offers the following observations and advice:

### *Begin with a holistic approach to your business*

Strategy evolves differently in enterprise-scale businesses and SMB. Within enterprises, strategy is generally a discrete process leading to a defined and documented set of conclusions. SMBs approach the issue differently. Within SMBs, strategy is often integral to the vision of the founders/principals, and imbued into everyday activities. As a result, SMBs have the advantage of continuous connections between strategy and operations. However, the lack of distance between the founder/principal and his/her strategy can make it difficult to plot formal extensions of core beliefs.

This is an important point, because while cloud can be a source for a point solution or a series of point solutions, it functions best as an integrated aspect of overall business strategy. The productivity benefits associated with automating a single task can disappear if the task automation is disconnected from related operations/activities, and the lack of a connection between cloud and business objectives can weaken the skills and scale-related benefits associated with cloud adoption – and consequently, the pace and magnitude of cloud payback. Used correctly, cloud functions as a core element of your business infrastructure...and correct use requires a vision for how cloud integrates with business strategy.

### *Take the time to understand the data that will be used and produced by cloud systems – its dependencies and implications*

Non-IT professionals reacting to business pressure or opportunities can be tempted to pursue direct paths to the acquisition of new capabilities: for example, I need more productivity from my (engineering, sales, HR) professionals, so I will source a cloud-based system to accelerate their throughput. This approach is understandable in context, but may not be sustainable in practice. One key element of planning for the cloud is to understand the implications of remote data and processing. Will your engineers have access to high-speed connections, or will they be left waiting for access to large files? Will the increased funnel visibility gained by your sales force be counterbalanced by the need for mistake-prone manual entry of orders once they finalize deals? Are there data dependencies between internal systems – for example, between customer service and sales – which will be 'broken' if one of the processes is moved to a third-party SaaS application? Is it actually legal for your HR department to store healthcare-related information in another jurisdiction? And how would your business deal with a data breach or other form of data disclosure? Developing a detailed strategy addressing this issue is probably beyond the scope of most SMB cloud planning processes (it is better addressed as part of the Governance, Risk and Compliance process, and is covered by another TCBC working group), but these questions should be at least raised and considered in the cloud planning process.

This guidance can be applied not only to SMBs, but also to individual departments within larger organizations, which may function as SMBs that access services (such as HR) shared with allied entities. In this case, the IT motion is commonly labelled as "shadow IT." Despite its negative connotation in the technology world, shadow IT is not necessarily a bad thing: at root, it is really just a means by which business professionals deploy IT solutions to address pressing business needs. However, the same basic rules that apply to SMBs apply to departments embarking on shadow IT – and this guidance regarding understanding of data dependencies is even more important, since the shadow cloud systems will likely use and contribute to data that is shared with other parts of the enterprise.

### *Insist on data portability*
One other aspect of data in the cloud is so important that it needs to be addressed separately: data portability. The guidance in this section is intended to help an SMB establish a viable cloud strategy – to build a complete and relevant set of understandings around cloud use, to select the right suppliers, to work effectively with those suppliers over the long term to meet current business objectives and to create new opportunities. But, it isn't always the case that these 'best laid plans' yield the anticipated results: suppliers can disappear, be acquired or pivot into new businesses, relationships can fray for many reasons, and/or your own business objectives and requirements may morph over time. If for any reason, it's important for you to change your cloud strategy, it will be *really* important for you to obtain a current, clean copy of all of your cloud-resident data, and to ensure that your supplier retains no rights to

sensitive information. It's reasonable to insist on this being a clear expectation of a relationship before you sign a contract, but it can be trickier to insist upon when the relationship begins to erode. Establishing adequate portability for your data in advance of committing to a cloud-based system is an essential step in SMB cloud planning.

*Build an understanding of the full scope of the solution before committing to individual services, and look for approaches that allow for assembly of off-the-shelf components*
It is easy to commit to a single cloud service. It can be difficult to connect multiple cloud services together – but if your firm ends up using multiple disconnected systems, you both lose the potential benefit of exchanging information across applications (which enables automated workflows and greater visibility via analytics), and increase the cost and complexity of managing your cloud environment.

There are cloud platforms that are designed to attract and integrate multiple applications: you can find this sort of capability associated with Microsoft's Office 365 and Dynamics applications, with Google Docs, with Salesforce's Force.com, and in other application marketplaces and exchanges. A competent cloud broker can assemble multifaceted solutions by working with APIs (application programming interfaces) that provide 'hooks' between different software packages. And standard data formats can facilitate the use of outputs from one program as inputs to others. If you begin with an appreciation of what you want to accomplish when cloud is integrated across your entire business, you – and/or a broker you work with – can make more informed decisions about appropriate platform technologies that will support integration and manageability.

*Build a thorough understanding of costs and payback sources before committing to a specific strategy*
Cloud can be used to replace existing IT capacity, or to provide a cost-effective means of sourcing new IT capacity, or it (especially, SaaS solutions targeted at line of business buyers) can be used to automate tasks that are currently manual or poorly automated. Each scenario has a different set of cost implications, which should be documented and reviewed by IT and non-IT management prior to finalizing a cloud strategy. What are the service costs? The cost of establishing robust, redundant connections to the cloud supplier? The cost of having a 'plan B' in case the supplier's service is interrupted? And what are the equivalent costs for a comparable on-premise solution?

Payback scenarios also differ by cloud solution type. In particular, solutions that replace existing IT assets generally require fewer IT staff than on-premise alternatives, and solutions that automate business tasks may free up time dedicated to manual activities performed by current employees. What is the impact of these changes? Will IT or business staff focused on now-redundant tasks be let go, to reduce headcount and compensation expense? Will they be redeployed to tackle initiatives that expand the profitability of the business – and if so, where will they report, and where will their expense be budgeted? The 'right' answer varies from environment to environment, but whatever it is, it should be clear and documented. A vague assumption that greater productivity will provide amorphous benefit is unlikely to produce verifiable returns – and the impact of the cloud strategy will be harder to establish (and very likely, less than optimal) if the cost/benefit analysis is not established before a cloud initiative is funded.

*If you are a development lead, insist on granularity*
The economics of cloud make it possible to acquire infrastructure inexpensively, and the lack of clarity in multi-tenant environments can prompt technical users to secure virtual private servers (VMs) and other dedicated resources to enhance privacy and reduce the impact of "noisy neighbours." However, the VM approach is fraught with overhead: if physical servers are generally utilized at sub-10% capacity, so too are virtual private servers. The real benefit of cloud comes from capitalizing on shared resources. Instead of relying on VMs, take the time to understand how standards like OpenStack enable emerging software-defined infrastructure options. In this type of environment, you can access and manage virtual components (servers, storage, networking) on a granular level. This has the benefit of reducing costs over the long term (since VMs may prove expensive to scale) and improving the durability of the code you develop (since it will be native to the software-defined architecture that will continue to increase in presence over time).

*If you are a business buyer, avoid infrastructure investments wherever possible*
The advice above works for developers, but the smaller a business is, the less likely it is to have dedicated staff developing custom applications to support unique processes. Most SMBs avoid heavy investment in infrastructure staff (including IT), can't afford the cost of developing or maintaining custom applications, and have in any event adapted their business processes to run on readily available infrastructure. Given this backdrop, why would an SMB invest heavily in its *own* infrastructure? Technology investments are best directed at the SaaS applications that enable front-line staff to be more productive.

Practically speaking, it's probably not wise to pursue a policy of no infrastructure under any circumstances. For example, while it makes sense to use cloud services for storage, backup and business continuity, companies with sensitive or operationally important data are probably going to want to have their own copies of that data, independent of its existence in a hosted solution. There are a couple of good reasons for this: it's important to have access to business-critical data in the event that your cloud supplier experiences a major outage or goes out of business, and experience has shown that migrations from one supplier to another are easier to facilitate if the data is held by the customer rather than the supplier. However, these are specific uses cases that respond to specific requirements. In general, investments in business-relevant applications will provide better and faster returns than investments in infrastructure that needs to be managed by internal resources.

*Understand that an investment in a cloud strategy entails a partnership with cloud suppliers*

In traditional infrastructure, IT services are delivered and/or managed by corporate employees, and there is an innate shared commitment that links IT delivery and IT service consumption. With cloud, this dynamic changes. Services that are used by your business on a daily basis are managed and delivered by third parties – often, by people you've never met, at locations that you'll never see. There are advantages to this: cloud suppliers can access skilled resources that your SMB would have trouble hiring and retaining, they are able to develop deep domain expertise, they benefit from scale beyond what an SMB can develop on its own. However, the interdependency is a factor in business performance, and as a result, should be a factor in business planning as well.

The working group was clear on the need to establish a two-way set of expectations as part of the cloud planning process. As a cloud customer, you should expect – and confirm – that your supplier has the services, resources and commitment needed to sustain a position as a long-term partner. At the same time, your organization needs to make appropriate commitments to training, integration of cloud capabilities within your operations, and to effective relationship management with (and across) suppliers. Both the cloud seller and the cloud buyer should be able to articulate a plan for building and nurturing a long-term partnership. An agreement predicated entirely on up-front cost will likely deliver near-term savings, but may not provide the type of ongoing support required for the higher levels of payback associated with longer-term cloud use. In relationships involving substantial commitments on both sides, a supplier should be prepared to listen to what the buyer needs, and explain two things clearly: their (the supplier's) understanding of the buyer's requirements, and how (if?) the supplier's products/services will address the buyer's needs. The buyer in turn needs to appreciate that cloud offerings are not static: cloud suppliers add new features and capabilities much more rapidly than was the case with tradition product vendors. Part of what a buyer should be listening for is the fit between current services and current needs, but another important part of the message is the supplier's trajectory: are they rolling out services that are aligned with your evolving needs, and at what pace?

*Spend time understanding the implications of a shift from 'hands on' to 'vendor management'*

The partnership structure articulated in the previous paragraphs describes a high-level understanding of what is involved in working with a cloud supplier, but internally, SMBs need to take a further step to navigate the move to cloud. One of the biggest operational differences between cloud-based infrastructure and on-premise infrastructure is that cloud demands a shift in management approach. In an on-premise environment, IT management is very task focused: the manager needs to ensure that patches are applied, backups are completed and tested, security products are connected, upgrades and new equipment are deployed, etc. Especially in SMBs (as compared to enterprise environments), IT management is a very hands-on endeavour.

Infrastructure management in the cloud is a very different process. With cloud, there is an ongoing stream of activity around patches, backups, security, upgrades and new deployments, but these tasks are the responsibility of the cloud vendor. In most environments, the IT manager will still need to preside over (a more limited set of) on premise systems, but his/her focus will be largely dedicated to ensuring that cloud solutions are meeting the requirements of the business. IT management –whether provided by a technologist or a non-IT business leader – doesn't need to become immersed in the core technologies used to support the business, but these managers do need to understand whether/how supplier SLAs are aligned with existing and emerging needs. They need to stay abreast of changes – within the business, within the current supplier, or with respect to supplier alternatives – that might affect the optimal set of supply agreements. In brief, cloud infrastructure management is focused on outcomes rather than activities – and since some of those outcomes are delivered by suppliers, the most important set of skills involves vendor management rather than technology management.

### Have a migration strategy

This advice seems self-evident, but many SMBs 'assume' rather than 'actively plan for' the migration from legacy to cloud systems. Most companies will understand that data needs to be migrated, and will build a plan for ensuring that the data is assembled, backed up, and moved to the new environment. Many (but not all) will allocate time and attention to testing the data after it is migrated, to ensure that the new systems are working with complete and accurate inputs, and are delivering complete and accurate outputs.

But while a data strategy is necessary for cloud migration, it isn't sufficient to supporting the cloud initiative. If legacy software is moving to the cloud, it needs to be tested as well, and the licenses need to be evaluated to ensure that the environment can evolve with business needs. The communications infrastructure needs to be scaled to ensure reliable access to the cloud system, and it may be necessary to deploy redundant capacity. Backup and restore and security processes need to be documented and tested. Governance, risk and compliance policies and processes need to be extended to cover new cloud considerations.[5] And technical staff (and in the case of SaaS, business staff as well) will probably require training on new system features.

Migration strategy has a human element beyond training as well. One issue that is often overlooked, for example, is the impact that cloud can have on management scope and responsibilities. Suppose, for example, that two IT staff members who were working on server configuration and support will now be reassigned to developing advanced IT-powered business capability within non-IT business units (or replaced with staff members who are better able to perform this role). Do these employees still report to the IT manager? Will the IT manager be able to provide guidance to the staffers in this new role, and/or perform reviews that fairly evaluate their performance and impact? And if not, what will this mean to the career arcs of the employees and the IT manager? In many cases, realignment of resources creates issues for several different employees, and in an SMB, this type of employee uncertainty can echo through the business. This may not be the kind of issue that prevents cloud adoption, but it is the kind of issue that can affect the success of the cloud strategy, and which should be considered in the migration strategy.

---

[5] GRC is covered by a separate TCBC Best Practices working group. Please inquire if you need access to this guidance.

*Consider what happens when you leave – before you enter*

Very few SMBs work through the scenarios around exiting a provider relationship before they begin working with that provider, but experience shows that this level of forethought is an important element of cloud planning. If a business uses enough cloud services, or uses them for a long enough period, it will hit a point at which it needs to move on from a supplier. This can be harder in the cloud than it seems. The cloud provider is holding your data, and retrieving that data and migrating it to a new supplier (as is highlighted in the data portability section) may be more complex than simply asserting ownership and demanding that the information be released or moved. If you have customized a cloud application, you may find that the cloud provider is more than simply a host – many cloud contracts convey ownership of modifications to the service provider, and you may be unable to take code modifications with you when you migrate to a new supplier. And while most major cloud firms are very professional in their customer dealings, some suppliers are not, and will either not assist or will actually impede actions that move business from their firm to another supplier. Understand and document how potential issues will be handled in the event of a move to a new source; look particularly at processes (do we have them documented, or do they live only in the supplier's corporate memory), data rights and access, the handling of modifications, and dependencies between systems to make sure that you can continue to optimize the benefits of cloud by working with the suppliers who are best positioned to help your firm.

*Predicate your final decisions on business rather than technology objectives*

As much as cloud is considered a technology option, it is also a tool that can be applied to improving business outcomes – and as businesses are measured by outcomes, it makes sense to prioritize key business objectives in your plans. Investments in cloud can – and should – be aligned to deliver better productivity, better customer conversion rates, faster cycle times, broader customer engagement, and/or similar benefits. Simply put: if you, your staff and your suppliers can't identify the ways in which cloud can help your business to achieve tangible gains, you're having the wrong conversations with the wrong suppliers.

Figure 3-5 illustrates the key issues in building an SMB cloud plan that is consistent with these best practices.

*Figure 3-5. Best practices in SMB planning*

❑ Begin with a holistic approach to your business

❑ Take the time to understand the data that will be used and produced by cloud systems – its dependencies and implications

❑ Insist on data portability

❑ Build an understanding of the full scope of the solution before committing to individual services, and look for approaches based on off-the-shelf components

❑ Build a thorough understanding of costs and payback sources before committing to a specific strategy

❑ If you are a *developer*, insist on granularity
❑ If you are a *business buyer*, avoid infrastructure investments wherever possible

❑ Understand that an investment in a cloud strategy entails a partnership with cloud suppliers

❑ Spend time understanding the implications of a shift from 'hands on' to 'vendor management'

❑ Have a migration strategy

❑ Consider what happens when you leave – before you enter

❑ Predicate your final decisions on business rather than technology objectives

*Source: TCBC/InsightaaS, 2016*

## Metrics and milestones

One of the most difficult pieces of guidance to find in the literature around cloud is 'what are the milestones, and how long should it take to move from one to the next?' While the working group doesn't claim to have a definitive model that will apply to all

SMB cloud initiatives, it did produce guidance that is helpful to calibrating SMB cloud initiatives.

---

*Figure 3-6. Cloud milestones for SMB planning purposes – the annotated version*

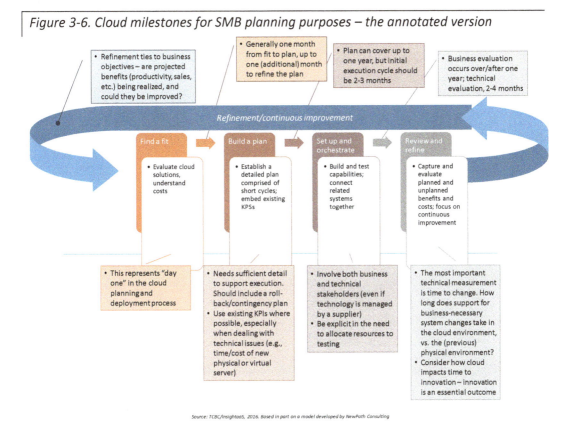

Source: TCBC/InsightaaS, 2016. Based in part on a model developed by NewPath Consulting

The model at the core of Figure 3-6 includes four steps, joined together in a cycle of ongoing refinement and continuous improvement.

The first step, "find a fit," describes the first step in launching a cloud initiative: the point at which a business sees a clear business and/or technical need for a cloud-based solution. This should be based (as per Figure 3-5) on a holistic view of your business, and should reflect an informed perspective on how data in the cloud can and should be managed. Management responsible for the cloud initiative should have invested the time needed to understand the scope of the proposed solution, the extent to which it is comprised of services that can be joined (e.g., via APIs) to create automation frameworks for more complex tasks in the future. Lastly, this step is not complete until the business and supplier have a common and documented understanding of the external costs involved, and the internal project owners have documented internal costs associated with the initiative.

The next step is to work with the provider to build a plan. Ideally, this framework will include some notion of a longer-term roadmap (covering multiple initiatives), and will drill down to a detailed plan that includes both delivery stages divided into short (anywhere from a couple of weeks to a month or two) execution cycles, and a rollback plan to support the business if the project is delayed or functionally inadequate. Where possible, the objectives in the pan should be linked to existing KPIs, so that the benefit of the cloud solution is apparent through the delivery process. In all, development of this plan should take 1-2 months, including refinement to ensure that the approach is well aligned with the needs, understandings and processes of the business.

The third step is delivery – set up of discrete capabilities, and (where appropriate/necessary) orchestration across these capabilities to provide support for multi-stage or complex processes. Initial delivery should be targeted at 2-3 months, so that the SMB receives near-term, tangible payback on the cloud initiative. The working group notes that in the rush to delivery, though, it's important to reserve time and resources for testing – modifying a live system is much more painful and costly than making adjustments to a system before it is in production.

Review and refinement helps to both prove and improve payback from cloud initiatives. On a technical level, the best way to assess cloud benefit is to evaluate how cloud has affected the time required to support business-necessary changes. Has cloud made it possible to improve agility by supporting development and rollout of new features? This should be apparent within the first 2-4 months of system deployment.

The 'bigger question' – has cloud improved our business outcomes? – is the most important objective of a cloud strategy. Each review cycle should include internal analysis of the effect the cloud system has had on the business processes it impacts. If the cloud initiative involves CRM, has there been a positive effect on sales volumes, sales cycle time and sales predictability? If it involves customer service, is there evidence that productivity has improved and that customers are happier? These types of improvements take time – often, years – to be fully apparent, but management can track relevant metrics on a quarterly or annual schedule, and can use the insights gleaned from this analysis to refine the system and associated business processes, and to ensure that their SMB obtains maximum benefit from the cloud.

## Reference sources

Reference sources that may be helpful in illustrating cloud planning context, business benefit and best practices for the SMB include:

- Keith Button. "Considering the Cloud." CFO Magazine, 2015. A good article that highlights some of the financial and other business considerations that are important to – and driving – cloud adoption.
- Aaron Dignan. "The Operating Model That Is Eating The World." The Ready, 2013. This post provides a remarkably durable view of how cloud affects industry-operating norms, and how this affects a strategy process that moves across purpose, process, people, product and platform.
- Data Driven Marketing: B2B inbound marketing metrics. Ascend2 and NetProspex, 2014. Many SMBs understand that extending cloud-based activity beyond internally focused applications to externally facing sales and marketing systems is an important cloud-related opportunity, but this is not a widely understood area. This report provides clear insight into current issues in inbound marketing.
- G2 Crowd. This site contains business software reviews that may be helpful to SMBs looking to identify or assess cloud applications.
- Advanced Cloud Application Adoption and Enablement: A TCBC Best Practices Document. Toronto Cloud Business Coalition, 2016. This is an article describing a report that outlines the keys to capitalizing on cloud applications. Prominent in the analysis is the importance of analytics and collaboration technology, which are (according to the report) central to the definition of "advanced cloud application."

*Chapter 4.*

# Delivering Cloud via Public, Private and Hybrid Environments

Essential guidance supporting decisions aimed at aligning cloud modes with business requirements

*Contributing community experts: Roy Hart (Seneca College), Jeff Cohen (KFC and Pizza Hut Canada), Tracey Hutchison (Cisco), Joel Steacy (VMware Canada), Craig McLellan (ThinkOn), Norman Sung (Red Hat), Marcus Cziesla (Red Hat)*

*Initial publication date: January 2016*

# Delivering Cloud via Public, Private and Hybrid Environments

## Definition and context

The TCBC Delivering Public, Private and Hybrid Cloud Working Group recognizes that a hybrid model for IT service delivery is the reality for most organizations, except, perhaps, for the smaller business that may find reliance on public cloud services a simpler option. But hybrid IT, or hybrid cloud environments, are also the most complex to manage: while legacy systems, processes and thinking may inhibit cloud adoption, different user groups that are increasingly involved in procurement decisions may opt for siloed cloud application delivery without regard for the organization's broader technical or overall process goals. A primary objective of the working group is to identify and address key issues in the acquisition and management of complex hybrid cloud resources, to inform and support further adoption.

Since its inception, the term 'cloud' has been variously interpreted depending on the user or provider's perspective; however, flexible use of the word has only added to the complexity surrounding the technology. To clarify, the working group has focused on adoption hurdles impacting use of cloud technologies that deliver highly scalable, on-demand services that can support new business models. These include: multi-tenant, public cloud services (SaaS or IaaS); private cloud, including on-premise and hosted deployments that feature

*The working group envisions cloud as an evolutionary process or roadmap towards the delivery and consumption of IT as a business services, as opposed to cloud as a collection of infrastructure components.*

automation, on-demand self-service for the end user, and metering capabilities that enable cost management; and simultaneous deployment of one or more of these, or hybrid cloud. The working group's definition of cloud does not extend to highly virtualized data centre environments or to IT managed services. These exclusions are based on a view of cloud that envisions an evolutionary process or roadmap towards the delivery and consumption of IT as a business service, as opposed to cloud as a collection of infrastructure components.

A good analogy that illustrates the working group's differentiation of cloud from other deployment models can be found in acquisition of different vehicle services. Buying a car (likened to traditional on-premise infrastructure) might entail a large investment but can help the consumer manage multiple requirements over time; shorter term needs for a new vehicle can be fulfilled with little upfront investment through car rental (IT hosting services); while hailing a taxi (cloud) allows the passenger to instantly manage unpredictable, sometimes short travel demands, or set up a scheduled ride program, paying only for the ride when it is taken and sharing cab expense with other riders. Each of these procurement examples offer different business outcomes, but the taxi provides the best opportunity for an individual to order up access to a pool of cab resources that have been optimized by an automated dispatch program.

The working group believes that there is a set of key issues that define the Canadian opportunity for cloud delivery. These issues, which span technology considerations and the interplay of business and IT requirements in the adoption of public, private and hybrid cloud in the Canadian marketplace, are as follows:

1. **Opting for various cloud deployment models**
   - When opting for one deployment model over another, how can the user organization prioritize the right decision factors?
   - How do the following affect decisions to run public, private or hybrid IT infrastructure?
     - Existing infrastructure
     - Data requirements
     - Type of application
     - Need to scale
     - Financial flexibility

2. **The role of provider location**
   - When sourcing a cloud supplier, Canadian organizations may face technical challenges such as latency – the need for speed of light in accessing data – but trust in a provider that resides outside Canada is the primary obstacle to public cloud adoption. What guidelines around data residency can be developed to support users sourcing domestic or international (US) infrastructure?

- How does the availability of local cloud resources affect the decision to build private infrastructure or contract public services?

3. **Developing cloud readiness**
   - What must IT do to prepare for cloud deployment: what steps can be taken to build infrastructure in a way that aligns with business need for agility and cost reduction?
   - How can business user expectations be managed, with respect to customization or other features/capabilities that may be different in on-premise, private infrastructure and public cloud services?
   - How is it possible to shrink the gap between the business user's cost/benefit analysis of cloud and the technologists' view of cloud value?

4. **Managing Shadow IT**
   - How can organizations monitor the use of cloud applications that may not be supported by IT in order to limit their potential risk impact?
   - What guidance can be provided to help companies reconcile the LOB's cloud agility needs with IT security and governance oversight?

5. **Cloud standards and promotion of data portability/systems interoperability**
   - What process, procedure, or technology can organizations deploy to support simultaneous management of multiple cloud environments?
   - What best practices work to ensure seamless access and simplify management of data and applications that might reside in on-premise infrastructure and one or more public clouds?

6. **Canadian specific challenges**
   - Do the lack of Canadian IaaS suppliers or the high cost of bandwidth relative to the US impact cloud adoption?
   - What steps can be taken to address the lag in Canadian cloud adoption?

These six issues are reflected in Figure 4-1.

---

*Figure 4-1. Defining the hybrid IT organization*

**Hybrid IT**
- Organizations deploy workloads on a combination of public, private and hybrid clouds, maintaining process consistency

**Traditional infrastructure**
- Legacy systems, processes and thinking inhibit cloud adoption

Six key issues

✓ Decision factors: scale, workload, application type, existing infrastructure, financial flexibility…
✓ Location: Latency, need for data residency…
✓ Cloud readiness: for IT: integration of self-service into private infrastructure; for users: alignment of expectations with real-world business options and constraints
✓ Shadow IT: methods of ensuring that user-driven cloud activities are connected with business standards for security, audit, control…
✓ Cloud standards: Processes, procedures and technologies supporting integration and management across multiple cloud environments, and between traditional and cloud environments
✓ Canada-specific issues: How does a relatively-small domestic IaaS supplier community and the relatively high cost of bandwidth affect Canadian adoption?

**User-driven cloud adoption**
- Siloed application delivery is not aligned with broader technical goals and processes

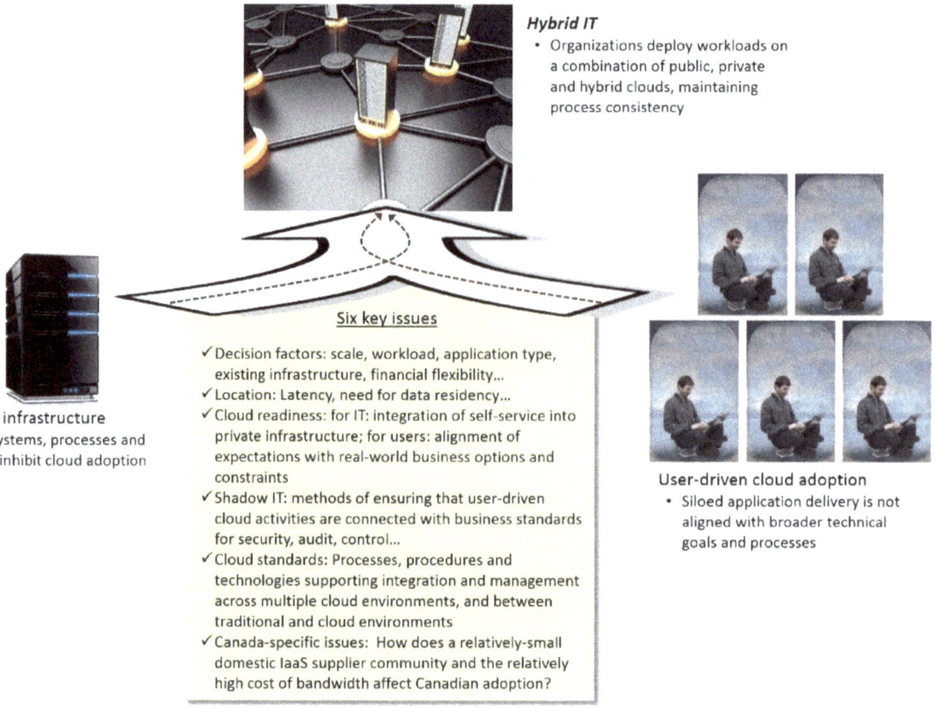

Source: TCBC/InsightaaS, 2015

---

## Business objectives and benefits

Confusion around cloud terminology, the use cases for various cloud modes and how these might work together has led to what the working group calls a "market education knowledge gap" in Canadian businesses, which contrasts with the understanding of US counterparts. Technical people in the industry have done a good job of outlining the potential for savings gained through high levels of virtualization and reduced maintenance/CAPEX via the shift of some share of virtual machines off-site to a hoster's infrastructure. However, less focus has been placed on communicating the broader opportunity that is available through optimal use of public, private and hybrid cloud, and their alignment with business issues and needs. It is the working group's contention that hybrid cloud – as opposed to remote hosting with some on-premise resources – can deliver new levels of organizational agility, market competitiveness, and support for innovation that extend beyond cost savings. These business benefits may be achieved through alignment of organizational objectives with the following cloud/hybrid cloud capabilities.

## Temporary workloads

"Cloud is fantastic with temporary workloads," observed one member of the working group, as it can support a business's fluctuating need for IT infrastructure. There are several good examples of situations where businesses require support for variable workloads, including seasonal business requirements or IT to support a particular market campaign, and test/dev environments where virtual machines can be quickly spun up (or down) to deliver temporary resources for the testing of new products and services in advance of launch to production. In these scenarios, the business pays only for resources used, when they are used. But cloud-enabled test/dev also enables more rapid time to market, and encourages a culture of innovation by reducing the cost of failure. With cloud, it is possible for businesses to 'fail fast' with less expense.

Cloud resources to fulfill variable need can be built as on-premise clouds, but also accessed through 'bursting' to additional infrastructure in third-party, public cloud services. Bursting is easier, the group notes, when the organization has already moved to cloud architectures, and when data resides in places that are accessible via cloud networks. Hybrid cloud – defined as "the best of both worlds" – can solve for both of these challenges, though the working group points to considerable process and technology change associated with the proper implementation of hybrid environments. While many organizations prefer to rely on public or on private cloud resources as there is uncertainty around the linking of internal and external resources, it is potentially the best approach for managing temporary workloads.

## Meeting on-demand requirements

Cloud's ability to deliver IT services on-demand is commonly viewed as an operational benefit, which provides the organization with fast and reliable access to data and applications. By shortening the time for IT procurement, delivery, installment and configuration required in traditional environments, cloud can have significant impact on an organization's ability to bring a product to market or enter new or adjacent markets to drive competitive advantage. On-demand resources can also generate significant cost savings, through reduced CAPEX and OPEX in public cloud deployments, while requiring payment only for those resources used. According to the working group, this approach is less ubiquitous than the business benefits would suggest it should be, as in some enterprises, accounts payable and procurement departments are not yet set up to handle on-demand service delivery. But from an operations and services delivery perspective, on-demand represents "the highest common denominator" for cloud.

## Self-service

The working group has defined automation/programmability and self-service, meaning the customer can access resources as needed through on online portal or web interface, as the "litmus test" for cloud services. Resources that are not self-service driven become managed services. Self-service provisioning offers two benefits: it can improve operational agility by offering different groups within the organization quick means to access IT resources, thereby reducing bottlenecks that build as traditional IT struggles with fewer staff and financial resources to fulfill increasing demand for IT resources; and it also enables departmental/business unit charge back for IT, to introduce more fiscal responsibility and better alignment of demand and budgetary resource for IT services.

## Scale

An organization's ability to quickly scale up or scale out IT resources when needed is an oft-cited benefit of cloud computing that relates directly to enablement of business growth. Scale via public cloud vs. on-premise build is in many ways a financial decision that must take into account business circumstances. For example, cloud can offer enormous flexibility to accommodate temporary workloads. In other cases, a financial assessment may indicate that large-scale need for resources over the long term would be better served through the building of on-premise, private cloud or virtual infrastructure. In this evaluation, an organization's preference for one form of financial structure over another may be a determining factor – for example, a preference for operating expense, which is more often the case in a smaller or mid-sized organization, or for capital investment, which is more readily available in a large enterprise with significant need for scale. As one member of the working group observed, "larger organizations are often CAPEX friendly, and OPEX allergic."

**Figure 4-2. Hybrid business objectives, benefits and requirements**

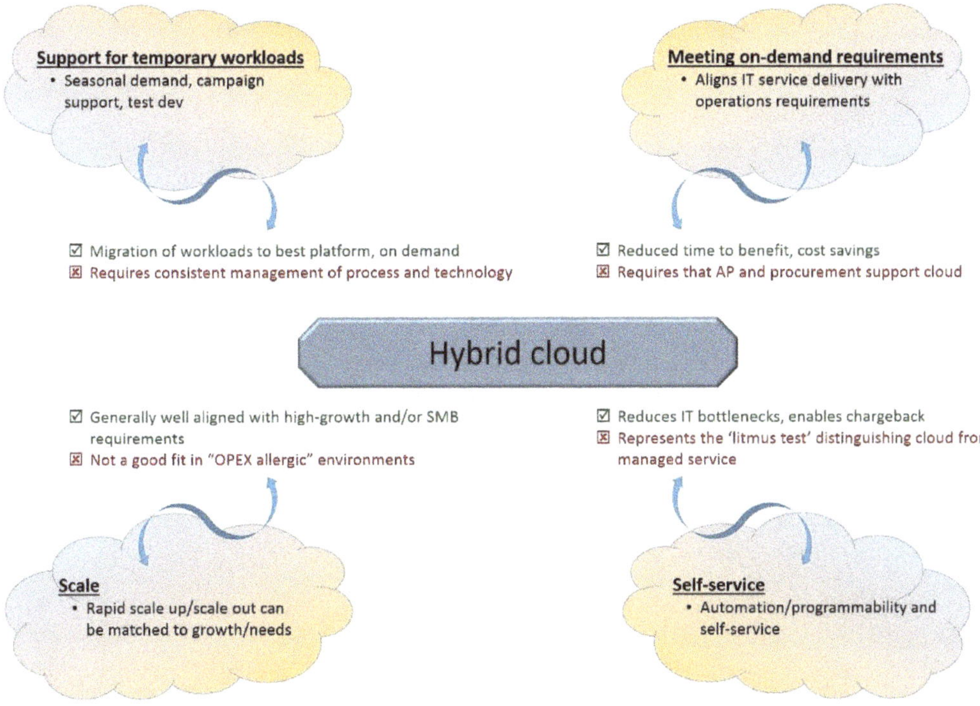

**Support for temporary workloads**
- Seasonal demand, campaign support, test dev

☑ Migration of workloads to best platform, on demand
☒ Requires consistent management of process and technology

**Meeting on-demand requirements**
- Aligns IT service delivery with operations requirements

☑ Reduced time to benefit, cost savings
☒ Requires that AP and procurement support cloud

### Hybrid cloud

☑ Generally well aligned with high-growth and/or SMB requirements
☒ Not a good fit in "OPEX allergic" environments

☑ Reduces IT bottlenecks, enables chargeback
☒ Represents the 'litmus test' distinguishing cloud from managed service

**Scale**
- Rapid scale up/scale out can be matched to growth/needs

**Self-service**
- Automation/programmability and self-service

*Source: TCBC/InsightaaS, 2015*

As the points above suggest, public cloud, private cloud and hybrid cloud approaches each offer unique business benefit to the adopting organization. While public services can deliver rapid scale for temporary workloads or support smaller businesses that find appeal in OPEX procurement models, private cloud can deliver scale at better cost in some circumstances, while hybrid cloud offers better, faster access to formerly siloed sources of information. In each case, cloud capabilities, including automation, programmability, self-service access to on-demand resources and consumption metering, can help transform IT from a cost centre to business enabler. The key to successful implementation is to identify the most appropriate cloud model for particular circumstances and leverage cloud capabilities to meet business objectives, while at the same time planning and managing to mitigate potential issues with cloud migration. In the best practices section below, issues such as the need to match workload requirements with the appropriate cloud technology, to address an organization's data residency requirements, to reduce management complexity and match user expectations of cloud with IT delivery to mitigate problems shadow IT, and to ensure hybrid cloud interoperability are discussed in greater detail.

## Best practice and process in delivering cloud via public, private and hybrid environments

### Opting for various cloud deployment models: key factors in the decision process

Cloud computing resources come in multiple varieties – on-premise private cloud, hosted private cloud, public cloud or hybrid cloud deployment. To ensure the deployment mode chosen is most appropriate to organizational circumstances, or can meet individual IT project requirements, adopting businesses must consider a number of decision criteria. For example, a large corporation with significant investment in IT infrastructure and skilled staff resources is likely to choose differently than would a small start-up organization. In the list below, the TCBC Delivering Public, Private and Hybrid Cloud working group has identified key decision factors that address infrastructure, scale requirements, and data and application needs in addition to different approaches that emerge out of business size. While the weight of these factors in decision making by different companies will vary according to the adopting organization's unique needs and situation, discussion of the criteria below may serve as a guideline for organizations planning for the optimal mix of cloud deployment models.

#### *Existing infrastructure*

Investments in existing IT infrastructure will play an important role in decisions around cloud computing and around specific cloud model adoption. A large, established enterprise that operates a highly sophisticated and highly virtualized environment will be best positioned to build out a private cloud and may need to leverage IT asset value over time. The cloud native start-up, on the other hand, may have less inclination to devote CAPEX to IT equipment or software licenses, and be more sensitive to the need for speed to market and the alignment between cost and use that cloud deployment can uniquely deliver.

The relative efficiencies of existing environments should also be taken into account: a 2014 NRDC study of US data centre infrastructure has found that if many of the large cloud server farms are highly efficient, these account for only 5 percent of data centre activity, while the other 95 percent of facilities are run by small, medium sized or corporate multi-tenant operators, where the average server runs at 12 to 18 percent capacity. The same study also found that average server utilization rates in highly efficient cloud service provider environments was 40 percent, a finding that indicates where most energy consumption and cost savings may be won. The working group estimates that public cloud deployment represents a quarter of the cost of running the same workload on in-house cloud infrastructure.

The working group recommends that cloud discussions begin with an assessment of current infrastructure, and the alignment of existing assets with business goals. In many cases, this discussion represents more migration path than a single decision: for example, an organization may operate with existing infrastructure, but rather than continue to make the same infrastructure investments on an annual basis, may transition to a hybrid IT environment, moving new workloads or projects to IaaS, while writing off aging infrastructure. While this path is not inexorable – the working group contends that hybrid IT, and hybrid cloud will be the dominant deployment model for some time to come – it is likely that a shift towards cloud will gather momentum, particularly in the small to medium sized company segments.

### Data classification
The type of data to be stored and processed in cloud infrastructure and applications and the security requirements associated with it are a critical starting point for discussion of cloud models. An organization's customer data, for example, is highly sensitive from both competitive and privacy perspectives and would require high levels of security that many organizations feel is best provided on site, or hosted in a private cloud. Similarly, information that is core to company operations, such as financial or PCI data, may be viewed as a good candidate for private on-premise or hosted private clouds, which promise higher levels of control and data reporting functionality. However, this view assumes that the user organization is able to execute the appropriate security requirements through reliance on internal resources, a proposition that may not hold in all cases. Many public providers have more robust governance, audit and security departments and functionality than do their cloud customers, and have managed to build competitive advantage based on their security capabilities. When looking to host sensitive data in public clouds, or to use public cloud infrastructure for bursting to additional capacity in hybrid scenarios, it is critical that the user do proper due diligence to understand the provider's security credentials and capabilities, SLAs for availability, and have security responsibilities on the part of user and provider clearly detailed in contractual agreements for each stage of data-in-motion. As one working group

member put it, "The more sensitive the data, the more important your choice of vendor is."

Other data sets may be less sensitive from operations, competitive or legal liability perspectives and hence better suited to a shared service model. As example, the working group points to communications or email applications, where there is no apparent value to hosting common data in private cloud infrastructure, and where financial/operational benefits available through outsourcing.  In the case of CRM or HR, data may be sensitive, but there are application service providers in the marketplace that are able to deliver security as well as specialized functionality.

Opting for cloud deployment models based on data type is a joint business activity that is best undertaken through the cooperation of security and governance groups and individual business departments within the organization who classify the data based on sensitivity and criticality, and with the support of engineering and operations workers who are better able to address technical infrastructure issues. In a smaller business, which is unlikely to staff these roles in-house, the working group recommends work with a third party specialist to consult on data classification and the security provisions that should be in place for different data types, and potentially with a specialist security provider that can monitor network systems and alert the cloud user on potential risk.

*Type of application*

Cloud application deployment and SaaS services offer the potential to improve agility in an increasingly broad array of business functions, and are now being adopted by many different departments across the organization. As recent research from InsightaaS shows, SaaS task automation is now applied to over 40 functions ranging from IT to corporate to customer-facing activities spanning IT, back office and front office requirements.

## Figure 4-3. SaaS automation options

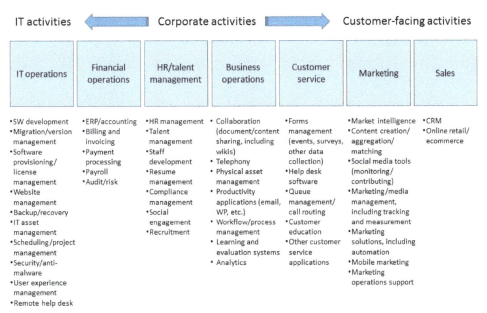

IT activities ⟵ Corporate activities ⟶ Customer-facing activities

| IT operations | Financial operations | HR/talent management | Business operations | Customer service | Marketing | Sales |
|---|---|---|---|---|---|---|

- •SW development
- •Migration/version management
- •Software provisioning/license management
- •Website management
- •Backup/recovery
- •IT asset management
- •Scheduling/project management
- •Security/anti-malware
- •User experience management
- •Remote help desk

- •ERP/accounting
- •Billing and invoicing
- •Payment processing
- •Payroll
- •Audit/risk

- •HR management
- •Talent management
- •Staff development
- •Resume management
- •Compliance management
- •Social engagement
- •Recruitment

- • Collaboration (document/content sharing, including wikis)
- • Telephony
- • Physical asset management
- • Productivity applications (email, WP, etc.)
- • Workflow/process management
- • Learning and evaluation systems
- • Analytics

- •Forms management (events, surveys, other data collection)
- •Help desk software
- •Queue management/call routing
- •Customer education
- •Other customer service applications

- •Market intelligence
- •Content creation/aggregation/matching
- •Social media tools (monitoring/contributing)
- •Marketing/media management, including tracking and measurement
- •Marketing solutions, including automation
- •Mobile marketing
- •Marketing operations support

- •CRM
- •Online retail/ecommerce

But to ensure that data and insight contained within these applications are not siloed, that the enterprise is able to take best advantage of the synergies available through orchestration of cloud assets, the working group advises adopters to consider SaaS deployment from the perspective of the application's ability to integrate with other business apps, processes or services. An application's integration points are critical in hybrid deployments as well: for example, the enterprise may need a cloud-based CRM or financial application to port data to an on-premise data warehouse, to enterprise management or project management applications or to another cloud-based application. Standalone applications may be easily deployed on cloud infrastructure; however, the need to integrate that application with many different environments, to set up a VPN, or source and code to APIs, can introduce considerable complexity and/or latency issues as data upload and download consumes additional time.

While integration capability varies from application to application, the working group lists unified communications, email, instant messaging and video, and some CRM tools with well-developed APIs as platforms with advanced interoperability capabilities. On the business side of the house, this list would include logistics and scheduling tools that are online and integrate to back end systems, as well as help desk software, monitoring software, and ITSM on the infrastructure side. Applications that are less well suited to cloud deployment would include programs that rely on tight integration, such as warehouse management systems that are closely integrated with financial systems, or POS applications that integrate with warehouse management and financial systems or other procurement apps.

## *Scale decisions*

Cloud's ability to enable user organizations to rapidly scale additional compute capacity is a widely touted benefit of the technology. While the addition of SaaS seats through online portals has become virtually instantaneous, at the infrastructure level, new virtual machine instances can be spun up very quickly to accommodate flexible demand for IT services. The working group believes that using a cloud provider to address scale requirements is generally easier than building automated provisioning and configuration internally: with many providers, the customer can easily set thresholds stipulating server utilization rates at which it's time to add more servers. No cloud infrastructure is limitless in terms of capacity; however, with more users and more infrastructure optimized for efficiency and resource pooling, the public provider is typically better equipped to service cloud-bursting demand than are internal environments. In addition, cloud scale may also be easier to achieve by running infrastructure and systems simultaneously in the same cloud. To illustrate, one working group member explained that if you host your website on public infrastructure and to achieve better performance use a content manager to help cache images across the country, scale will be much easier to reach if the public provider also hosts the content delivery network.

Decisions around scale potential on different cloud platforms should also be informed by financial considerations. While public cloud offers impressive flexibility, there is a scale at which this option may not make sense from an accounting perspective, and the working group advises organizations to make the appropriate financial calculation. For example, if study shows that it is less costly to buy hardware and build the internal cloud needed for 2,500 and 3,000 Linux hosts, then when 15,000 hosts are needed – for a longer period of time – the decision for on-site, private cloud is even more clear. In smaller environments, hosted services are likely more economical, especially for temporary workloads; however, the economics will be different for an organization with 65,000 users and thousands of servers.

## Financial flexibility

Beyond issues of scale, an organization's decision for public, private or hybrid cloud will depend on preferences or requirements in financial structuring. For many businesses, the ability to 'pay-as-you-go' or pay for resources that are consumed when they are consumed, that is available via subscription models offered by public providers will provide financial flexibility that is vital to operations. Other, typically larger organizations, however, may prefer to avoid this type of operational expense as it impacts profit and loss on a monthly basis. The CAPEX involved in building private cloud internally may represent a better proposition for companies that wish to capitalize expense over a three to five year period, and for large public companies in particular, which may deduct equipment expense directly from the bottom line to demonstrate greater profitability on a quarterly basis.

A key addendum to the CAPEX approach, however, is operational cost, a factor that is often neglected when organizations are determining the optimal cloud delivery mechanism. True cost, the working group notes, would need to include an assessment of utilization rates with existing infrastructure and associated energy expense (40 percent utilization is the average for cloud service providers), as well as set up labour and ongoing maintenance expenses as contributors to the overall cost of cloud projects. While true cost is difficult to determine with exact certitude, it should also include potential loss associated with risk, or with the internal IT department's relative ability to address uptime, compliance or security requirements. The cost of downtime varies greatly from business to business – estimates range from Gartner's $5,600 per minute to the Ponemon Institute's $7,900 per minute – but can cause significant financial distress, while the fines and loss of trust/reputational risk resulting from data breech may also extract heavy penalties that should factor into decisions over cloud delivery capabilities. Beyond the "sticker price" of driving workloads into cloud, the working group noted higher value factors that can have significant potential impact. Sticker price comparisons, for example, may not account for the challenges in ensuring transparency from security or compliance experts within the organization who may operate based on different assumptions and according to different incentives. The group's belief that treating public cloud services as commodity is misleading as it encourages neglect of these important operational cost factors and risk.

Related to this discussion of OPEX vs. CAPEX models for funding IT resources is the shift within many organizations away from resource procurement by the IT department to the business unit manager who may make purchases, of SaaS applications in particular, out of operating budgets. This outreach to third-party cloud-based providers is designed to circumvent bottlenecks that may occur in internal IT service delivery, when IT is unable to meet business expectations for speed and ease of deployment. As drivers of company revenues, marketing and advertising divisions, for example, are making an increasingly vocal argument that as users of the application and owners of the data, and as holders of necessary budgets, they should have increasing responsibility for IT purchases. In many larger organizations where security and governance policies have been extended to cloud scenarios, adoption by individual business units is permitted as long as policy requirements are met.

Figure 4-4 aligns these best practices considerations to illustrate the different points at which specific enterprise contexts and objectives may indicate movement to a public or private cloud approach, as well as the 'wild cards' that impact each decision point.

### Figure 4-4. Navigating the public/private/hybrid decision process

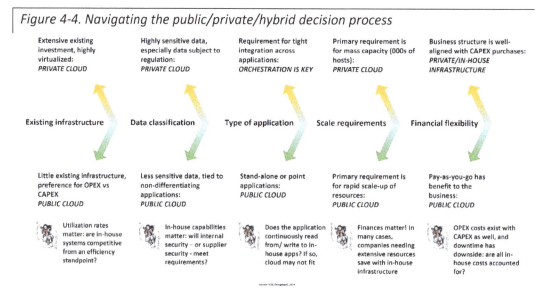

| Extensive existing investment, highly virtualized: *PRIVATE CLOUD* | Highly sensitive data, especially data subject to regulation: *PRIVATE CLOUD* | Requirement for tight integration across applications: *ORCHESTRATION IS KEY* | Primary requirement is for mass capacity (000s of hosts): *PRIVATE CLOUD* | Business structure is well-aligned with CAPEX purchases: *PRIVATE/IN-HOUSE INFRASTRUCTURE* |
|---|---|---|---|---|
| **Existing infrastructure** | **Data classification** | **Type of application** | **Scale requirements** | **Financial flexibility** |
| Little existing infrastructure, preference for OPEX vs CAPEX *PUBLIC CLOUD* | Less sensitive data, tied to non-differentiating applications: *PUBLIC CLOUD* | Stand-alone or point applications: *PUBLIC CLOUD* | Primary requirement is for rapid scale-up of resources: *PUBLIC CLOUD* | Pay-as-you-go has benefit to the business: *PUBLIC CLOUD* |
| Utilization rates matter: are in-house systems competitive from an efficiency standpoint? | In-house capabilities matter: will internal security – or supplier security - meet requirements? | Does the application continuously read from/ write to in-house apps? If so, cloud may not fit | Finances matter! In many cases, companies needing extensive resources save with in-house infrastructure | OPEX costs exist with CAPEX as well, and downtime has downside: are all in-house costs accounted for? |

## Evaluating hybrid management strategy

The five decision criteria highlighted in Figure 4-4. demonstrate some of the issues that determine whether private, public or hybrid might represent an appropriate strategy for the enterprise. There is another set of issues, though, that is equally important to implementing best practice in cloud delivery strategy: the availability of appropriate supply sources, the extent to which a company's internal practices and culture align with cloud, the means to building optimal hybrid IT or hybrid cloud operation and management. These issues serve as the underpinning to executing on the decision process shown above, while impacting the success of cloud deployment.

## The role of provider location

Few topics in cloud have elicited more, or more persistent discussion, than the location of the cloud provider's data centre facility, and potentially, the customer's data. At a technical level, cloud economies of scale depend on workload balance across infrastructure devoted to servicing end user departments and branch locations in the case of private clouds, and in public clouds, on the balance of workloads across regional boundaries. In public environments, location is essentially immaterial from a technology perspective, and cloud operates most efficiently through the creation of vast pools of compute capacity that can optimize sharing of resources, and with it, the cost of computing for adopting organizations. The more sharing of resources, the greater the potential benefit to customers. This promise has been reflected in the commoditization of Infrastructure-as-a-Service resources, and recent price wars amongst the large, global suppliers. But while both demand for cloud services and investment in resources have dictated the construction of massive public cloud offerings south of the border, for the Canadian market, access to these global clouds presents challenge on the legal, perceptual and networking fronts.

In Canada, there are two federal privacy laws that impact data storage: the Privacy Act, which imposes obligations on federal departments and agencies to protect citizens' privacy rights by limiting the collection, use and disclosure of personal information, and the Personal Information Protection and Electronic Documents Act (PIPEDA), which sets ground rules for use of personal information by private sector organizations in the course of commercial activities. On June 18, 2015, Canadian Parliament passed into law an amendment to PIPEDA, the Digital Privacy Act, which introduces new data breach notification requirements. This Federal legislation applies to commercial operations across Canada, except in the case of provinces (such as British Columbia, Alberta and Quebec) that have implemented their own private sector privacy legislation.

As these laws relate to cloud, stricter controls on the use, access and management of data contained in Canadian legislation relative to the US legislation have meant that several government agencies, including healthcare organizations, have imposed local data residency requirements – or the storage of data within Canadian, or even provincial jurisdictions. The conviction that Canadian data is safer on Canadian digital ground has been reinforced by passing of the US Patriot Act, which allows US authorities greater right to subpoena and access data than does Canadian legislation, and by the revelations of ex-CIA agent Edward Snowden, who provided evidence of the National Security Agency's determination to take advantage of its right (or wrongs!) to monitor the data transmissions of international governments and citizens as they cross US territory.

If privacy and security requirements in governmental legislation are clear, decisions over choice of cloud provider for businesses operating in Canada have been less so due to factors such as the paucity, until very recently, of enterprise-scale Canadian service provider facilities, the continued vulnerability of US company data to subpoena by US authorities when these opt to store data in Canadian facilities, and a general gap in understanding of the scope of legislation and its applicability to an organization's data assets. For example, while the government of British Columbia's FOIPPA legislation requires that government data be stored locally, this is not necessarily the case for private sector data. And while provisions of the US Patriot Act have served as bell weather on many data privacy discussions, Canadian authorities have similar access rights to Canadian information. One point that is clear though, is that misperceptions around legislation have had the impact of inhibiting cloud adoption, a finding that was underscored in research conducted by the Canada, US and Mexico Trilateral Committee on Transborder Data Flow, an Industry Canada-led initiative that brought together senior government leaders, business representatives and members of the federal privacy commission to look at legal restrictions or impediments to cross border data flow.

In situations where conflicting legislation may apply, the working group advises that businesses inform cloud data strategy with the opinion of a third party legal expert, who may shed light on legal requirements for protection of personal data, and who may be able to help with mechanisms to support international data transfer, such as safe harbor, model clauses and binding corporate rules. A next step should be creation of an inventory of the type of data that may be involved, and its classification based on sensitivity to Canadian privacy legislation requirements. For example, there may be commercial applications that are suited to delivery via a SaaS-based, international service, while other applications containing sensitive information may be better hosted on-premise or in Canadian hosting facilities.

Data residency issues have been interpreted by the service provider community as new opportunity to service a unique market requirement. In the last half decade, a number of global providers have made significant investment in the establishment of domestically-based cloud infrastructure to service customers looking to house data in Canadian facilities, while Canadian providers have also established hosting and other infrastructure services. Some of these now offer data storage/management in multiple global locations, and allow customers with international operations to control placement of data in specific locations. When choosing a provider, the end user must know where data will be stored, where the provider's data centres are located, and, if necessary, establish that the data is not leaving the country.

Another issue that is important to provider location is network service delivery capability. As the working group notes, the "network time for data round trip" may be critical, depending on the type of application that is moving to cloud hosting, depending on the time sensitivity of the application. There are technical requirements for collaboration platforms, for example, which require that the app run within a certain microsecond time frame to ensure quality of voice service, or to avoid problems such as jitter, which may be impacted by the distance data needs to travel. Similarly, online transaction processing applications in financial or ecommerce applications might also be sensitive to business loss due to latency.

## Developing cloud readiness: change management in people, process and technology

Preparing the user organization for cloud involves change management planning and activity at three different levels: successful implementation will depend on transition in people, process and technology. Each cloud project is unique, and change in and between these areas will vary depending on existing infrastructure and the goal of cloud migration. However, the working group points to one constant requirement across organizations, which is the need for a shift from a traditional *Field of Dreams* IT mentality, which said "build it and they will come," to an approach that seeks to align IT resource delivery with internal business customer needs. Cloud planning will likely begin with an assessment of legacy infrastructure, but decisions must also be based on an evaluation of the potential benefits to be derived from deployment of cloud business process, which is developed through collaboration between IT, information management groups and business constituencies, including the user groups. The role of IT in the new cloud paradigm is to explain costs and technical requirements, and to ensure that cloud meets corporate culture needs and corporate steering guidelines. As one working group member put it, "when internal customers want something, the answer can't be 'no' anymore."

According to the working group, though developing cloud readiness from a technology perspective requires consistent focus, for most organizations, the biggest challenge lies in transitioning people and process. As a result, it is the group's belief that organizations should begin by defining what are the objectives are of moving to cloud. Is the primary goal a low cost alternative for IT infrastructure that has reached end of life, is cloud designed to managing the organization's fluctuating/seasonal demand for IT resources, or is cloud migration a means to building business agility – through advanced applications such as mobility or test/dev environments that enable a 'fail fast' approach to product and service innovation? Answers to questions like these can help determine the most appropriate cloud delivery model, but also form the basis for organizational readiness activities, including the prioritization of business functions or applications for migration to cloud, and the selection of cloud platform or cloud service provider. In terms of business readiness for cloud, it's important that the adopting organization understand internal budgets for cloud infrastructure and applications – and the potential for procurement via business units rather than IT – how new service provider subscription billing models can be accommodated in more traditional accounting systems, and what support offerings are available from the provider and which must be developed – or added as new skilled resources – to enable internal service delivery.

A next stage involves technical implementation, including the steps required to prepare infrastructure, develop application awareness and transfer data for transition from a traditional IT environment to one that is hybrid or cloud enabled. In cases where the adopting organization has legacy infrastructure – the so-called 'Big Iron' systems – deployment of x86 or cloud native applications may present technical issues; however, high levels of server/storage virtualization within the Canadian marketplace mean that many enterprises have already transformed infrastructure and are prepared for the shift to cloud and for build out to high availability. A mismatch between the hypervisor that an application runs on and the cloud platform a provider runs may also introduce hurdles, requiring some form of integration, as can disparity between on-premise and public cloud hypervisors. In hybrid scenarios, other key issues in workload mobility are network readiness (virtualization), and the ability to execute network security provisions.

A critical piece in developing technical readiness involves identifying which applications and workloads will run easily in cloud and which will not. At an operational level, workload evaluation is important to determining the most appropriate cloud delivery model. For example, high compute, high availability and low latency applications, may be better suited to deployment in a dedicated, bare metal offering in public cloud than to multi-tenant infrastructure in which resource sharing can introduce delays. Application designers within the user organization must also determine whether an application is 'self-aware' and resilient enough to work logically in a distributed fashion in the cloud environment. Applications that are single threaded, that not aware of where they are running, that may not survive a dropped link in a shared environment or a move to another server, that were written in older coding languages and which are not cloud sensitive, may require rewrite in modern languages such as CC++, Python or JAVA, or may simply need to remain on-premise in traditional infrastructure.

But the working group stresses that the alignment of technology system change with process change represents the biggest challenge for adopting organizations. Issues that are often overlooked, but which need to be addressed include management of CMDB (change management database), change control, ticketing systems, approval processes (for access to cloud apps and data), data classification to determine sensitivity and storage in different cloud modes, and in the case of self-service, deciding who has access and what are their permissions. Cloud platforms deployed without supporting process change are of limited utility: cloud will not deliver the anticipated benefits when it is not used by people.

By engaging business constituencies in cloud strategy and planning, and by building the support around cloud platforms needed to encourage the full incorporation of cloud data and apps within business processes, organizations can shrink the gap between the business user's cost/benefit analysis of cloud and the technologists' view of cloud value and utility. This exercise involves two additional inputs: the creation of training enablement and other programs and activities to support end users and encourage their smooth transition to optimal use of cloud applications, and the management of business user expectations with respect to customization or other features/capabilities that may be different in on-premise, private infrastructure and public cloud delivery of IT services. For example, while customization specific to business processes may be common to on-premise application development by in-house architects and developers, even when hosted on an external cloud, this may be limited with an off-the-shelf, shared SaaS application. In these cases, business users must be educated on the cost benefit of SaaS, and be willing to introduce the appropriate user training and business process change. For the technicians, on the other hand, one member noted "If you own the application, your need for modification for [private] cloud is probably less than if you are deploying customer data into a SaaS app and have to figure out how to wedge your round customer data peg into the SaaS square customer delivery mould."

## Managing Shadow IT

Ease of cloud procurement has had an ambiguous legacy. While the business manager's new-found ability to order up SaaS applications or to spin up new VMs via online portals with credit card in hand may deliver the speed and agility that line-of-business executives are looking for in IT service delivery, this approach generates a host of complex questions that may impact organizational health. Consider, for example, the case of developers who set up a quick website running on public cloud infrastructure to capture prospect lead information, who realize later that capturing personal information requires the security policies of the corporate cloud, but are unable to port the virtual machines back on premise because the code used for public cloud is different than for on-premise infrastructure. For the organization, the outcome is security/privacy risk, delayed launch of the project, and potentially, higher cost as the fees associated with infrastructure solutions are often incremental, increasing with the introduction of features and seats. 'Shadow IT' (or 'stealth IT', as it is sometimes called) involving the use of IT systems and solutions inside an organization without corporate approvals can entail unintended, and undesirable consequences on each of these fronts, but is a phenomenon that continues to grow with the practice of assigning business units with their own technology budgets.

What accounts for this seeming indifference to the security and governance requirements set out by information managers within the corporation, which the IT department has been responsible for until now? One response to this question describes the harried IT department, struggling with declining budgets to meet the increasing technology demands of business, which is unable to keep pace with the required innovation. Another cites business unit impatience for the latest, consumer-oriented applications as the source of unnecessary risk that must be controlled. In the working group's view, control over shadow IT is a horse that has left the gate: however, with the proper framework and strategy, it is possible to bring the organizational views of business and IT together to simultaneously serve the agility and governance needs of the business as a whole. Components of this strategy may include:

*Identify shadow IT solutions.* As a starting point, organizations should have better understanding of what cloud solutions are in fact running within the corporate environment. This may be achieved through the use of tools/appliances that monitor organizational systems and networks for rogue deployments, and tools that can monitor various clouds to spot utilization by different groups or individuals.

*Reach reasonable compromise.* Armed with information on who is using what cloud service, the company may approach Line-of-Business to reach agreement on process for cloud service adoption. The intent is not to insist that IT perform a complete assessment complete with architectural and security review, which may take up to a year to perform, but rather to encourage business to notify IT when cloud solutions are deployed to enable IT to take appropriate steps around security and access.

*Designate certain IT activities for execution by specific groups.* While the build and maintenance of cloud infrastructure and the multi-year roll out of large, cloud-delivered applications are likely best addressed by IT, smaller, and more contained, departmental projects that SaaS-based delivery has made simple to manage are best deployed via business unit efforts and budgets.

## Cloud standards and promotion of data portability/systems interoperability

A long standing obstacle to greater adoption of public cloud in the Canadian marketplace has been a perceived loss of control over data. This perception arises out of concern for the security of corporate data and applications, but also speaks to issues around data portability. Depending on the provider, data may in fact be more secure in the cloud supplier's environment; similarly, it may be more or less easy to retrieve data on conclusion of a cloud engagement depending on contractual agreements and provider capabilities. A key touted benefit of cloud is the ability to "shop around"; but to avoid vendor lock in, the cloud user must have some means to recover data and applications.

Data portability is also critical from another perspective. As organizations move more and more applications and services to the cloud, they will need to have some mechanism for sharing data across applications to enhance collaboration across business units. Migrating data across functional areas, such as billing, logistics, financials, sales, marketing and HR, can enable the delivery of new sources of information to individual departments, and allow leverage of corporate data to ask new questions that can improve operational performance or create new approaches to product/service delivery and/or market opportunity. The importance of sharing data extends to businesses with a mix of private clouds, private and public clouds, or groups of SaaS applications. It has been estimated that 90 percent of organizations now have some workloads in the public cloud, and an increasing trend is towards adoption of several cloud applications that have been purpose built for specialized functions. Orchestration of these clouds through integration and data sharing offer potential to break down information silos, improving efficiencies across the IT function, and also unlocking additional business value for the organization.

The key means to establish interoperability between clouds is through APIs, application program interfaces that allow the creation of software connectors between different cloud applications or systems. While many organizations have found it necessary to maintain specialist staff to manage this integration, many established clouds, such as Microsoft's Azure or IBM's Bluemix PaaS, have clearly defined APIs that are typically based on OpenStack, in order to ease integration for customers. Many IaaS providers will have built API extensions for the major platforms. In addition, some of the larger, more full-service providers will have built out partnerships with SaaS or other providers, engineering integrations with these to create an ecosystem of service clouds. By onboarding these partners, the service provider manages the integration piece on behalf of customers. Levels of integration offered by the cloud provider then, in terms of programmatic APIs or through service partner ecosystems, are a key piece of intelligence that should inform the user organization's cloud adoption strategy and procurement decision making.

Interoperability questions also play at the system level, particularly in hybrid environment scenarios. While one approach to enabling organizations to migrate workloads between their own private infrastructure and public/private/or multi-tenant environments is to build a virtual LAN interface that can be managed and disconnected once it is no longer in use, increasingly, vendor organizations are developing specialized management tools that support seamless workload mobility. In some cases, these tools are designed for the delivery of specialized functionality – Disaster Recovery-as-a-Service, for example, provides an increasingly popular management interface to solve for the organization's resiliency requirements – while others promise real time migration of virtual machines and workloads without disruption of production operations. For providers, these services have the added benefit of supporting the quick onboard of customer applications and data to their cloud platforms. An additional use case for seamless workload mobility operates at the developer level: a cloud provider's ability to offer the scale and service automation needed by the developer community, such as database-as-a-service, automated provisioning of OS and memory, or services that allow the transfer of workloads from test/dev to production environments or from in-house clouds and back to public cloud resources again, should be important criteria in the decision to access specific PaaS services, and in platform selection.

In cloud architectural design and in cloud vendor selection, user organizations may also want to weigh the importance of open cloud standards against the benefits of proprietary systems that are engineered to work together. As the working group notes, "openness, open source and OpenStack are all different topics" that relate to different areas of the IT stack. While openness may refer to the ability to move a database of content to another system or application, an OpenStack environment runs at the infrastructure level, allowing the IT operations team to move virtual machines via the hypervisor – some of which are open and some not. Whatever the level, in the case of open source business apps, or open protocol operating systems and infrastructure, a key requirement is the implementation of distributions that have been tested and hardened to provide the reliability and continuity required in enterprise deployments.

Figure 4-5. Key issues in assembling a cloud platform

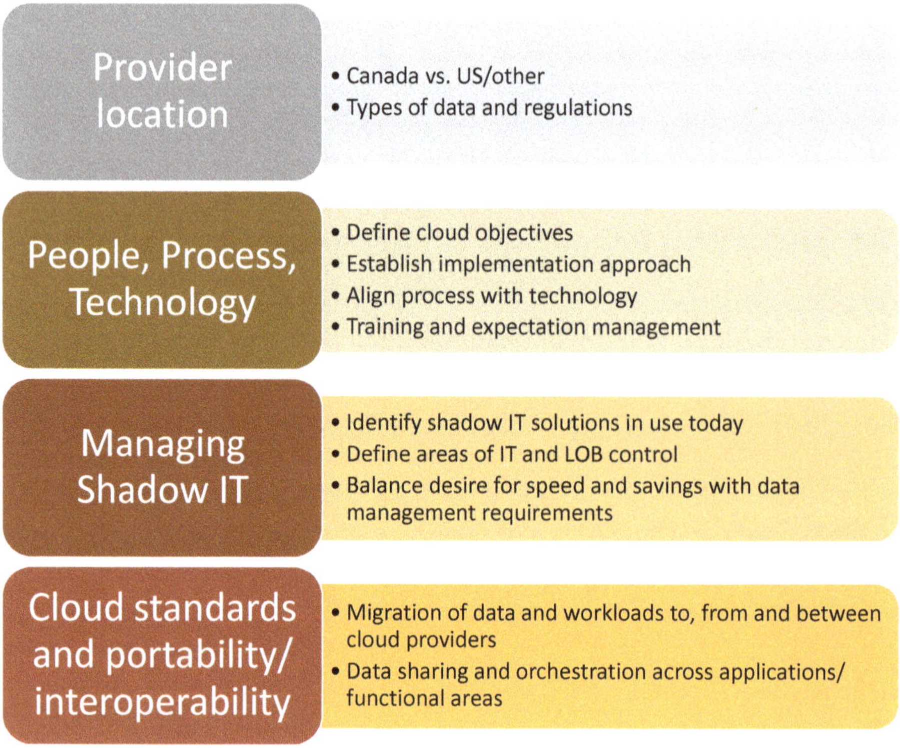

| Provider location | • Canada vs. US/other<br>• Types of data and regulations |

| People, Process, Technology | • Define cloud objectives<br>• Establish implementation approach<br>• Align process with technology<br>• Training and expectation management |

| Managing Shadow IT | • Identify shadow IT solutions in use today<br>• Define areas of IT and LOB control<br>• Balance desire for speed and savings with data management requirements |

| Cloud standards and portability/ interoperability | • Migration of data and workloads to, from and between cloud providers<br>• Data sharing and orchestration across applications/ functional areas |

*Source: TCBC/InsightaaS, 2015*

## Canadian specific challenges

An oft cited Canadian cloud adoption hurdle is the high cost of bandwidth in Canada relative to that in the US. While in theory pricing could potentially influence an end user consumer's willingness to access cloud services, it is the working group's belief that costs do not introduce barriers at the business level. From the perspective of a business sourcing Canadian versus global cloud resources, the same Canadian bandwidth and costs would apply, leveling the playing field for Canadian and other providers. Similarly, when decisions are made around building on-premise resources versus accessing infrastructure through the cloud, bandwidth factors are seldom isolated from other operational costs and requirements. For example, in an organization where everyone works in the same office with the same LAN and limited external exchanges, moving to the cloud may entail additional, unnecessary charges. However, in the more connected environments that are the norm today, businesses typically have already contracted bandwidth services. Bandwidth, in other words, is simply a cost of doing business in the digital world.

In the Canadian context, another argument holds that more moderate Canadian adoption rates are related to lack of supply. However, specific challenges to the healthy growth of cloud markets have had more to do with go-to-market strategy on the part of local providers than with actual delivery capability. Data residency requirements, whether real or perceptual, have buttressed the generation of domestic demand for domestic supply, as have government client preferences for locally-sourced cloud solutions as a means to job creation and the development of greater economic sustainability. As noted above, Canadian and global providers alike have made significant investment over the past half-decade in the installment of domestic cloud infrastructure to service customers looking to house data on Canadian premises, and some of the more advanced services now offer data storage/management out of multiple global cloud locations to service multi-national needs. The result has been over, rather than under supply of cloud infrastructure, leading to a commoditization of IaaS services here and south of the border. All the while, a major provider of infrastructure services, which benefited early on from the efficiencies associated with cloud scale, continues to dominate the pricing landscape and with it, the Canadian market for cloud infrastructure. To counter this influence, a number of Canadian providers have focused on the development of value added services, and new distribution channels: "IaaS is just an entry ticket," one working group member added.

Cloud's key value proposition has been ease of use. Cloud promised to be easy to find, easy to use and easy to pay for. In the working group's view, more modest adoption rates for cloud in Canada relative to the US are in no small measure associated with less sophisticated marketing activities here, leading to a lack of user engagement with cloud, and to lack of awareness of the more advanced features that can deliver on the transformative promise of cloud. Virtualization may serve as a technology foundation for cloud, but through alignment of cloud orchestration, automation and service charge back, companies may lay the foundation for transition to the digital business of the future.

## Metrics and milestones

As a general statement, success reporting is achieved by comparing business outcomes against business goals: the measurement mechanism evolves once these two values are understood. In cloud implementation projects, this general principle applies, with one proviso: complex hybrid cloud environments require multiple frameworks and metrics for different types of cloud, capable of supporting evaluation by different constituencies. A clear statement of objective with SaaS adoption, for example, is likely to align with improvement in a business function, and the outcome may be productivity improvement, which translates to cost savings. But the cloud technology itself may also be an input to improvement at the application layer, as cloud enabled dev/op methodologies, elastic infrastructure resources and preconfigured PaaS development environments support 'fail fast' approaches that serve to shrink time to market for new products and services. While there is some overlap, in this example, success is measured by business management in terms of improvement in business function, but at a technology level, through time savings: with cloud, a project that could take weeks can be achieved in days.

Measuring cloud implementation success at the infrastructure level involves a different set of evaluation criteria that can also inform choices around appropriate deployment modes. For example, system uptime is a critical requirement that is always challenging and especially hard for the small to mid-sized business to achieve; it may be easier for some organizations to contract with a cloud provider equipped with the latest technology and skills expertise that allows the vendor to offer 99.9% uptime in SLAs. To assess a provider's ability to deliver on these SLAs, a number of services are now available that monitor the uptime or application performance of multiple cloud provider platforms, comparing these metrics in a single platform that the adopting organization can use to evaluate different public services. Next generation monitoring tools also exist to measure application uptime and response at different layers of the infrastructure, whether the app is running on-premise, in a private hosted, or a public cloud environment. As one member of the working group noted, while these approaches require investment, "this is where we need to go" to ensure the application is delivering expected value, and these tools should be put in place at the onset in cloud implementation.

According to the working group, cost, quality (uptime), responsiveness and time to market are "the big four" measures of cloud project value, which allow users to assess the performance of different deployment models. Hybrid scenarios with built in data portability function as the optimal testing ground, where the user can learn, experiment with proof of concept, and respond appropriately to specific adoption models. If the expected returns in terms of cost, quality, responsiveness and innovation speed are not available within a set time frame, then new strategy to build additional cloud resources can be developed, and data readily transferred to new hybrid modes.

> According to the working group, cost, quality (uptime), responsiveness and time to market are "the big four" measures of cloud project value, which allow users to assess the performance of different cloud models.

## Reference sources

Additional references that readers can use to better understand the key issues that impact decisions around adoption and management of public, private and hybrid cloud delivery include:

- Mary Allen. "Building Bimodal Bridges." InsightaaS, August 2015. This article examines Gartner's theory of bimodal IT, the need to address the distinction between innovation and core system management/operations, and techniques that can be adapted for real-world use.
- Understanding Hybrid Cloud Deployment Models – Wikibon Whiteboard. December, 2015. This video describes six different models of hybrid cloud deployment.
- Cloud Business Models, Metrics and Imperatives: A TCBC Best Practices Document. The Toronto Business Cloud Coalition, 2015. This Best Practices document from the TCBC Cloud Business Models, Metrics and Imperatives working group contains guidance on the metrics and measurements used by non-IT business management to evaluate cloud initiatives (member-only access).
- Cloud Standards Customer Council. Interoperability and Portability for Cloud Computing: A Guide. November, 2014.

- Data Center Efficiency Assessment. Scaling Up Energy Efficiency across the Data Center Industry: Evaluating Key Drivers and Barriers. Natural Resources Defense Council, 2014. This report highlights links between multi-tenant data centres and utilization rates, and between utilization rates and energy efficiency. It also provides recommendations for metrics and use of DCIM.
- Jill Dyche. "Shadow IT is Out of the Closet." Harvard Business Review, September 2012.
- Office of the Privacy Commissioner of Canada. The Personal Information Protection and Electronic Documents Act (PIPEDA).
- Phil Lee. Challenges in global data residency laws – and how to solve them. Fieldfisher Privacy and Information Law Blog, September, 2014.
- Paul Lewis. A Question from the High Iron: Innovating with Shadow IT. LinkedIn, August 2015. This blog post takes the position that shadow IT "isn't really a problem. It's where actual business problems get solved," and urges IT departments to provide a cloud on-ramp that facilitates line of business use of new systems to address business issues.
- What is OpenStack? Opensource.com

*Chapter 5.*

# Advanced Cloud Application Adoption and Enablement

Essential guidance supporting decisions aimed at aligning cloud modes with business requirements

*Contributing community experts: Paul Gragtmans (ET Group), Arturo Perez (Solsteace), Norman Sung (Red Hat)*

*Initial publication date: March 2016*

# Advanced Cloud Application Adoption and Enablement

## Definition and context

The phrase "advanced cloud application adoption and enablement" covers a wide swath of the cloud technology landscape. It's intuitively clear why understanding and articulating best practices in this area is important to the overall TCBC mission of accelerating cloud use and adoption, but it is also important to be focused enough in the definition to ensure that it is possible to deliver real value through this document.

One factor that complicates the definition of "adoption and enablement" is the trend for innovation to occur first in the consumer space, and then spread to the enterprise. Tools like Dropbox and Skype are widely used within the enterprise – in fact, research has shown that the type of file sharing enabled by Dropbox is seen by businesses as the most important collaboration capability, ahead of functions like video conferencing and voice communications. But these tools penetrated businesses at the user level: they weren't introduced to the enterprise by IT, and they typically aren't managed by IT. In fact, users often push back on IT attempts to rein in or control use of these types of tools, or to substitute corporate-approved alternatives. Consumer apps don't prioritize integration or (in many cases) enterprise-grade security, but they do prioritize user experience, and this is proving to be a compelling driver of adoption and use.

Another complicating factor in defining "advanced cloud applications" is the trend towards building applications that enhance the value of other systems, creating a type of cascading effect. For example, monolithic enterprise applications like ERP and CRM are out of scope for this "advanced cloud application" analysis, but collaboration capabilities that (greatly) enhance the value and ROI of these core applications by adding collaboration (for example, for help functions) and analytics (to understand the best ways to support these applications) are both in scope and important examples of how cloud apps create value for the firms that invest in them.

One outcome resulting from these factors is the need to develop business-grade cloud applications that capitalize on the viral acceptance of prominent consumer technologies and serve the objective of creating additional value for these in-use applications, rather than attempting to displace them. Microsoft's Skype for Business is a good example of this approach. Formerly known as Lync, Skype for Business offers enterprise-grade capabilities, but is designed to connect seamlessly with the millions of users who have installed the consumer version of Skype. With this approach, Microsoft is attempting to provide businesses with an application that can provide rapid ROI (collaborative applications tend to provide compelling returns on investment) while also leveraging, rather than seeking to replace, a viral consumer technology. Will this work? It's hard to say – Skype for Business addresses an IT management need, but from a user perspective, it's possible to view Skype for Business as an architected solution to a distributed web problem. Overall, though, it is clear that the IT management problem will become more pronounced with time, as the pace of consumer app introductions far exceeds the rate at which new business-grade applications are introduced to the cloud. In today's market, innovation starts with the consumer, and that innovation shapes business user expectations. Advanced cloud business applications need to be as innovative as consumer apps, and need as well to offer capabilities that deliver positive ROI on investments in adoption and enablement.

## Key characteristics of advanced cloud applications

The TCBC Advanced Cloud Application and Enablement working group determined that a workable definition of "advanced cloud applications" would include the following characteristics: cloud based, providing remote (to the user) management and seamless delivery regardless of location; native support for mobility, so that the application can be accessed on any device; embedded collaboration capabilities, allowing app users to share questions and/or work products with colleagues or customers; rich communications tools to support the collaboration function; and embedded analytics/dashboarding capabilities, allowing the business to understand use of the application, and potentially, to explore methods of enhancing the value of the app. These characteristics are illustrated in Figure 5-1.

Figure 5-1. Advanced cloud applications: key characteristics

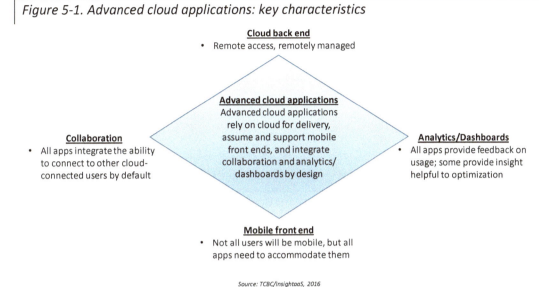

**Cloud back end**
- Remote access, remotely managed

**Advanced cloud applications**
Advanced cloud applications rely on cloud for delivery, assume and support mobile front ends, and integrate collaboration and analytics/ dashboards by design

**Collaboration**
- All apps integrate the ability to connect to other cloud-connected users by default

**Analytics/Dashboards**
- All apps provide feedback on usage; some provide insight helpful to optimization

**Mobile front end**
- Not all users will be mobile, but all apps need to accommodate them

*Source: TCBC/InsightaaS, 2016*

## Reference sources

Additional references that readers can use to better understand the key issues defining advanced cloud applications and adoption and enablement issues include:

- Mary Allen. The InsightaaS Collabmobilicloud series, 2015. This series of whitepapers combines analysis by InsightaaS with deep market data (much of which is sourced from California-based Techaisle Research). It explores the connections between collaboration, mobility and cloud, which are viewed as a single solution area by many buy-side managers.
  - Collabmobilicloud: A New Work Era - Provides an excellent description of how and why collaboration, mobility and cloud are (from a user point of view) all part of the same trend
  - Collabmobilicloud: Merging User Perceptions – A data-rich report that includes a great Techaisle graphic on midmarket cloud application adoption
  - Collabmobilicloud: The Security Continuum – This whitepaper deals with the issue of security in an innovative way – it uses a fictitious account of "a day in the life" of a utility employee to highlight many of the threat sources around collabmobilicloud.

- Collabmobilicloud: Empowering the End User – Trends towards use of multiple technology types has led to a perception that end user devices are collectively interchangeable and individually unimportant – but is this the case, or is device strategy important to productivity outcomes?

- Collabmobilicloud: Interplay in IoT – This whitepaper expands on the scope used in the previous collabmobilicloud documents by examining how the combination of mobile, cloud and collaboration technologies support IoT – itself, an advanced cloud application.

- Paul Gragtmans. "Does Rich Communication accelerate the velocity of collaboration?" ET Group, 2014. This post highlights the connection between rich communications tools and collaboration success. If (as the working group believes) collaboration is an essential element of advanced web applications, then the richness of the tools used to facilitate collaboration has a direct impact on the value and impact of the applications.

- Paul Gragtmans. "Is True Collaboration a 2 Pizza Team Rule?" ET Group, 2013. This post highlights a belief shared by Thomas Edison, Jeff Bezos and Mark Zuckerberg – that small teams (and those focused on 'higher order' outcomes) are more productive than large, complex organizations. This has an implication for evaluation of cloud applications: if you plan to use them to support small teams, some features (such as the richness of communication) become more important than others (e.g., the number of connected users supported), which may affect evaluation of/commitment to different applications and application strategies.

- Gartner Says Demand for Enterprise Mobile Apps Will Outstrip Available Development Capacity Five to One (Gartner Group, June 2015). Mobile access is a core (and expected) attribute of advanced cloud applications. However, it is becoming difficult for businesses to match demand for new mobile-enabled applications to supply of the skills required to deliver these applications. Gartner sees wearables and IoT accelerating this discrepancy over the next four years.

- Leigh Shevchik. "What You Need to Know About the Booming Enterprise Apps Industry." New Relic News, 2013. This brief post is somewhat dated, but it contains interesting data that provides at least some context for an understanding of how mobile application enablement is evolving in the enterprise.

## Business objectives and benefits

The key to successful adoption of advanced cloud applications – or any business technology – is rooted in the ability to address business objectives and deliver tangible benefits. Focusing on the 'why' of advanced cloud application adoption and enablement helps position best practices in a business-relevant context.

As Figure 5-2 demonstrates, the business drivers and benefits associated with advanced cloud application adoption and enablement run the gamut from the ability to identify new opportunities to the need to keep pace with competitors and customers. At a high level, the key issues are:

- Can your organization's IT infrastructure keep up with the pace of consumer innovation? Can you deliver "order in chaos" by embracing key consumer apps and evolving your business environment to reflect the new capabilities and growth opportunities unlocked by this innovation?
- Can you capitalize on the dashboarding/analytics embedded within cloud systems? Can you use this insight to evolve current processes or to develop new products, markets, or marketing approaches?
- Can you capitalize on the high ROI potential of collaborative applications, through compressed process times (for example, for customer problem resolution or new product introduction) or by reducing the friction around ad hoc internal collaboration?
- Can you build a portfolio of cloud apps that combines the ability to enhance existing apps (as in the example of using add-ons to enhance help and support) with the ability to provide new options for collaboration, analytics and automation of business processes? And can you build the IT capacity to optimize this portfolio?

*Figure 5-2. Key business drivers/benefits of advanced cloud application adoption and enablement*

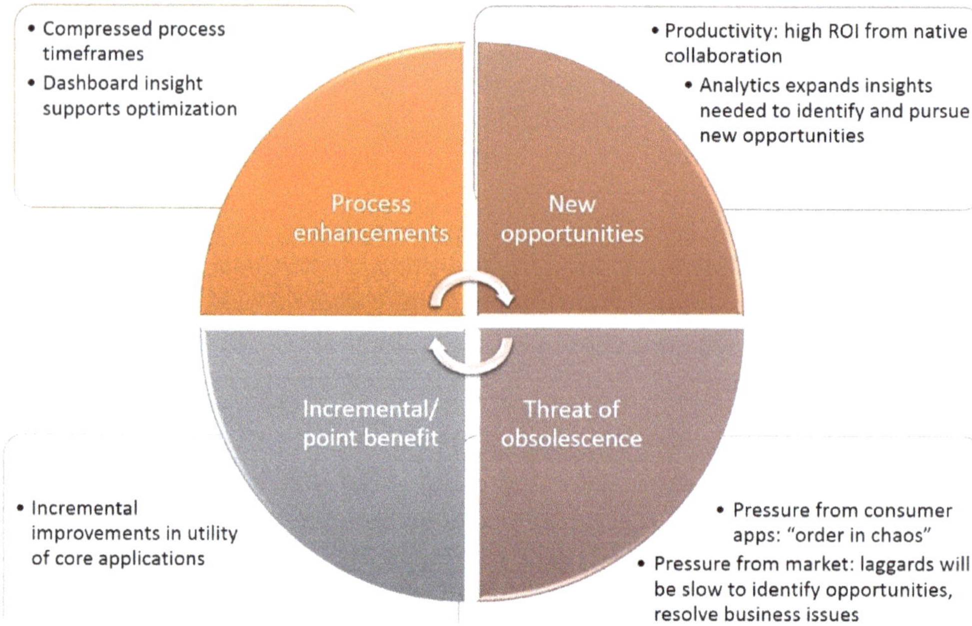

- Compressed process timeframes
- Dashboard insight supports optimization

- Productivity: high ROI from native collaboration
  - Analytics expands insights needed to identify and pursue new opportunities

**Process enhancements**

**New opportunities**

**Incremental/ point benefit**

**Threat of obsolescence**

- Incremental improvements in utility of core applications

- Pressure from consumer apps: "order in chaos"
- Pressure from market: laggards will be slow to identify opportunities, resolve business issues

*Source: TCBC/InsightaaS, 2015*

Figure 5-2 demonstrates the key issues involved in business adoption of advanced cloud applications, but it also suggests some of the obstacles faced by corporate IT in an environment that is shaped by the pace associated with consumer apps. The steps needed to effectively embrace enterprise technology are different from the "process" used by consumers. Enterprises need to address the four core issues shown in the Figure by creating portfolios that are based on tools, rather than by centring (or continuing to centre) their strategies on monolithic applications that are slow (and hard) to evolve. In particular, IT departments that fail to react to compressed business timeframes and related user expectations risk being ignored by users who view IT as an impediment and opt for unauthorized alternative apps. It is very important that IT not allow this tension to escalate into a struggle for control: the key objective is to create a productive work environment, and IT actions that users see as arbitrary and focused only on power maintenance will erode the trust needed for collaboration in pursuit of the broader business goal.

## Reference sources

Additional references that readers can use to better understand the key issues defining advanced cloud applications and adoption and enablement issues include:

- Clayton Christensen. Seeing What's Next. Perseus Distribution, 2004. A successor text to The Innovator's Dilemma and The Innovator's Solution, Clayton Christensen's Seeing What's Next is lauded for its inclusion of business model innovation discussion and examples.
- Nicholas Carr. The Big Switch. WW Norton, 2013. Nicholas Carr (of "IT Doesn't Matter" fame) examines the implications of cloud computing for business and society at large.

## Best practices in advanced cloud application adoption and enablement

*Speed. Agility.*

The discussion of what constitutes best practices in advanced cloud application adoption and enablement begins with speed, or more accurately, the difference in pace between traditional applications and cloud apps. Traditional enterprise software – big ERP packages, or CRM packages, or similar applications – tends to be delivered in suite form. Over time, very large applications create new options for internal users, but the cost of developing these options is very high, and the pace of delivery tends to be very slow.

There are reasons for the deliberate pace of new software rollouts in enterprises, relative to the frenetic pace of consumer apps. Essentially, developers of consumer apps take responsibility only for the app, not for the entirety of the user environment. Corporate IT management, though, has responsibility for the totality of the user's experience – support, integration, and security. IT has a further obligation to support corporate imperatives: integration across a wide range of legacy applications that have been knitted together over time, security that embraces not just the user but back-end systems and core data, a responsibility to provide for auditability and regulatory compliance, testing of new capabilities before they are rolled into production to ensure compatibility within the corporate environment, a need to keep investments within budget constraints, etc.

However, the fact that there is a rationale for a deliberate approach to new applications doesn't mean that a deliberate pace is the *only* approach that is supported by reality and logic – and in fact, it is increasingly clear that corporate IT needs to find ways of attaching the core attributes of security, integration and auditability/compliance to a methodology that is more closely aligned with the breadth and pace of an app store than a traditional enterprise software environment. The ground rules, as Figure 5-2 shows, have changed: *speed* is a critical factor in success, and success itself is measured in *agility* – the ability to react rapidly to new demands or opportunities by introducing new advanced apps, and without breaking the user environment or disrupting IT's ability to support necessary corporate objectives.

It seems clear that over time, businesses will evolve to a software approach that includes three major elements.

1. *Core systems of record.* In (at least) enterprises and other established businesses, current core systems of record – the complex ERP suites and similar software that is the source of essential information on transactions, employees and customers – will likely remain as systems that are closely managed by internal staff, and often, on internal platforms. Younger/smaller businesses will, in most cases, skip the path to these monolithic applications, and build businesses on cloud-native core applications.

2. *Task automation.* Regardless of which approach a business takes to core systems of record, automation of the tasks and processes within/across a process, a department or an enterprise will increasingly be delivered by a portfolio of cloud-native apps. These applications, as is shown in Figure 5-3, will be a mix of replacements for existing task automation apps, new apps that enhance existing apps, and new apps that automate tasks (or entire processes) that are currently not automated or poorly/partially automated. In practice, many of these apps will provide an "on steroids" treatment for activities that rely on discrete, manually maintained Excel sheets, delivered via the corporate equivalent of an app store. In the future, with the growth of artificial intelligence, it is possible (likely?) that some of these apps will perform tasks rather than simply provide support to human workers.

3. *Advanced cloud (and mobility) enabled functionality.* Underlying the core and task automation systems will be a set of applications delivering capabilities that capitalize on the unique attributes of the cloud and mobility. It is clear that analytics will be central to this third category: advanced cloud apps (as is shown in Figure 5-1) all contain some analytics/dashboarding capabilities; enterprises will look to expose and connect this insight, using it to fuel advanced systems

that help manage IT (through better performance data) and business operations (through better insight into opportunities for improving efficiency, market reach, product positioning, etc.).

The working group sees analytics as a particularly important piece of the overall puzzle. All businesses have structured data today, especially within their core systems of record. Increasingly, these businesses are able to access additional data sources that might arise from customer interaction or other market inputs (for example, from social media), and/or from operational data (for example, from the performance data drawn from production equipment via an IoT/Industrial Internet construct), and/or from external sources that might affect demand in different ways (e.g., weather data, economic trends). To stay competitive, enterprises in all sectors will need to stay abreast of information that identifies priority actions within the business, or requirements to adjust market/customer strategy, and/or which discovers segments that have common needs that can and should be addressed by adjusting product configurations or packaging. These analytics systems need to obtain information from multiple sources – individual person to person (H2H) interactions, automated data streams, alerts triggered by anomalies in machine to machine (M2M) communications, etc. – and the actions identified through the analytics systems need to be communicated through a similarly-wide range of communications, in the form of management recommendations developed by data scientists, analytics-based staff guidance issued via mobile devices, or more automated communications via social media, H2M instructions, and/or other formats.

Figure 5-3 presents a framework that is aligned with the need to anticipate the "pull" of new application opportunities. It illustrates the different ways that cloud is (or is not) used within the software portfolio, and supplements this view by positioning it within three broader sets of objectives: the business objectives that drive investment in advanced cloud applications, the technical objectives that represent the technology goals supported through advanced cloud applications, and the business outcomes that result from effective deployment of advanced cloud applications within the enterprise.

*Figure 5-3. Building a software portfolio based on advanced cloud applications*

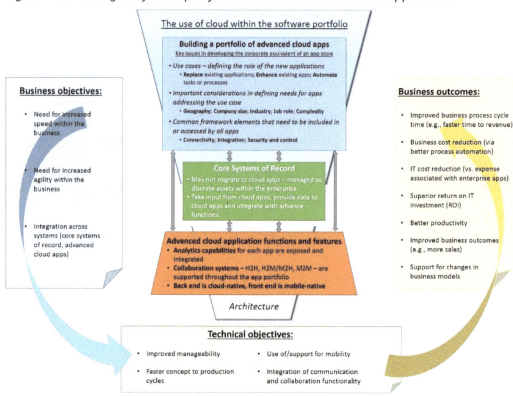

Source: TCBC/InsightaaS, 2016

## Reference sources

Additional references that readers can use to better understand the key issues defining the development of a software architecture connecting a portfolio of advanced cloud apps with ore systems of record and advanced functionality – especially analytics – include:

- Rethink application possibilities and align to desired business outcomes
  Avenade, 2014. This whitepaper, based on a survey of 200 US companies with annual revenue of more than $250 million, finds that "IT Decision Makers (ITDMs) are reporting an increased expectation from their businesses around three dimensions; firstly on user experience and design; second on a move towards faster shorter development cycles; and third an increased pressure to

drive transformational digital applications." It deals explicitly with cloud and mobility.

- Geoffrey Moore. Confessions of a Serial Authorpreneur. 2015. Via a serial blog, noted business expert Geoffrey Moore ("Crossing the Chasm") "addresses the operational changes needed to enable an established enterprise to commit to a new category and rapidly scale its business to a size at parity with its existing product lines."
- Marty Parker. "Communications Enabled Business Processes." UC Strategies, 2012. This seven-part series by Marty Parker (the link is to the first of the seven, "Optimize Resource Utilization") examines the business benefits associated with superior integration of communications tools with business processes and applications. While the series is oriented towards suppliers, it offers real value to buy-side managers as well.

## Advanced application adoption and enablement in practice

### Examples of (and lessons learned from) cloud application adoption

Given the breadth of solutions included under the "advanced cloud application" banner, it is difficult to generalize about adoption practices. By highlighting a few examples, though, we are able to demonstrate some of the key issues associated with adoption success.

### *Salesforce*

Salesforce is the exemplar for cloud applications, and with good reason – it is not only the leading cloud business solution, but also the application that proved that cloud was not merely some kind of 'on ramp' to sophisticated on-premise suites.

Salesforce was unique in identifying and exploiting opportunities in software use and design. Some of the innovations associated with its CRM systems include:

- *Targeting business management.* The entire industry is moving towards greater control/oversight over IT projects by non-IT executives. Selling to this group seems like a sensible approach today, but in 1999, when Salesforce was founded, it was a revolutionary idea. Giving business executives access to relevant systems designed to support their objectives was the role of IT, and business executives were expected to wait in the development/deployment queue until it was 'their turn' for new system support. The fact that Salesforce targeted the senior sales executive – typically, a peer of or at least, the strongest position outside the C-Suite – was helpful, as sales executives generally have much more internal influence than IT executives. In the broader context, though, this model of providing functionality that addresses a current need, with better-than-internal-standard quality, immediate or nearly immediate delivery and a much lower cost than a comparable internally deployed system, blazed a trail that thousands of other advanced cloud applications would follow.

- *Embedded expertise.* Enterprise-scale software benefitted from templates and consulting supplied by firms with deep understanding of both industry and functional needs. This kind of best practice support was not available to SMBs until Salesforce provided it to its customers. The onboarding process for Salesforce incorporates the selection of features that are associated with practices designed not only to automate but also to elevate sales practices.
- *The expansive platform.* There are senses in which Salesforce was and continues to be unique, and its presence as a platform application sets it apart from almost all other cloud applications. There are three main advantages to building a position as a platform. One is that other firms that use the same software can exchange information; this is helpful, for example, in channel and alliance relationships where there is utility in sharing visibility to opportunities. Another is that new staff often come with experience with the software gained at previous employers, which reduces time to benefit for new hires using the system. And the third – and least common in cloud software, and software generally – is that a platform attracts third-party development that provides extensions to the core package's functionality. In an important way, Salesforce echoed the advantages of its major suite-oriented competitors (such as SAP) by providing the opportunity for modular expansion, while simultaneously retaining the pay-for-what-you-use, pay-as-you-go, instant-on benefits of cloud. This capability both enables Salesforce to compete with SAP and Oracle in enterprise accounts, and made it unique in the SMB market.

## Location-based intelligence

Location-based intelligence systems capitalize on the cloud phenomenon of *mashups*, connections between multiple applications that allow a core solution to deliver context and functionality drawn from external sources. Most systems that rely on geographic data – including GPS systems, Uber (for matching drivers with customers), and many other applications – connect with multiple databases in order to present a rich experience that reflects insight into a specific location.

One example of a cloud-resident location-based application is Location Hub from DMTI Spatial, a Markham (Ontario) based company that was acquired by European shipping solution vendor Neopost in 2013. Location Hub combines data from dozens of different sources to deliver a fast and highly accurate perspective on physical locations via a SaaS application. This application can in turn be connected with other systems to provide critical business input. It is used by an underwriter to improve decisions on accepting risk on mortgages, and by other financial institutions to support fraud management systems. In one particularly interesting example, Location Hub was used by an insurer to identify locations in Calgary that were in need of urgent assistance in the wake of the 2013 flood, prioritizing claims processing and dispatch of contractors.

UK-based Network Rail is another firm that harnesses cloud and location-based solutions delivered via mobile devices to improve delivery of core business services. Using the cloud-based FeedHenry mobile middleware platform from RedHat "to build apps quickly and flexibly and roll them out to the business," Network Rail has increased the agility of its IT staff and the ability of its business operations to engage in activities ranging from predictive maintenance to crisis management.

### *Digital signage*
Digital signage is not seen as a cloud application, but the development of the digital signage market/industry provides an interesting analogy for the ways in which cloud evolves and alters buyer options and expectations.

In a presentation, Paul Gragtmans of ET Group (a member of the advance application adoption and enablement working group) described digital signage as progressing through a series of delivery expectations. This path – from "playability" to "manageability" to the ability to use different (and lower cost) players, and finally, to wide-scale integration – parallels many of the key points in the evolution of cloud applications.

At first, the key issue for digital signage was its ability to deliver on basic functionality: the ability to create and display content. Suppliers who weren't able to meet this basic benchmark were shaken out of the market, so the creation and display of content is considered the 'ante' in digital signage, much as the ability to deliver useful output and manage associated data is a core requirement of cloud systems. Interestingly, there are some remaining differentiators in this area, including being "open" to use/incorporation of different kinds of content (e.g., social feeds). Cloud systems can also achieve a limited measure of differentiation by being able to work with different kinds of data and/or data from a wide range of sources.

In the next stage in digital signage market evolution, *manageability* became a key concern. Was it possible to display different content on different screens? Would it be possible to fine-tune screen content in real time? These kinds of issues recur in cloud as well. One of the important benefits of using cloud lies in its ability to deliver analytics that help identify opportunities for application, network and/or process optimization – and a key area of cloud differentiation is suppliers' ability to enable clients to react rapidly and effectively to cloud's manageability advantages.

The third stage of digital signage market development revolves around player-agnostic systems. In the early days of digital signage, performance was a significant problem; to smooth out disjointed images and provide a better experience, suppliers tended to build proprietary software and dedicated processors into their displays. Over time, this became expensive and complicated for digital signage users. They now prefer to find suppliers who can work through industry-standard browsers rather than proprietary display logic; in addition to reducing lock-in and cost, this simplifies management and allows for inclusion of any content that is compatible with a browser. Cloud, of course, also benefits from use of adaptive browser interfaces, enabling display of content on any PC, tablet or smartphone. This is a critical issue in driving user adoption: a browser-based solution doesn't require the user to install an app (or multiple device-specific apps) on a PC or smartphone, increasing the opportunity for casual use that may lead in turn to more intense use of the solution.

Perhaps the most compelling parallel between the two markets, though, is the final stage in Gragtmans' presentation, which highlights the importance of integration. Digital signage that can be integrated with (for example) emergency notification and response systems can perform entirely new functions: it can direct people to safe exits in the event of a fire or other safety issue, and can be combined with input from security cameras to provide on-premise, real-time guidance to first responders. The integration benefits of cloud are not generally drawn so starkly in terms of emergencies and safeties, but the underlying comparison holds. We are in the midst of a period in which diverse cloud applications offer greatly enhanced value through integration. At present, this integration tends to be achieved via a common platform – for example, through interconnections between applications developed and run on Force.com. It's likely, though, that – as was the case with digital signage – we will see pushback on this type of proprietary approach, and market incentives for suppliers to offer expanded integration options (for example, via APIs) to help businesses to integrate multiple cloud solutions to address complex process requirements. It's also likely that, as is the case with digital signage, integration and more sophisticated manageability will unlock new opportunities (such as context-aware advertising) that could not be captured with earlier-generation technology. IT strategists plotting an enterprise cloud strategy, like those responsible for digital signage strategies, need to assess not only current capabilities but also the impact of future advances in manageability, greater system openness and vastly broader integration when evaluating the ways in which an advanced cloud application can enable new capabilities within the business over time.

## Issues that are important to the adoption and enablement of advanced cloud applications

These examples highlight some of the issues that are most important to successful adoption and enablement of cloud applications – expertise (and entire services) embedded in software, the ability to capitalize on and combine innovation and capability from multiple sources, the ability to evolve from a minimum viable product (MVP) to enhanced functionality over time, and a technology vision that is aligned with the ultimate business goal for deploying technology. Other issues noted by the working group include:

- *Focus on applications with compelling metrics.* Users and executives will primarily gauge the success of new application adoption by two issues: speed and impact on the business. Relative to on-premise software, cloud applications should always provide an advantage in terms of time from decision to initial user access, but the most important measurement of speed is time to benefit. The business benefit itself is generally assessed in terms of cost savings or increased revenue, and/or in terms of better connection to customers, prospects or other target communities. Businesses that evaluate potential new applications in terms of speed and impact and which prioritize applications that can rapidly deliver compelling payback will earn support and trust from executives and end users.

- *Emphasize agility and integration, and de-prioritize adherence to existing corporate IT policies governing software development.* This advice seems counter-intuitive: why would an organization choose to ignore existing policies for new application introduction? The basic rationale revolves around the importance of disruption arising from cloud. Corporate IT policies governing new software systems are generally designed to give IT control over the pace of new software introduction, allowing IT to move at a measured pace towards new capabilities. However, cloud software doesn't progress in an orderly fashion. Cloud allows for the rapid and simultaneous adoption of new capabilities across the enterprise. Companies that are good at capitalizing on this potential are able to innovate rapidly; those that are not risk falling farther and farther behind. IT needs to step beyond its desire for control and view innovation and integration as its key outcomes, not as tasks that can be slotted into an ever-lengthening priority queue.

- *Understand the connection between the broad trend towards digitization and the requirement to be effective in enabling cloud applications.* Many traditional business domains are being reshaped by cloud applications. The CEO of a major Canadian bank recently told employees that the institution was becoming a technology company that delivers banking services, and identified ApplePay as a major threat to the business. The chairman/CEO of GE was famously quoted as saying, "If you went to bed last night as an industrial company, you're going to wake up this morning as a software and analytics company." And the concept of 'Uberfication' is used to describe the ways in which new businesses use cloud applications to attack established competitors. Businesses need to be proactive in capitalizing on the process and market benefits unlocked by advanced cloud applications (by taking advantage of new automation opportunities and/or relevant services that are provided as SaaS applications), while also staying aware of opportunities to package their own outputs with or within cloud applications – and while also being diligent about understanding how new cloud software-based competitors might undermine current market positions.

## Concluding guidance

The working group volunteered some summary guidance to help managers understand keys to successful adoption and enablement of advanced cloud applications, approaching the issue from both a business and a technical perspective.

From a business perspective, the advice is to make sure that you have an economical path to a compelling outcome, promising a measurable, meaningful return on your financial investment and time commitment. The starting point for adopting a new application has to be a business objective that warrants the effort required to transition to a new system.

> *Make sure that you have an economical path to a compelling outcome, promising a measurable, meaningful return on your financial investment and time commitment*

From a technical perspective, the key issue is the underlying infrastructure. Before adopting an advanced cloud application, be sure that your infrastructure will adequately support the application itself (will your environment support applications that depend on pervasive virtualization and automated management?) and will also adequately support the users of the application (to ensure a positive user experience). Also, recognize that cloud applications are intended to scale: the idea of starting with a limited set of functionality and a limited number of users and increasing users, features and connected applications over time is core to the entire concept of cloud applications. Initial infrastructure weaknesses or constraints are likely to become even more apparent – and deleterious – over time.

## Reference sources

Additional references that readers can use to better understand best/proven practices in adopting and enabling advanced cloud applications include:

- Mary Allen. "Building Bimodal Bridges." InsightaaS, 2015. This article examines Gartner's theory of bimodal IT (with a distinction between innovation and core system management/operations) and ways that it can be adapted for real-world use.
- Apple Developer Enterprise Program (Apple). This easy-to-follow marketing overview demonstrates how a corporate "on ramp" to mobile app development/enablement works.
- Paul Blanchard Configero. Presentation to Atlanta Salesforce User Group (Configero via SlideShare, 2012) – slide deck used in a 2012 presentation

illustrates potential user complaints (slide 9) and important tactics for improving Salesforce performance within the enterprise (slides 11 and 13).

- Paul Lewis. A Question from the High Iron: Innovating with Shadow IT. LinkedIn, August 2015. This blog post takes the position that shadow IT "isn't really a problem. It's where actual business problems get solved," and urges IT departments to provide a cloud on-ramp that facilitates line of business use of new systems to address business issues.
- Michael O'Neil and Mary Allen. "Life in 'interesting' times." InsightaaS, 2015. One of several InsightaaS posts exploring the use of SaaS-enabled location-based intelligence systems.
- Danny Palmer. "Enterprise mobility brings Network Rail agility 'never before conceived to be possible'." Computing, 2015.
  "How Mobile Apps are Keeping Network Rail Moving." FeedHenry, 2013. This article and video provide insight on Network Rail's use of cloud and mobile infrastructure.

## Metrics and Milestones

As is generally the case with enterprise technologies, it is difficult to establish precise payback timeframes for advanced cloud applications. However, there are some guidelines that can be used to establish initial expectations. These vary by the application objective:

- If you are adopting an application that is expected to reduce costs – such as a technical application automating IT processes – you may realize benefits immediately, and should expect to see tangible improvements within 60 days.
- If you are adopting an application that is intended to help the business to generate more revenue, you are relying on a combination of changing technology, changing user behaviour, changing business processes and potentially, changing customer behaviour; additionally, returns are subject to the length of a normal sales cycle, which can vary very widely. This is clearly a more complex set of conditions than is found with applications focused on cost reduction. In this case, assuming a normal sales cycle of up to 60 days, initial benefits should be apparent within 3-6 months, and should continue to build for at least the first year. Applications focused on generating revenue in businesses with longer sales cycles will require more time to yield benefits.

- New applications that are focused on improving productivity – including, and notably, new collaboration platforms – are more complex to adopt than cost-reduction applications, but are easier to control than applications focused on revenue generation. Companies adopting productivity applications can expect to see first tangible returns in a 60-90 period.

Please note that the starting point for each of these timeframes is application launch, not project launch: the development and testing of an application generates enthusiasm and awareness, but the 'clock starts ticking' when the application is in production, not when it is first approved or available for testing and review. It can be difficult to maintain this perspective, since excitement is highest at the outset of a new project, but initial success (and potentially, the need for corrective measures) should be gauged by appropriate timeframes. This same guidance holds true for traditional monolithic software suites as well – but fortunately, the time from project launch to production is greatly compressed with cloud!

## Course corrections: where to look if benefit expectations are not met?

While the timing guidelines above can help management to set expectations for advanced cloud application ramp-up, they beg a second question: where should a business look for remediation if benefits are not realized within these timeframes?

As with the 'concluding guidance' in the previous section, there is merit in looking at both technical and business issues to identify why anticipated benefits are not materializing. Some of the questions that should be asked when investigating under-delivery are aligned with issues that were likely covered in the planning process. The technical questions are easy to anticipate and evaluate: is the infrastructure platform sufficient to deliver the performance needed by the users? If not, is this an issue of back end capabilities, or of the ability to deliver a compelling user experience via endpoint devices used by business staff?

The business issues are somewhat harder to analyze. Most often, advanced cloud applications fail to meet benefit expectations because the users and processes have not evolved to capitalize on the benefits offered by the solution.

To provide a non-technical simile: It is best to envision a cloud application as a tool that has a defined purpose, like a deli slicer, rather than one that is highly configurable, like a Swiss Army Knife. The tool can't be neatly adapted to a wide variety of use cases: if the user wants to open a can rather than slice deli meats, he/she needs to find a different tool, as the slicer can't be adapted to a non-standard use case. In the same vein, the tool provides benefit when processes and users change to capitalize on its capabilities. In the example of a slicer, the business benefits when the machine is used instead of a knife to make rapid, consistent cuts in a block of cheese, greatly reducing the time needed to fill an order. The tool doesn't deliver optimal benefit if the deli's business process still requires a user to sharpen a knife before unwrapping the cheese, however, or if the user decides to use the knife instead of the slicer.

To bring the analogy back to evaluating shortfalls in cloud application benefits, there are several business-level issues that may be responsible for underperformance. At the process level, is the application appropriately aligned with the needs of the business – was the actual requirement for rapid fulfillment of cheese orders, rather than for a mix of cutting and can-opening? Has management evolved workflow definitions and expectations to capitalize on the potential of the application – has it eliminated steps associated with phased-out technologies or manual processes (e.g., 'sharpen the knife first' even if the slicer is used to prepare the customer's order), and adjusted throughput expectations (the application equivalent of expecting deli workers to fill cheese orders in a shorter time)? And on the user side, have the new users received the training and support necessary to drive a migration to use of the new tools, or are they defaulting back to traditional behaviours (use of the knife rather than the slicer)?

This discussion illustrates the importance of the basic operating model factors of *people, process and technology* on advanced application success. Figure 5-4 illustrates how these areas should be approached to understand their impact on delayed or weak benefit realization from advanced cloud applications.

*Figure 5-4. Examining cloud application underperformance: key issues*

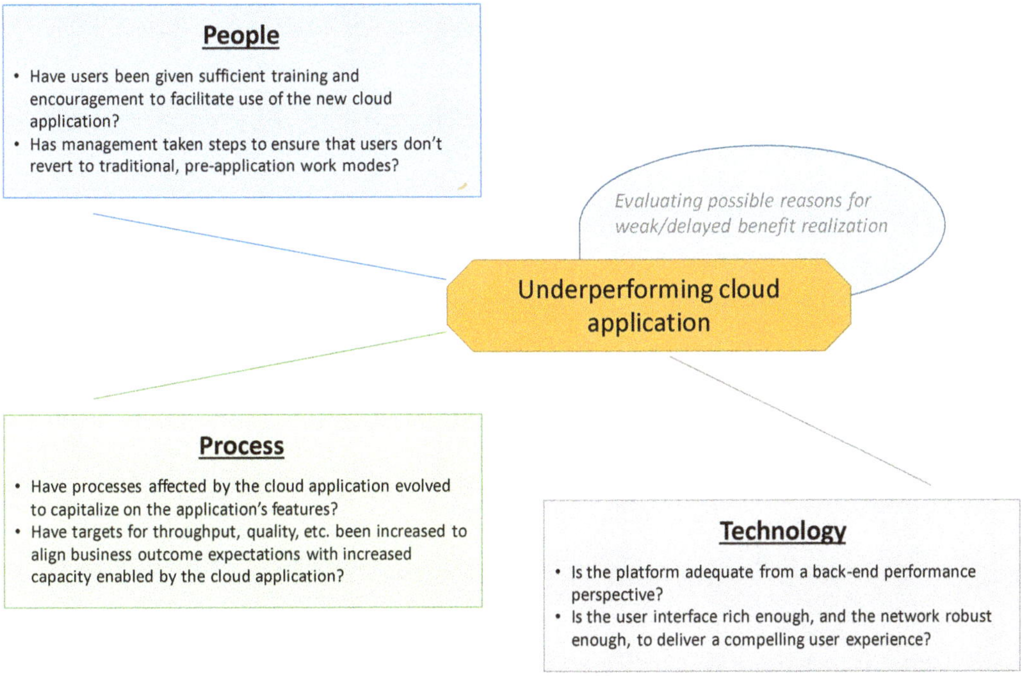

**People**

- Have users been given sufficient training and encouragement to facilitate use of the new cloud application?
- Has management taken steps to ensure that users don't revert to traditional, pre-application work modes?

*Evaluating possible reasons for weak/delayed benefit realization*

**Underperforming cloud application**

**Process**

- Have processes affected by the cloud application evolved to capitalize on the application's features?
- Have targets for throughput, quality, etc. been increased to align business outcome expectations with increased capacity enabled by the cloud application?

**Technology**

- Is the platform adequate from a back-end performance perspective?
- Is the user interface rich enough, and the network robust enough, to deliver a compelling user experience?

*Source: TCBC/InsightaaS, 2016*

As Figure 5-4 illustrates, it is possible for any of people, process or technology to be the root cause for weak performance of advanced cloud applications vs. expectations, and there are certainly plentiful examples of all three issues derailing anticipated benefits. As a starting point, the working group urges that management step back and look at the 'big picture'. What has – and hasn't – changed in the processes and activities surrounding the new application? It's always hard to identify changes that *haven't* occurred, but which might have been expected…but this is often the best first step towards finding root causes of underperformance and making the adjustments needed to obtain best payback on corporate investments in adopting and enabling advanced cloud applications.

## Reference Sources

References that help identify issues in aligning advanced cloud application metrics with business objectives include:

- Carl Aspler & Associates. Seven Suggestions for Leading Successful Change, 2012. Drawing on his experience with GE, change management expert Carl Aspler describes the "E=QxA" equation: the effectiveness of a change is the product of its technical quality and its acceptance by staff members. Aspler's work focuses on the 'people' component of the factors shown in Figure 5-4; in the references work, he notes that while successful projects had sound technical quality, "98% of all changes evaluated as "unsuccessful" at GE also had good technical solutions or approaches.

- "Gartner Says That by 2017, 25 Percent of Enterprises Will Have an Enterprise App Store. Gartner Group, February 2013. To be fair to Gartner, this forecast is a couple of years old, which may explain why the hype around enterprise app stores is exceeding their appearance, at least within the Canadian business community. However, the observation is directionally correct: enterprises are looking to establish a measure of control over mobile apps, and corporate app stores provide a means of offering users choice without exposing core infrastructure to unmanageable security and auditability risks.

- Cloud Business Models, Metrics and Imperatives: A TCBC Best Practices Document. Toronto Business Cloud Coalition, 2015. This Best Practices document from the TCBC Cloud Business Models, Metrics and Imperatives working group contains guidance on the metrics and measurements used by non-IT business management to evaluate cloud initiatives.

*Chapter 6.*

# Cloud Governance, Risk and Compliance (GRC)

Essential guidance on extending corporate GRC practices to the cloud

*Contributing community experts: Andrew Nunes (Fasken Martineau DuMoulin), Dave Collings (Do IT Lean), Matt Ambrose (PwC), Stefano Tiranardi (Symantec), Roy Hart (Seneca College), Jerrard Gaertner (University of Toronto, Ryerson University)*

*Initial publication date: February 2016*

# Cloud Governance, Risk and Compliance

## Definition and context

When the answer to "cloud?" is 'yes', what is the next question? Based on recent experience, it appears that the answer involves 'governance'. In most cases, there is no real debate about whether cloud will be used. Cloud is deployed in a clear majority of businesses today, and in fact, many organizations have moved to a "cloud first" mandate. Legacy issues around security and data residency still demand attention, but for the most part, the debate around cloud management has evolved to a discussion of how cloud use and expansion should be governed.

There are currently no generally recognized governance guidelines that a Canadian business can refer to as a means of identifying the process needed to establish effective governance and controls over new cloud-based workloads, or even over the migration of current workloads to the cloud. However, there are principles that apply more broadly to governance, risk and compliance that can be (and are) extended to the cloud.

Defining the key terms in the process represents a meaningful first step in this process. Governance in our context refers to the policies established by the board and senior management, and the oversight process for these policies. Controls are the processes used by management – in our context, IT management – to effect the governance policies. Compliance defines a set of objectives that are an important component of the overall goals that the controls are designed to achieve. And risk in its various forms (business risk, technology risk, risk associated with regulations and laws, etc.) poses a threat to compliance, and is addressed systematically via the controls. This seems an abstract construct, and there is clearly quite a lot of real-world activity that tests the limits of and connections between each area. But this initial understanding establishes a framework that can be used to develop more concrete guidance.

Looking at the abstract terms through the lens of cloud exposes a key issue. The descriptions above suppose that the business has control over the various elements considered by and important to the policies and controls. But with cloud, an important part of the framework is outsourced to a third party – the cloud provider. And with the expanded use of cloud, it is likely that a business will have multiple third parties incorporated within its operations. It isn't possible to actively manage the activities of a single large cloud provider, much less a portfolio spanning multiple IaaS, PaaS and SaaS suppliers. As a result, the controls need to be extended to the cloud provider, and the provider needs to be vetted for capabilities that are important to effective operation of the controls.

As cloud becomes more common, the decision to locate a workload in the cloud is viewed as merely an operational issue. But this decision is different in kind than decisions about the selection and deployment of new servers, routers, storage or applications. It is possible to position cloud as an operational decision, but only if the governance and control structure is strong enough and broad enough to provide an effective means of integrating cloud into the practices required by the enterprise's board and senior management.

*Figure 6-1. The governance framework – extending beyond the cloud*

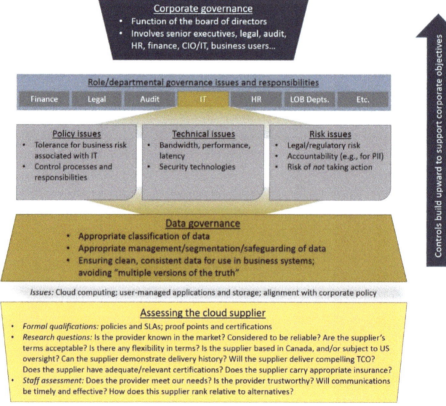

Source: TCBC/InsightaaS

As is noted above, there is no single clear and concise source of guidance on cloud governance in Canada. Figure 6-1 provides meaningful insight, though, because it illustrates several key points: that oversight and direction starts at the executive level, with a definition of what the business sees as essential policy and risk issues; that these requirements apply across all roles and functions within the organization, including IT; that IT needs to manage policy, risk and technical issues with respect to data governance, regardless of whether the data is resident within the organization's physical premises or offsite; and that part of IT's responsibility in a cloud or hybrid environment is to ensure that providers are subject to and supportive of the controls used to implement corporate policy objectives.

Reference sources

Additional references that readers can use to better understand the key issues defining advanced cloud applications and adoption and enablement issues include:

- About Governance of Enterprise IT, IT Governance Institute. Overview of the COBIT 5 principles for enterprise IT governance, with links to additional resources.
- Cloud Computing for Small and Medium-sized Enterprises: Privacy Responsibilities and Considerations. Office of the Privacy Commissioner of Canada, 2014. General information and FAQs on cloud computing for small and medium-sized enterprises including privacy responsibilities and considerations.
- Modelling Cloud Computing Architecture Without Compromising Privacy. Information and Privacy Commissioner of Ontario, 2010. This document, developed as part of then-Commissioner Ann Cavoukian's Privacy by Design (PbD) initiative, discusses the impact of the "blurred perimeter" of cloud and the PbD principles developed to address the issue.
- Privacy in the Clouds. Information and Privacy Commissioner of Ontario. Background document on the issues surrounding privacy and the cloud, also issued as part of the PbD initiative.
- Cloud Controls Matrix v3.0.1. Cloud Security Alliance, 2014 (no-cost registration required). Spreadsheet template providing a detailed description of the issues important to effective governance of cloud-based systems.

- [SDP Specification 1.0](). Cloud Security Alliance, 2014 (no-cost registration required). Report provides a description of the need for and functioning of a software-defined perimeter.

## Business objectives

If GRC for the cloud is (as Figure 6-1 suggests) positioned as the extension of corporate governance to cloud systems – and not as an independent category – then the business objectives relating to cloud GRC are consistent with those that drive GRC more broadly.

## Governance

At the highest level, *governance* refers to the role of a firm's board of directors, who are charged with representing shareholders by exercising oversight on business operations. This general heading covers the executive team (senior management, legal, HR, etc.), the objectives that they are pursuing, and the management framework used to document the activities and outcomes that are important to these objectives.

In today's corporate world, business operations are heavily dependent on IT operations, which are in turn increasingly dependent on cloud. This cascade creates a chain through which an issue that begins in the cloud can become a senior management or board issue. As a result, IT management needs to be cognizant of the connections between corporate governance and IT practice.

- *Cloud specific issues:* In cloud, "governance" has two meanings: it references the organizational structure and process described above, but the term is also (and more often) used in cloud circles to describe oversight of data management and security processes.

  The discrete use of the word "governance" in the cloud context is understandable, as processes around data and security that impact the lives and evaluation of IT efficacy are affected by cloud, and the term conveys an implication that formal processes are mandatory. However, the working group is clear in its belief that tighter connections between cloud and corporate governance would benefit all parties, for several reasons, including:

    o  In terms of movement and location of data, and the accompanying issues surrounding audit, cloud introduces new governance issues. These tend to fall into IT's lap, but they are not IT issues – the affect (and should be exposed to) HR, legal, and senior management. Alignment of cloud and corporate governance positioning cloud as a subset of broader corporate policies and structures enables predictable oversight for business-relevant issues.

- o It's fair to argue that because companies increasingly rely on IT, putting IT in the cloud will create unique corporate issues that are of importance to the CEO. An informal process that relies on cloud-specific governing issues 'bubbling up' via the CIO or CTO is not an optimal means of aligning enterprise-level interests.
- o Customer contracts may govern information lifecycle management requirements, acceptable storage locations for data, and other cloud-relevant issues – but it may not be reasonable to expect IT to monitor new contracts for clauses of this sort. Linking cloud to corporate governance helps to increase visibility on issues spanning IT and non-IT operations.
  - Note – this issue may also have implications in businesses that use cloud-based email or other cloud-based document storage and exchange media.

## Risk

*Risk* refers to the management of issues that could have a negative impact on the business's ability to deliver value to its shareholders. Risk takes many forms. Business risk varies by industry and in some cases, by company: it can include portfolio exposure (for financial institutions), supply chain volatility or production interruptions (for goods-producing firms), infection or practitioner shortages (for health care providers)...each business context contains risks that might threaten the viability of a particular type of business. There are broader categories of risk that apply across industries as well. For example, most companies have some level of IT-related or data-related risk (relating to interruption of IT service provision or data leakage), and many have regulatory risks (which might involve data, allowable capitalization levels, environmental factors, etc.).

- *Cloud specific issues:* In IT circles generally and in cloud specifically, "risk" is most closely associated with security and business continuity: it is understood that breaches, malware and IT failures have a negative impact on corporate reputation, relationships with customers and other stakeholders, and on the ability of the business to operate. IT organizations within publicly traded enterprises are also aware that they need to demonstrate controls that mitigate risks, especially with respect to release of financial data.

Enumerating these concerns, though, is different from identifying each as a "cloud-specific issue." Each is an *IT* issue. Using the cloud to deliver IT has some specific implications for how the risks might arise and how they need to be controlled/managed. But there's a parallel between risk and governance. The section above notes that cloud governance should be aligned with overall corporate governance. Here, we see that cloud risk aligns with overall IT risk (which in turn, is a subset of the corporate risk profile).

At a tactical level, however, there are some differences in how controls are established in the cloud. If an issue requiring physical intervention occurs with an on-site system, or if a compromised system needs to be shut down, it is possible for IT staff to act quickly and effectively. If this same issue involves equipment hosted in the cloud, what are the steps to resolution? Adequate controls may require the firm to obtain supplier sign-off on clear remediation and escalation processes – potentially, up to and including the right to dispatch company staff to take on-site actions if the supplier can't respond appropriately to a risk source. It should be noted, though, that both contractually defined system access and the ability to dispatch corporate staff may be problematic in some cases – for example, the laws governing cloud contracts may vary across countries, and in any event, the geographic location(s) of a cloud supplier's data centre(s) may limit the extent to which the client can take physical or even programmatic action to isolate a compromised asset.

There are cloud-specific risks at an operational level as well, especially the risk of lost connectivity (due either to outages in the network or at the cloud supplier) that affects process throughput. A manufacturer, for example, may need ongoing access to design or ERP systems to sustain production, or a call centre may require access to customer-specific data. What steps need to be taken to mitigate this cloud risk? The working group noted that redundancy can be used to ensure that work doesn't come to a halt in the event of an outage: redundant communications systems can (and should) be used to connect cloud-based resources to production facilities, and there may be merit to having at least a limited redundant set of core data available on site in some environments.

Lastly, there are regulatory risks specific to cloud that merit their own notice. Data housed in an unstable jurisdiction, or in one that doesn't provide stringent protection of intellectual property, may be difficult to retrieve and protect. This isn't an issue for local data centres, but as one working group member observed, "Not everyone operates like we do in North America."

## Compliance

*Compliance* refers to an enterprise's ability to demonstrate that its operations are in accordance with regulatory requirements. Firms subject to regulation – including all publicly traded firms, and organizations in industries such as finance, government, communications and healthcare – have to be able to track compliance with applicable laws and regulations, and need the ability to quickly respond to any issue that threatens to make them non-compliant.

- *Cloud specific issues:* There are two different compliance-related cloud issues: the need to include cloud processing and transmission as part of compliance exercises, and the impact of cloud use on compliance tasks.

  The first issue – the need to account for cloud as a component of processes subject to compliance – centres on the need to certify the integrity of processes and data. For example, it may be necessary to show that financial results have not been tampered with, which would require a firm to establish the integrity of each possible link to the ERP system. If the ERP system (or a system that is linked to it in a meaningful way) is based in the cloud, then there is a need to account for the hosting environment(s) and transmission paths. This issue could arise with any system that affects finances, or domains subject to regulation (such as health care).

  The second issue involves complexities that cloud can introduce into the audit process itself. IT is an important source of insight for auditors and regulators, who often need to track the data in or generated by a process. How would the need to query a cloud provider affect the cost of an audit, or the time required for its completion? It is certainly not common to factor "increased costs relating to audit" into the overall financial evaluation of a cloud solution, but it is possible that in some situations, cloud will have a material impact on audit and compliance costs, which affect the overall value of a cloud solution.

Because cloud operations can be opaque – difficult or impossible to query or audit – enterprises are often sensitive to how cloud might affect their ability to assure compliance with relevant strictures. To be fair, there are many different types of audits, and cloud would have no negative impact on a number of them: for example, a manufacturer might undergo four audits a year (financial/accounting, ISO, insurance, fire), and in many cases, cloud would have either a somewhat positive effect (e.g., in demonstrating offsite backup for insurance and fire) or no real impact (generally, ISO). Where cloud did pose an obstacle to a thorough audit, though (certainly possible with financial/accounting), it would add to the cost and complexity of corporate compliance.

## Aligning cloud with overall GRC business objectives

The business objectives of GRC have been defined as follows[6]:

- Protect and enhance business value by fostering a risk aware culture, support informed decision-making, and address multiple compliance and assurance layers;
- Enhance operational efficiency by rationalizing risk management, controls, and assurance structures and processes, as well as intelligent use of IT and data management structures;
- Provide a proactive and dynamic approach by enabling the organization to more quickly, consistently, and efficiently respond to challenges arising from evolving risk profiles and rapidly changing regulatory requirements; and
- Support a linkage to strategy by enabling the organization to meet compliance objectives while improving performance to be use of an integrated framework and support the strategic objectives.

While these items describe business outcomes, they connect directly with IT objectives as well. IT provides support for "informed decision making" and the visibility needed to assess risk and provide assurance of reasonable corporate practices. As is noted in the

---

 [6] Eric Krell, "Four Objectives for Effective GRC." Business Finance, 2011.

second bullet, IT is an essential component of risk management, and becomes even more central as businesses evolve from traditional to technology-based business infrastructure. IT is viewed as a key means of enabling rapid response to many different business requirements, including those imposed by regulators. And in advanced organizations, IT is the point at which the guidance embedded within strategic frameworks is translated into corporate capabilities.

Cloud plays a key role in advancing IT's ability to deliver on these outcomes; therefore, the business objectives for cloud GRC can be directly connected to the business objectives for an entire enterprise. Where cloud does become 'different' is in the development of the specific tools and practices used to extend enterprise GRC to the cloud. In many organizations, these practices provide the key to helping senior management to appreciate how their companies can obtain the benefits of cloud without incurring increased risk, obviating existing governance principles or impairing the corporation's ability to comply with laws and regulations.

## Reference sources

- New technology-based outsourcing arrangements. Office of the Superintendent of Financial Institutions, 2012. A memorandum connecting the 2009 "Outsourcing of Business Activities, Functions and Processes" with "new technology-based services such as Cloud Computing."
- Steven B. Kerr. Regulatory implications of cloud computing. Fasken Martineau. PowerPoint-format document traces cloud-related regulations issued by the Office of the Superintendent of Financial Institutions (OFSI) and their implications for cloud strategy.

## Best practices

At a fundamental level, appropriate GRC practices begin with *accountability*. Who is responsible for what aspects of the complex chain that involves policy, technology and legal risk? GRC relies on oversight of a documented set of standards and policies – and this in turn relies on defining what's important, and who's responsible for ensuring that required steps are taken, and that necessary follow-up occurs.

The cross process, enterprise-wide nature of cloud can make it difficult for firms to assign unique responsibility for specific process steps to individuals or individual departments. Take as an example management of personally identifiable information

(PII). Companies have a legal requirement to safeguard this information, so legal needs to be involved in setting and reviewing policies and practices. Release of the information would create brand damage (and possibly, liability), so senior management needs to understand the efficacy of the policies and practices well enough to defend them, if need be, to shareholders and other stakeholders. The information is processed by and stored in IT equipment, so the CIO and his/her staff need to establish both data management practices and put effective IT security solutions in place to safeguard against unauthorized electronic access to the data. Business users collect the information through the course of transactions and/or other customer interactions, so they need to be included in the policy and procedure definitions, and finance will have access to this data for invoicing purposes, so they need to be included as well. Inclusion of staff members in any documented process likely requires training (and proof that training has occurred), so HR would need to be involved in sourcing appropriate training materials/courses and documenting successful completion of the training by staff and/or management.

Looking at Figure 6-1, we see that accountability for PII involves each of the groups included in the "corporate governance" group shown at the top of the Figure, with the exception of Audit (who may well need to sign off on whatever process is ultimately used to protect PII). And the example as defined above only references internal resources. When cloud is included as part of the infrastructure, each of the parties involved in the chain has additional, externally-facing responsibilities: IT needs to demonstrate that supplier practices meet internal security standards, HR needs to be satisfied that supplier staff either have no access to PII and/or can be shown to be trustworthy, audit needs to be satisfied by the degree of insight that it can obtain into supplier activities, etc.

To provide a structure to this cross-functional set of responsibilities, the working group proposed the process outlined in Figure 6-2.

*Figure 6-2. Core steps in the cloud GRC process*

**IDENTIFY**
- Identify cloud-specific risk issues.
  - Note: cloud GRC doesn't replace corporate GRC; it represents an operational system that can be incorporated within the broader GRC risk framework

**ARTICULATE**
- Articulate the nature of risks and how they are to be addressed
  - Note: this requires both SOP and contingency plans for each issue identified above

**ASSIGN**
- Identify roles/individuals with responsibility for specific issues
  - Note: Try to ensure an appropriate allocation of tasks/responsibilities between the user organization and the cloud service provider(s)
  - Note: Include individuals with oversight responsibility for the process itself

**DOCUMENT**
- Understand and clearly document remedies in the event of performance issues
  - Note: realistically, most suppliers will occasionally have issues in meeting performance standards. What happens when these occur? Do SLAs meet your needs?

**REVIEW**
- Review the assumptions, actions and responsibilities with stakeholders
  - Note: Review documented assumptions and actions with business process owners, legal, etc. to understand whether process and remedies are appropriate/adequate; also, probe to see if there are any business risks that haven't been considered, but which might be relevant to cloud user

**ALIGN**
- Update the understanding of risks, actions and accountability; align with overall corporate governance policies
  - Note: obtain signoff from business process owners after updating GRC assumptions and policies based on feedback from the review stage; align with/incorporate into corporate GRC practices and documentation

*Source: TCBC/InsightaaS, 2015*

## Applying the GRC steps to real-world cloud challenges

The process described above contains a number of steps that respond to very specific issues and conditions within a particular enterprise – which makes providing general guidance on its application challenging. However, in the interests of providing some tangible illustration of how GRC is applied to cloud, the working group developed the following scenarios:

*Management of sensitive (/regulated) data*

1. *Identify:* Given the preoccupation with the security of cloud resources, it's very likely that management of sensitive (and/or regulated, in some contexts) data will need to be included as a cloud GRC topic. One issue that should be investigated is the ability of the organization to react rapidly to data leakage. For example, if internally housed data was inadvertently exposed via a web portal that is hacked, it would be reasonable to have "take the database offline immediately" as an important component of the response. Is this possible with a cloud provider – will IT have the access and control needed to accomplish this task? Another data management issue might pertain to back-up. How is data that is critical to operations (or subject to regulation) maintained? What backup and restore procedures are in place? Can these procedures be extended to a cloud provider – and if so, how can they be tested, how often should they be tested, and who is responsible for ensuring that the tests are conducted and are successful? Should the data be backed up to both the client's location and to the cloud provider's facilities? How many locations should be used for backup, and how often should the data be replicated and/or reconciled?

   - Note – it may be the case that a supplier will not accept responsibility for issues that are included under a company's overall GRC policy. Where this happens, a buyer faces a choice. They can of course refuse to move data or workloads to the cloud. They can decide that the GRC requirement isn't critical, and agree to proceed with the cloud supplier anyway. Or they can look to reconfigure the way in which they are using the cloud provider to mitigate concerns associated with the supplier's ability to meet the internal GRC standard. Enterprises choosing either of the latter two options should be sure to document the ways in which they are (or aren't) aligning with GRC objectives, so that they are able to account for these processes/decisions in the future.

2. *Articulate:* Continuing the discussion of back up/maintenance of sensitive/regulated data: if data processed by and stored at a cloud providers' facility includes data that is critical to operations, it should probably be replicated in real time or near-real time to a remote facility operated by the

client, and possibly, to a remote facility operated by the cloud provider as well. All copies of the data should adhere to a common and reasonable backup schedule, using backup processes and technology that is tested on a regular basis. Additional systems should be used to ensure consistency of data across versions, so that if the user is forced to rely on a replicated copy, there is confirmation of consistency between the replicated and 'live' versions of the data.

3. *Assign*: With respect to data management, the CIO will probably have responsibility for ensuring that internal and cloud-based data management processes and technologies are appropriate and consistent. If there is a regulatory requirement for some of the data used/stored by the system to be retained for a period of time, audit will likely want to ensure that this data is safe and available if needed. In both cases, the buyer requirements will need to be recognized in the supplier's SLA – meaning that legal may need to be involved as well to ensure that the SLA meets the business objectives.

4. *Document*: As is noted in Figure 6-2, realistically, most suppliers will occasionally have issues in meeting performance standards. At this step, it's important for whomever is responsible for a step in the process – in this example, the CIO, audit, and/or legal – to examine the remedies outlined in the cloud supplier's SLA, and to determine if these remedies are sufficient to the purposes of the business. If they are not, the business needs to design, document and operationalize a process to address this gap. The multiple back-up scenario above might well meet corporate needs for data retention. However, how (if at all) can liability associated with leakage of sensitive data be addressed?

5. *Review*: Once the process is drafted and documented, review the outcomes with all key stakeholders, including business process owners, legal, and other executives/oversight sources if/as appropriate. Are there exceptions to general assumptions that need to be specifically addressed? For example, depending on industry/context, PII, engineering blueprints and/or other types of IP might qualify as data types with unique processing requirements. Are they excluded from cloud workloads, and/or handled differently in the cloud?

6. *Align*: Once all parties have been heard from, document the GRC process, obtain sign-off from relevant stakeholders, and align/integrate the cloud-specific policies with the overall corporate GRC corpus. This ties together the "corporate memory," adding (in this example) an understanding of how data in the cloud is

treated, and how threats to data in the cloud are managed, to the overall corporate policies on data management.

*Responding to a breach*

The six-step approach can also be applied to a scenario in which a breach has occurred. In this case, the steps might work as follows:

1. *Identify:* The first step in understanding how to respond to a breach is to identify the affected parties. Whose data has been released? And what response/disclosure/notice is required?

2. *Articulate*: Once the source and scope of the breach and the response requirements are understood, the next step is to draft communications targeted at key constituencies. This step highlights the cross-functional nature of GRC requirements: from a technical perspective, a breach is IT's concern, but responsibility for articulating the response resides in other parts of the organization.

3. *Assign*: Expanding on the observation regarding broad responsibility for articulating the corporate message(s) after a breach, response is a cross-functional issue. IT will have a role to play: it will need to understand what went wrong, and what can be done to mitigate current damage and prevent additional leaks. Marketing/PR will be involved in communicating to the community at large, while sales and customer service will likely have to reach out to specific customers to discuss the causes and implications of the breach and to articulate the remediation steps that the enterprise is taking. Legal will need to be involved as well, both to examine corporate exposure and to understand the extent of cloud supplier liability.

4. *Document*: IT's understanding of the scope, causes and remediation of the breach, and the messages drafted for use by marketing/PR to communicate with the public at large, by sales/customer service to communicate with customers, and by legal for communication with both internal executives and cloud suppliers, need to be clearly documented. In response to a breach, it's important that every internal resource charged with external communications conveys a clear and consistent message.

5. *Review*: Before the communication plan is enacted, senior management needs to review and approve the corporate position with respect to breach causes and effects and remediation efforts. This may well include input from executives

representing key departments, such as legal, and will likely include some executive-level discussion with the various staff members responsible for external communication.

6. *Align*: The executive team needs to ensure that the content and process of communications around the breach is consistent with corporate messaging objectives. Once all parties have been heard from, document the GRC process, obtains sign-off from relevant stakeholders, and align/integrate the cloud-specific policies with the overall corporate GRC corpus. This ties together the "corporate memory," adding (in this example) an understanding of how data in the cloud is treated, and how threats to data in the cloud are managed, to the overall corporate policies on data management.

## Final guidance

The working group was asked to discuss the question, "If you are contemplating moving a workload to the cloud, or trying to develop or enhance your approach to GRC for workloads already in the cloud, you should consider…" Responses included:

- The scope of assignability of responsibility, and the roles of each involved role/area. Understand that while cloud workloads are (generally) managed by IT, GRC is a corporate issue, involving many different areas of the enterprise, and different levels of management throughout the organization. As one group member said, "Make sure you have the right people at the table, and make sure you have a Plan B."

- Variability in terms and conditions, across suppliers and with respect to internal requirements. Large, established suppliers tend to issue "long, detailed contracts leaving you with very little wiggle room to negotiate," especially if you are a small or midmarket customer. Smaller/newer suppliers may also offer "cookie cutter" contracts (in many cases, downloaded from the internet), but may well be more willing to negotiate SLA terms and conditions, which can help align SLAs with internal GRC requirements.

- Limits on remedies, and the overall impact of cloud reliability on business continuity. Be cognizant of the gap between the supplier's obligation in the event of an outage and your real costs and requirements. For example, if your supplier goes down for two days, what is the financial impact on your business, and how much of this loss is your supplier obliged to cover? What effect would an outage have on your operations, and do you have a means of providing for business continuity if a supplier goes down?

- The extent to which a supplier is obliged to provide proactive monitoring and reporting. The group's members were clear on the importance of having cloud suppliers perform self-monitoring, and on the need to have the supplier proactively report any service interruptions or other issues. Ideally, this self-reporting should trigger remedies called for in the SLA: for example, if a customer is to receive a credit in the event of downtime, the supplier should monitor availability and automatically issue the credit if its systems go down – it should not wait for the user to identify an outage and to submit a claim for the credit.

- Developing a model/template to guide your cloud supplier management approach, and/or engaging a firm that can provide a relevant framework. One group member's firm works with customers on developing GRC strategies. It uses a model that considers suppliers (their reputation, capabilities, references, etc.), the terms of the SLAs/formal agreements, the extent to which the cloud supplier(s) are aligned with internal requirements and with external needs (e.g., safe and reliable delivery of systems impacting customer success and satisfaction), appropriate monitoring processes and metrics, and options (the "plan B" referenced above) for alternative service delivery in the event of a breach, outage, etc.

## Metrics and milestones

The final issue covered in TCBC Best Practices documents is metrics and milestones. However, it is very difficult to credibly establish either an appropriate measurement for GRC, or the markers that indicate that a steady state has been achieved. Apart from a general consistency with corporate GRC, the measure of cloud GRC is having clear responsibilities and action plans appropriate to the needs of the organization, and the specifics of this approach are necessarily tied to a host of issues – location, culture, industry, regulatory environment – that will vary widely across organizations.

Similarly, there's no clearly defined point at which cloud GRC can be said to be complete. As one working group member noted, you're never really 'done' with any vendor management program. As cloud expands and evolves, so too will the need to define the ways in which suppliers of connected or overlapping services need to respond to system outages, and the responsibilities of internal staff – within and outside IT – in working with these suppliers in a predictable manner that is consistent with enterprise GRC requirements.

*Chapter 7.*

# Cloud Security, Privacy and Reliability

Essential guidance on how to identify and assess key issues relating to cloud security, privacy and reliability in a business environment

*Contributing community experts: Don Sheppard (ConCon Management Services), Stefano Tiranardi (Symantec), Chris Vernon (Symantec), Brandon Kolybaba (Cloud A), Ed Dengler (CIPS), Sangam Manikkayamiyer (Symantec)*

*Initial publication date: February 2016*

# Cloud Security, Privacy and Reliability

## Definition and context

Cloud security is rightly attracting the attention of security professionals who work with infrastructure, applications and solutions, as well as the interest of business and information managers and members of the board members.

While media accounts of high profile data breaches are feeding the perception that cloud technologies are inherently insecure, from a legal or statutory perspective, an organization's use of public cloud services may entail delegation of responsibility for corporate data to a third-party, and with it a loss of control that is different in kind from that in traditional IT environments or in outsourcing relationships. In contracts with outsourcing providers, audit rights, review rights, or other procedures may be established to ensure compliance with certain laws; however, with public cloud services there is less transparency, and the customer's ability to prove that security parameters are executed properly is not as certain.

Security barriers to greater adoption of cloud, then, represent a multi-pronged challenge. Apprehension continues to exist over the service provider's security capabilities in some communities. Though these capabilities may, in fact, be more robust than what end user organizations, and smaller companies in particular, can deliver out of their own resources, security will not serve as a competitive differentiator for the provider until market misperceptions around multi-tenancy risk are addressed. Regulatory exposure is another link connecting security concerns with hesitancy in cloud adoption. Cloud security and governance issues arise from the user organization's real need to demonstrate control and adherence to statutory obligations. A third area of concern lies in the need for good corporate processes for preparing and transmitting data to the cloud provider. Beyond the provider credentials, cloud users need to understand and implement efficient means of ensuring the security of data in motion.

IT security is a vast topic area that has been subject to much misinformation, particularly as it relates to the cloud component. Since many of the security technologies that are deployed in traditional environments and in cloud are the same, the TCBC Cloud Security Working Group's goal is not to describe all solution approaches, but rather to help IT and business leaders to understand what security issues are relevant in a cloud context, what are not, how these might impact cloud adoption, and how cloud-related technologies may in fact contribute to security functionality.

The Working Group appreciates the availability of multiple comprehensive definitions and descriptions of cloud security developed by organizations such as the ISO, the Cloud Security Alliance, and NIST, and is not looking to reproduce this effort, but rather to identify and address key security challenges that are hampering adoption of cloud in the Canadian marketplace.

*Figure 7-1. Cloud security and reliability: key areas of focus*

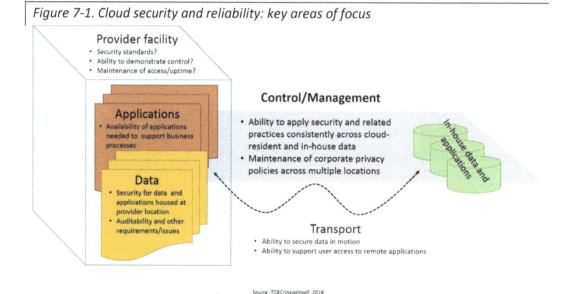

Source: TCBC/InsightaaS, 2016

Under this broad agenda, the Cloud Security Working Group looked to develop guidance in the following subject areas:

1. <u>Cloud security overview</u>

   - A high-level overview of cloud security frameworks that is accessible to senior and middle management within user organizations. This overview is intended to educate management on the risk associated with cloud computing, security strategy and policy requirements, and on the range of technology solutions available in the marketplace to support better procurement decisions and alignment of responsibility for security process and practice with provider and internal resources.

- The overview is also intended to inform IT professionals looking to understand security issues that are unique to cloud. It provides summaries that focus on specific security technologies and processes that are important in a cloud context. These technologies and processes include, but are not limited to, data access technologies, identity management (including single sign-on), data encryption, data retention cycles, and data management and provisioning.

## 2. Data privacy

- Scoping data privacy requirements, including issues around data classification, retention schedules in cloud contractual agreements, perceptions of data residency needs and the legislation/legal process that may influence this are examined from both the cloud provider and cloud user perspectives.

## 3. Data portability

- Corporate strategies for porting data to cloud providers and between clouds will vary based on what component of the stack is being addressed, as well as the size of the business. A lifecycle approach to data transport that addresses the adopting organization's need to prepare, securely transmit and recover data from the cloud provider is required, as is understanding of different security responsibilities in IaaS and SaaS environments and between customer and provider, as well as clarity around SLA terms and critical application requirements.
- A view of cloud networking, which considers not only the requisite technologies but also due diligence the user organization around cloud provider capabilities and terms can help to mitigate security risk. What are the relative advantages of using virtual private networks vs. Internet-based public networking, and what factors play in efforts to ensure data portability via interoperability in cloud network infrastructure?

Figure 7-2. Cloud security, privacy and reliability: challenge and opportunity

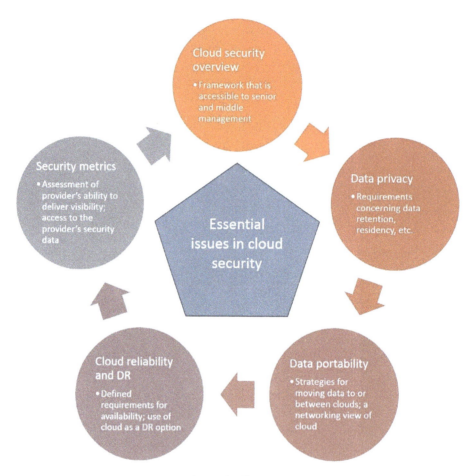

Source: InsightaaS/TCBC, 2016

4. <u>**Cloud reliability and DR**</u>

- Solving for a lack of clarity around cloud provider/customer understanding of cloud reliability and resiliency needs though better definition of availability requirements will help user organizations align cloud delivery with user/process needs.
- Cloud is providing new levels of redundancy to enable modern approaches such as DevOps or to provide more cost efficient means to ensure reliability such as disaster recovery-as-a-solution.

## 5. **Security metrics**

- What steps can the user organization can take to assess a provider's ability to provide adequate visibility and knowledge into the security performance of cloud infrastructure, platforms and applications? What constitutes due diligence in this area, and what metrics should be in place to ensure provider compliance with SLAs?
- The cloud customer's timely access to security data about the provider's physical infrastructure can help the adopting organization measure, evaluate and mitigate risk. What kind of report capabilities are needed to help address these security challenges?

## Business objectives

Cloud computing has effectively demonstrated its contribution to organizational agility. By supporting the rapid adoption of new technologies and their orchestration in new IT/business oriented architectures, cloud can help users develop new capabilities, improve process efficiencies and/or reduce costs more quickly than competitors. However, each new application creates a need to secure users, data, and the environment with which that the solution integrates. Organizations that continue to view security as an onerous requirement will produce a governance framework that is too slow and unwieldy to keep pace with these emerging opportunities. On the other hand, firms that understand the connection between business success and effective IT security, which build the robust frameworks needed to capitalize on these opportunities, will be quicker to adopt and profit from the new agility that cloud can deliver.

A conventional view holds that IT security is a cost centre – a "necessary evil" that knowledgeable and responsible organizations put in place to protect themselves against risk. In an evolving threat landscape, where the attackers are likely more sophisticated than the targeted user organization, this proposition has become increasingly challenging. Cloud service providers offer a service alternative: having made investment in security expert staff resources, technology and certifications, these are able to deliver a level of security that may be difficult for the enterprise to match, and hard for smaller businesses even to aspire to. As the CSO of one major service provider put it, "The unemployment rate in cyber security is zero, and will be zero for the foreseeable future." In relationships with third party providers, customers may directly access security services support, or contract for the delivery of other applications/services where cloud acts as an enabler of security. In addition, cloud providers can deliver a more cost-effective solution to the organization's need for business continuity and disaster recovery capabilities.

From a business perspective, however, conventional wisdom – and legislation – holds that a business cannot totally outsource its risk: whether information resides on premise or is hosted by a third party, at the end of the day, legal liability for the data remains with the business. And the penalties for failure have become increasingly onerous. While in some high profile cases of data breach legal liability has extended to officers of the company, financial losses associated with data breach are mounting due to increasing fines from regulators, and higher costs for information risk insurance. Ultimately, the greatest risk is to business reputation, the basis for trust between buyer and seller and potentially the weightiest source of financial loss. In our highly competitive global market, intellectual property is the foundation for many companies' success, and information is a critical asset that can deliver competitive advantage – assuming adequate protection is in place.

In a world of increasing threats and with higher penalties for security breaches, a business' primary objectives must be to identify and reduce security risk, and to mitigate the impact of failures.  In cloud scenarios, this involves understanding:

*Changing threat vectors*
Data loss will always be a problem, whether it hails from a virus, a computer or cloud exploitation. However, the threat vectors – the path or a tool that a threat actor uses to attack the target – change in migration to cloud, introducing new security challenges, particularly in organizations that are new to cloud deployment. A new class of attacks emerges in multi-tenant public clouds that the user organization should be aware of – for example, new hacker opportunity to target multiple virtual connection points into the provider's physical hardware. Additionally, in the transition to cloud, or in hybrid cloud scenarios, many businesses are challenged to define an integrated security strategy, or to implement the appropriate tools needed to manage the security integration required in multi-cloud deployments.

At a technical level, there may also be new issues around notification of security threat or breach – is the provider responsible for alerting the customer of a potential security problem, and how does this change in IaaS, PaaS and SaaS models –  that if left unaddressed entail additional risk for the user.

## Need *to augment IT* security *policy*

Key to effective IT security is a sound foundation in policy that touches physical, human and technology processes. A key to effective security management in a cloud deployment is to map existing risk polices to the cloud environment, incorporating additional detail on policies and procedures within the overall security framework as needed. This addition is especially important when the organization is accessing new functionality from the cloud provider. Equally important, though, is provider transparency and the user's visibility into the current status of policy implementation, which may be more complex in a cloud provider environment.

These requirements are likely to vary with the size of the organization. Large enterprises, for example, are likely to have sophisticated policy, procedure, and compliance processes in place. As a result, large enterprises may be better positioned to manage security for on premise environments and to provide detailed security strictures to third-party providers. Small and mid-size firms, especially those that are not in regulated industries, may lack the understanding and processes needed to define the security attributes and responsibilities of a cloud supplier. Managers within organizations of all sizes should understand that while the need to tackle the security management issues that arise with cloud deployment is a common imperative, the levels of sophistication that are required to manage cloud-specific risk vary across different sizes and types of businesses.

The translation of risk avoidance to business benefit is a proposition that is generally not well understood. Though cloud security is rarely viewed as a direct driver of business growth, its absence certainly entails increased business vulnerability. For the cloud provider that can educate the market on the superiority of its security controls – and demonstrate an ability to reduce the complexity of security requirements for customers – the advantage is clear. For the user organization, better cloud security enables the use of cloud – with all the agility and costs savings benefits that brings – while delivering to the provider, the market reputation and reward for operating in a manner that inspires the trust which a less-fortunate, less-secure competitor may lack.

## Best practices and processes in cloud security, privacy and reliability

### Cloud security overview

A fundamental question in the TCBC Security Working Group's discussion of cloud security best practices has been, is cyber security different in cloud and traditional IT contexts, and if so, in what ways? As in many complex topics, the answer to this question is yes and no: while many of the same approaches, activities and technologies can be brought to bear in building traditional infrastructure environments, with on-premise private cloud or even cloud service provider offerings, as noted above, the use of shared resources in multi-tenant infrastructure, loss of control over data and applications, and process change involved in cloud adoption introduce their own unique challenges. So while guidelines such as the NIST Framework for Improving Critical Infrastructure Cybersecurity or the ISO/IEC 27001 information security standard offer comprehensive recommendations to inform risk management that can be applied across all types of environments, the working group's cloud security overview is aimed at helping business managers, and even IT leaders that may be new to cloud, understand the specific security issues associated with cloud adoption. As one working group member put it, "fundamentally you would need the same security, methodologies and protocols, but you need to implement them in a slightly different way," while ensuring that mid-level management to the VP level understand the risks, and means to risk mitigation in cloud migration.

The working group's view is that security in cloud and traditional IT environments is the same in another respect: in both contexts, building structure around security strategy, policy and programs is key to effective risk management and reduction, and in the case of cloud to reducing adoption barriers. This structure may be developed through a "Prevent, Detect and React" approach that offers protection across the threat continuum and adjusts to prevent further, additional risk.

*Prevent*

The 'prevent' imperative spans activities aimed at preventing security risk or failure, which includes definition of an appropriate security framework, strategy and policy that determines acceptable risk levels and appropriate liability coverage. Most importantly, in cloud scenarios, it establishes responsibility for execution of security for different application and infrastructure components.

To a great extent, the type of cloud deployment will determine responsibilities. In cases where there is on premise cloud infrastructure, responsibility for key aspects of security will likely fall to internal security experts, while in public cloud scenarios, service providers will likely manage security requirements on behalf of customers. In between these ends of the cloud spectrum are many shades of grey, where responsibility must be worked out through discussion with the cloud provider. For example, in the case of an external third party that delivers specialist security services for cloud-based infrastructure and applications (on premise or off, or in different hosting arrangements), the provider may assume responsibility up to the network edge, but not beyond. In this case, an organization's 'prevent' approach would rely on a combination of supplier and internal capabilities.

The best strategy for determining responsibility for security components considers this issue from a proactive point of view, and organizations that are creative in establishing who/what proactive entities are charged with discovering vulnerable areas, identifying new technical solutions and ensuring that these solutions are implemented are likely to obtain the best protection. Who manages proactive strategy and execution; who asks what is the state of company information security and how can it be improved; is the cloud provider merely an implementer; and at what point does the provider's responsibility end are questions that managers need to ask as they work to ensure that appropriate security is in place. In the working group's view, answers to these questions are likely to change, depending on the size of the business.

'Prevent' also operates at a technical level, and the working group has identified the following as specific point solution technologies that should be taken into account in the development of security methodologies for cloud deployment:

- *Data access technologies*, including secure networking and mobile device management.
- *Identity management and authentication*, including single sign-on technologies that allow the end user to access multiple clouds in a secure manner. ID and access management functionality to authenticate access to remote cloud services may be acquired through third party provider services.
- *Data encryption* for data at rest in cloud storage repositories, and for data traversing networks between clouds, in hybrid cloud scenarios and from user devices to the provider or user's private cloud environment.
- *Data retention cycles*, or policy and policy around archival requirements and the provisions that should be made for the secure and permanent deletion of data that is no longer kept, including deletion of cloud encryption keys.
- *Data management and provisioning*, such as the classification and prioritization of data based on security and privacy requirements, its separation into security

domains and associated decision-making around secure cloud storage, including choice of on premise or third-party cloud service provider.

### *Detect*

If prevention is about stopping threats in the first place, detection involves putting in place mechanisms that identify and alert the organization to a threat that is actually occurring. These may include:

- *Intrusion detection* systems – a device or software application that monitors the network or system activities, including applications, for malicious activities or policy violations and reports suspicious activities or traffic to a management station.

- *Infrastructure monitoring* – management and analysis of loss, via an information security operations center (SOC) responsible for the monitoring, assessment and defence of enterprise systems, including cloud. A SOC ensures security incidents are properly identified, analyzed, communicated, defended, investigated and reported. In some cases, security monitoring may be provided by a third-party specialist, who offers Security-as-a-Service to multiple customers.

### *React*

'React' means having the plans and tools in place to address security risk when a problem arises. For example, specific plans must be in place to manage a denial-of-service (DOS) attack against the organization's infrastructure. In cases where the cloud infrastructure is delivered by a third party, the plan must identify who (customer or provider) owns which security components, what actions will be taken, and how much effort the cloud provider is obliged to make, according to the cloud service agreement.

Plans must be in place at the people and process levels as well. If a business unit manager has made questionable decisions during procurement of SaaS services in the world of shadow IT, or has neglected provisions for data protection, then HR policies must be in place to educate this individual. Similarly, organizational issues may arise in the rogue use of unsanctioned cloud applications by staff looking for consumer-oriented tools, which can have security consequences. While platforms for discovering and monitoring this kind of activity are beginning to appear, shadow IT may difficult to control at both the technical and organizational levels; a better approach may be to welcome decentralized procurement of cloud resources, provided that the organization's security and privacy policy requirements are addressed through HR education programs and, if necessary, disciplinary policy.

In the group's view, security strategy should be designed with the assumption that a breach will occur, with due attention given to the implementation of 'prevent, detect and react' policy and technology. To illustrate the functioning of these three security components, the working group uses the case of a security breach via an insecure access device as an example.

Prevention would mean that any device in the organization comes pre-installed with anti-malware software on it. Detection would involve the identification of any penetrations through network testing that could pick out this type of code traversing the network. 'React' would mean no longer allowing the suspect device on the cloud network.

*Figure 7-3. Cloud security overview: key considerations*

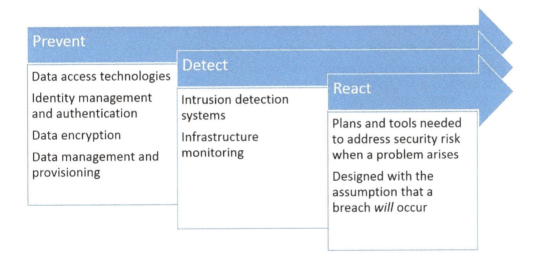

*Source: TCBC/InsightaaS, 2016*

For the end user organization, the best cloud security lies in moving beyond the simple adoption of security technologies to include discussion of security requirements at a strategic management level. Managers – both business and IT – who can discuss security limits, borders and parameters with a third-party cloud provider, outlining responsibility for the deployment of technology solutions, including for specific components in different implementation scenarios (does responsibility extend to data at rest, data in motion, to the applications, or to servers or the network as well?) will be better positioned to ensure protection of the company's information assets. And users who can extend the discussion to assign responsibility for the proactive development of new approaches to cloud security to internal staff resources or the provider will be best able to address risk at a time of rapid evolution and expansion of the threat landscape.

There is considerable variation in the value-added services available from different cloud infrastructure providers in terms of functionality and price for security services, and in the security protocols adopted by different application service providers. The working group advises organizations to learn as much as possible about provider certifications and security guarantees, to ensure these are specified in contractual agreements, and where possible, to build in advance planning for future requirements. While 'future proofing' the cloud agreement is difficult, changing an existing contract six months down the road when a new security challenge is identified may be even more difficult. Depending on the organization and its resources, this kind of forward thinking around security may not be possible at a local level. The small to mid-sized business, for example, may not have the required security expertise in-house, and is advised to consult with a security specialist – before, rather than after, a problem is discovered. Ultimately, responsibility for data protection resides with the user organization – whether cloud is on premise or hosted by a third-party provider – and liability for loss is an important business driver for cloud security awareness, good practice and knowledge of provider capabilities, contracts and commitments.

## Data privacy

Data privacy is a complex issue that should be viewed as part of a company's responsibility to staff, partners and customers, and in terms of the organization's obligation to protect personal information according to legal and regulatory frameworks. While data privacy requirements fall with equal weight on organizations that rely on traditional IT infrastructure and on those that take advantage of cloud services, these obligations have taken on added significance in the cloud context due to structural characteristics of the North American marketplace that has evolved around the delivery of cloud technologies. Until very recently, the greater availability of capital in the US to build large, shared infrastructure resource pools or successful SaaS offerings has dictated the creation of cloud-based businesses south of the border that now command dominant market share. But while cloud economies of scale have tended to bolster the position of the large cloud providers, optimization of their offerings depends on the sharing of workloads across company, regional or country boundaries. For many potential Canadian customers, discomfort with the loss of control over data resulting from the use of public cloud services has been exacerbated by concern over the ramifications of data storage outside Canadian borders.

For organizations using or considering use of public cloud services, understanding the legal obligations around the location of personal data – and awareness of differences in Canadian, US and European legislation – is an important component of cloud privacy/security strategy.

In Canada, two federal privacy laws impact data residency: the Privacy Act imposes obligations on federal departments and agencies to protect citizens' privacy rights by limiting the collection, use and disclosure of personal information; and the Personal Information Protection and Electronic Documents Act (PIPEDA) is a set of ground rules for the use of personal information by private sector organizations in the course of commercial activities, which applies to operations across Canada, except where provinces (British Columbia, Alberta and Quebec) have introduced their own private sector privacy legislation.

The perception that controls on the use, access and management of data contained in Canadian legislation are more stringent than that in US law has led many businesses to conclude that their data is more vulnerable in the US, or even that data storage in the US is somehow in violation of Canadian privacy laws. The conviction that Canadian data is safer on Canadian digital ground emerged out of the US Patriot Act, which allegedly allows US authorities greater right to subpoena and access data than does Canadian legislation, and reinforced by the revelations of ex-CIA agent Edward Snowden, who provided evidence of the US National Security Agency's practice of conducting surveillance on the data transmissions of international governments and citizens. The recent European Court of Justice ruling that a year 2000 "safe harbour" agreement with the US is no longer valid due to differences in the levels of protection available in US and EU privacy law have expanded the relevance and complexity of this issue, especially for organizations that operate on a global basis. Canadian customers, for example, who wish to house data in a European data centre, may be subject to the provisions of the US Freedom Act if the cloud repository is owned by a US company.

The applicability of Canadian, European and/or US privacy law as it relates to cloud and data residency depends largely on the particular circumstances of an individual business and its regional reach. Companies that operate internationally with a need to store data in multiple jurisdictions may need to deal with conflicting privacy/data residency requirements; the specific classes of data that are to be hosted in global cloud facilities may raise privacy questions for the adopting organization. While interpretation of law is best left to specialist legal opinion, a few points are worth bearing in mind.

Though privacy legislation applies to personally identifiable data only, many organizations have neglected to take advantage of cloud technologies on the assumption that all data is subject to this body of law. While good practice involves ensuring protection to all commercially sensitive information, it's important not to invoke privacy legislation as pretext for rejecting all cloud services – or all those delivered out of facilities outside Canadian borders. And if US authorities' right to access citizen's data outlined in the US Patriot Act has led many businesses to conclude that data should stay in Canada and even on premise, Canada and the US have agreements in place providing for the cross border subpoena of data: Canadian security agencies have access rights to Canadian information that are similar to those of their US counterparts.

Ultimately, the gaps in understanding about data residence are a product of the lack of case law that would test the limits of legislation, and would inform market perceptions of vulnerability resulting from data residency and cloud storage decisions. For example, while several of the larger US Internet service companies have recently gone public with revelations that they cooperated with agencies such as the NSA over data access, others have refused to comply with warrant requests for customer information – so far without legal consequence. Though cloud-based contravention of privacy laws has not been tested in Canadian courts either, confusion and speculation over their application in cloud contexts has served as a primary cloud adoption hurdle, despite the opinion of privacy experts. Former Ontario Privacy Commissioner Ann Cavoukian has concluded, for example, that privacy and cloud are not fundamentally at odds with each other, rather it is possible, to build "privacy by design" into cloud and other IT systems through adherence to better information management policy.

Lack of clarity around cloud security and data residency issues has also served in the past several years as a source of opportunity for large, global firms as well as new domestic providers who have set up cloud businesses in Canada to capitalize on market uncertainty surrounding this issue, and to capture burgeoning customer interest in sourcing locally based cloud services. But for cloud adopters, the working group believes a better approach is to develop a good strategy and process for identifying what their personal information actually is, how many copies they have, and deciding where different classes of information, including sensitive corporate data, should reside – on-premise or in cloud – and for ensuring visibility into what data is being shared with whom. Adopters should also understand different data management issues associated with different cloud services – IaaS or SaaS.

SLAs with the cloud provider are an important mechanism for ensuring that the process and policy are executed in cloud, and the working group advises the creation of a checklist of items affecting data privacy and security to be included. This list would focus discussion between customer and provider on issues such as:

- Contractual agreement over the length of time data is to be retained in cloud and rules around its disclosure
- Where provider data centres are located and where customer data could potentially transit
- Data classification to ensure protection of personal or sensitive business information, including mechanisms for data encryption
- The division of responsibility for tasks between customer and provider for security in specific areas of the cloud network, including access control, incident monitoring, auditing and compliance.

*Figure 7-4. Data privacy: key considerations*

Contractual agreement: data retention and disclosure

Data location: where data centres are located, transmission paths

Division of responsibilities: customer and provider security responsibilities across the cloud network

Data classification: identification and treatment/encryption of sensitive data

*Source: TCBC/InsightaaS, 2016*

Summarizing, the group advises the extension of sound data security and privacy practices developed for local data storage to cloud repositories. Though this may be challenging in SaaS environments where standardized application providers may resist customization, security technologies such as encryption can help solve many privacy issues. As one member put it: "Data residency is not going to be a problem in 10 years. If you do security correctly, data privacy does not matter."

## Porting data in cloud networks

The ability to securely port data is a fundamental requirement in cloud computing, which is defined at its simplest level as ubiquitous network access to a shared pool of configurable computing resources (by the US National Institute of Standards and Technology). While security is critical in all IT environments, the need to move data and applications between on premise and cloud provider repositories in hybrid scenarios, to support cloud bursting or SaaS and PaaS-based deployments, or simply to access remote cloud storage via a multiplicity of devices/operating systems through networks with varying levels of security, introduce additional challenge. But in parsing security risks associated with cloud data transmission, understanding of the particular risk and remediation required in the use of different cloud delivery models is critical, as are grasp of security requirements at different levels of the cloud stack.

At a high level, in cloud infrastructure relationships, data encryption is the primary security technology used by IaaS customers sending data to service provider clouds, and since data is transmitted over the Internet, encryption is often reinforced with a secured VPN connection. In ideal scenarios, agreements are put in place specifying where responsibility for the security of data transmission begins and ends in the cloud network for both the customer and the cloud supplier. "Does the SLA say that the provider is only good to his doorway or does he take it to the customers' doorway?" one working group member asked to reinforce the importance of this kind of statement of demarcation.

In SaaS scenarios, where the provider hosts user data, the customer typically relies on agreements specifying that the provider is responsible for security provisioning. In hosting arrangements, such as SaaS, or in environments where the provider is responsible for operating systems management and maintenance, security often comes down to trust in the vendor and in policies and procedures that have been put in place to provide protection against data breach. As one (security provider) member of the working group noted, "when we replace applications that people have in-house, they always say 'if we are going to replace this internal application that we have full control over with one that requires network connectivity, it comes down to the SLA. The SLA is critical, as is trust in the vendor."

So what do cloud adopters aspire to in SLAs addressing cloud-network data to ensure application availability? According to the working group, this varies according to the size of the customer organization. While smaller companies focused on realizing cloud benefits show greater tendency to take security arrangements for supporting the exchange of data at face value, larger organizations have the staff resources to examine the provider's back end infrastructure, to request reports on how the provider fared in meeting SLAs for uptime, to view the provider's security certifications, and to review data sheets describing auditing and control mechanisms in place in the provider's data centre. More thorough research into provider security and reliability are also a function of the application – and more likely when the application that forms part of the cloud network is a critical piece of the customer's infrastructure.

Ultimately, however, a key requirement is to ensure that the security techniques and mechanisms on both sides of the wire – at the end user premises and at the provider's end – are compatible, are aligned, can work together and are capable of being managed by the provider, the customer, or a third party security provider to support data portability. In SaaS relationships, this is typically achieved through APIs that create interoperability between on premise and cloud systems, through use of open source technologies that support interoperability, or potentially through the specification of interoperability standards within the SLA. In addition to security standards that may also apply to create interoperability in cloud networks, cloud standards that may support the organization's security and risk management needs include: Cloud Auditing Data Federation (CADF), developed by DMTF to define open standards for cloud auditing, LDAP, OAuth, OpenID Connect and SAML, which enable third party ID and access management functionality, and US FIPS 140-2, a standard that specifies the security requirements in cryptographic modules used in security systems. In 2016, the ISO plans to publish its standards document on Service Level Agreement framework and terminology in cloud computing.

## Cloud reliability and disaster recovery

Ensuring access to a service is a fundamental need that can be supported through cloud technologies that bolster IT delivery reliability. In scoping requirements for cloud service uptime, a good starting point is to differentiate between concepts of reliability, resiliency, high availability, disaster recovery and their impact on business continuity, which all contribute or refer to service access but mean different things. Currently, there are no standard definitions of these terms, though the ISO is now engaged in committee work to establish metrics that can gauge performance for these various service characteristics. As one working group member put it, "there are as many definitions for reliability as there are vendors selling reliable things. There are differences between cloud reliability, cloud service reliability, overall facility reliability and individual instance reliability." Despite this lack of consensus, the working group advises that it is possible for customers and providers to agree on an interpretation of individual terms, and to introduce this as documentation in the SLA. With mutual understanding of terms, it is possible to specify service delivery expectations. As further guidance, the group suggests including legal oversight on these arrangements, with penalties specified, and a policy on enforcement of penalties established to provide the customer with some leverage, greater guarantee that the service is working as it should, and more predictability in terms of cost.

To monitor performance in meeting SLA service quality and uptime specifications, the provider can deploy standardized third-party audits that entail the inspection of security controls, and that map these back to the service agreement in order to report to the customer on achievement of the SLA. However, conversations with the provider around SLA expectations and penalties are often difficult to have, in particular for an SMB that typically has less buying clout than its enterprise cousin, as deviation from standard SLAs and compensation are challenging for the vendor to manage. In many cases, the objective of the vendor is to not include penalties, while the objective of the customer writing the RFP is to have large penalties: as one working group member put it, "the contract is a negotiation of the ends towards the middle."

While helping to establish a common language from a contractual perspective, negotiation over SLAs also enables the delivery of varying service levels depending on the application: high availability may be required for mission critical applications, for example, while lower availability may be appropriate for an application that is less sensitive to issues such as latency. Different use cases may require the same levels of redundancy; however, each business case could involve different levels of disaster recovery, with price acting as a corresponding variable. For cloud service users, an important first step is to create realistic expectations around real service needs, matching this to budgets for different levels of cloud redundancy or scalability.

In the emerging DevOps world, where cloud provides for continuous delivery of compute resources to support innovation in an iterative development cycle, and where code can be provisioned virtually instantaneously with the required compute, networking and storage, notions of reliability and DR take on different meaning. To illustrate new approaches to older concepts of reliability, one working group member pointed to the example of General Electric Corp., which has committed to multiple cloud providers for different services and in the case of failure of one service will move an application to another provider to ensure redundancy. To support applications with high redundancy needs, the company deploys across three clouds simultaneously to mitigate risk. To take advantage of this kind of tactic, however, a methodology must be in place that begins with Agile methods, uses code that is engineered to support continuous integration and deployment, and relies on the coordination of development and operational resources. With full cloud automation, and a fault tolerant architecture that powers instant migration between cloud providers, reliability is delivered out of the unique characteristics of cloud technology itself.

Cloud is also enabling new forms of disaster recovery (DR). Cloud-based DR comes in two varieties: resources to burst to if in-house computing is compromised, and a DR feature that is provided as part of a cloud offering – for example, DR-as-a-Service capability that is built into SaaS applications. Based on the pay-as-you-go model, cloud-based DR is less expensive than traditional DR offerings as the customer pays only in case of disaster, rather than a monthly contingency fee. In thinking about cloud-based DR, users should consider the provider's ability to ensure real time synchronization, the quality of the DR in terms how long it takes to recover data and apps, how far back the customer must reset in order to recover, how many copies of the data are kept in other places, and in what other countries. Potential users should also weigh the impact of various security technologies on DR capabilities: while it provides good security for data transport, the working group notes that encryption is "not a silver bullet" and can in fact impact availability as decryption of web application data using a key may introduce delay in restoring systems.

## Security metrics

Measuring security performance presents a philosophical challenge. Can the absence of a thing (security breach) be counted? Typically, metrics are used to measure success against a defined target, which in the security world has proved difficult to quantify. However, this exercise has become increasingly prevalent with the development of systems that monitor infrastructure and applications to count items such as the number of attacks that were 'prevented' over a certain period, the accuracy of threat detection in 'detect' activities, or the time to threat remediation in 'react' scenarios. Metrics are now understood as the key to shifting perceptions of security from a necessary evil (expense) to an enabler of business outcomes.

But how do security metrics apply in a public cloud context, and what can be measured that is unique to this environment?

The primary mechanism for measuring against established targets in provider relationships is the SLA, which may specify how much of the customer system is encrypted, or guarantee vendor disclosure of metrics such as the number of DDOS attacks stopped on a monthly basis, or the number of failed login attempts. For specific applications, providers may deliver reporting on metrics as a separate deliverable: in one SaaS-based email security application, for example, stats on mail filtering, spam camping and domain camping are made available to customers in a separate database. In many ways, the level of detail provided around how these metrics are used will determine their value. For example, while reporting that counts DDOS attacks on the provider might suggest some vague notion of security effectiveness, a clause in the SLA that promises remediation in seconds, minutes, hours or days (and penalties for not meeting that target) would result in development of tangible business intelligence and deliver tangible business benefit.

Due to the multiplicity of cloud offerings, consensus on the metrics that should be used to assess performance or the penalties that can be applied for failure to achieve SLA targets is likely to remain elusive. In this event, it may be possible for the customer to contract a third party service for assessment and monitoring of the provider services. As with the SLA, however, the working group advises caution in the use of these services. While a full service assessment, such as that provided by the Cloud Security Alliance's STAR registry, offers proven value, simple feedback on cloud provider uptime may not provide useful or actionable information when aligned with SLAs: a five-minute response to an incident may still be considered uptime according to some definitions, even though it disables the mission critical application. Similarly, a server may respond to a ping, but the DB server and the email server have been down for a month – in this instance, is the service up or down? Or a provider may be 100 percent uptime, but when hit with a DDOS attack is only able to deliver service that is so slow it is basically useless. Definitions are a critically component in metrics around business continuity, and best practice in this area begins with agreement on what is being measured, who is responsible for measurement, and where it is applied, i.e. at the solution, individual service level, or against specific resources within the cloud service.

In assessing the cloud provider's security capability, another set of metrics may apply. Specs on the vendor's physical security systems, for example, or the Tier status of its data centre facility, or the provider's security certifications may provide valuable insight into security capabilities that can be used by the customer to demonstrate compliance with regulatory or auditing requirements.

Accuracy and the security of the provider's billing system is another important area to monitor, especially as cloud shoppers move from one provider billing model to another.

## Reference sources

Reference sources providing additional insight on cloud security best practice issues include:

- Ann Cavoukian. Privacy in the Clouds. A White Paper on Privacy and Digital Identity: Implications for the Internet. Information and Privacy Commissioner of Ontario.
- Ann Cavoukian. Privacy by Design. The 7 Foundational Principles.
- David Chinn, James Kaplan and Allen Weinberg. Risk and responsibility in a hyperconnected world: Implications for enterprises. McKinsey Insights & Publications, 2014.
- Cloud Standards Customer Council. Cloud Security Standards: What to Expect & What to Negotiate. October, 2013.
- Cloud Standards Customer Council. Interoperability and Portability for Cloud Computing: A Guide. November, 2014.
- CSA. The Notorious Nine Cloud Computing Top Threats in 2013.
- CSA. Security Guidance for Critical Areas of Focus in Cloud Computing, v3.0. 2011.
- CSA. SecaaS Implementation Guidance. Category 7// Security Information and Event Management. 2012
- CSA. CSA Security, Trust & Assurance Registry (STAR).
- CSA. Cloud Security Alliance Announces Key Initiative in Development of Cloud Security Standards in Partnership with ISO/IEC
- ENISA (European Union Agency for Network and Information Security). Procure Secure: A guide to monitoring of security service levels in cloud contracts.
- Samuel Gibbs. "What is 'safe harbour' and why did the EUCJ just declare it invalid?" The Guardian, October 2015.
- ISO/IEC 27001: 2013 Online Browsing Platform.
- The ISO27K Information Security Standards.
- ISO/IEC 17788. Cloud computing: Overview and vocabulary. 2014.
- ISO/IEC 17789. Cloud computing: Reference architecture. 2014.
- NIST Framework for Improving Critical Infrastructure Cybersecurity, version 1.0, February 12, 2014.
- National Institute of Standards and Technology. The NIST Definition of Cloud Computing. September, 2011.
- National Institute of Standards and Technology. US Government Cloud Computing Technology Roadmap, volume 1.

- Michael O'Neil. Success and profitability: Security and the value of IT/business solutions. August, 2014.
- Don Sheppard. "The ins and outs of cloud service level agreements." ITWorld Canada. August, 2015.
- Eric Simmons. Cloud Computing Service Level Agreement. ISO/IEC Standardization. NIST Cloud Computing Program.
- Symantec. Securing Data in the Cloud.
- Symantec. Securing Your Enterprise in the Cloud.
- United States of Secrets (parts one and two). Frontline. PBS, 2014.

*Chapter 6.*

# Cloud Skills Requirements and Development

Essential guidance on identifying and developing the skills that are essential to capitalizing on cloud

*Contributing community experts: Alex Sirota (NewPath Consulting), Timothy Ubbens (American Express), Pam Maguire (Global Knowledge), David Sabine (Berteig Consulting), Nima Honarmandan (Berteig Consulting)*

*Initial publication date: March 2016*

Cloud Skills Requirements and Development

# Cloud Skills Requirements and Development

## Definition and context

In traditional, on-premise approaches to IT, the definitions of roles and skills requirements are reasonably well defined. Business leaders have functionality requirements; business analysts translate these needs into functional specifications; IT assigns the request to a priority queue, and when it is time to tackle the project, identifies the best technical approach to meeting the requirement – often, based on technology that is already installed within the company's IT environment, to capitalize on existing investments in hardware, software and skills. In some cases, the solution will require either new technology or an advanced understanding of existing technology, in which case the IT department will invest in skills (via training or by engaging outsourcers/consultants) to deliver the new system; this investment in new skills will be additive to planned IT training investments needed to develop or maintain certifications or general facility with core installed technologies. Additionally, the new solution may require that business users become familiar with additional or enhanced system features. In some cases, the business will invest in formal training, either by engaging external trainers (likely, from a consultant or from the software provider), or by having a member of the IT department develop a training course for the business staff. More typically, though, new feature instruction will occur via on-the-job training: in some cases, a document outlining new features is circulated, and support staff are given training in how to respond to calls from users, while in others, the entire approach may be ad hoc.

It wouldn't be accurate to say that cloud entirely disrupts this existing set of processes – but cloud certainly alters many of the key premises on which it is based, and as a result, demands a different definition of skills requirements and development.

The most important departure is the premise that business solutions are designed/defined and developed/deployed by IT, as part of a managed queue and with limited technical input from the business process owner. Cloud has enabled and accelerated a broad trend towards greater business management involvement with, and oversight of, development and delivery of solutions addressing business challenges and opportunities. Fully 35 years after the introduction of the IBM PC, basic demographics demonstrate that most business leaders and staff members spent at least some of their childhoods and most of their adult/professional lives 'hands on' with technology: this group will be less reliant on, and less apt to rely on, guidance from IT with respect to the pace and direction of new process automation.

Cloud computing (and the expanding set of business services delivered via the cloud) enables business management to exert much greater control over IT/business solutions. At some level, even in the traditional "waterfall" definition of system delivery used above, there is a need to connect two types of insight: understanding of what the business needs (functional requirements and the benefits associated with meeting those requirements), and understanding of what technology can deliver, how this delivery can be achieved, and the cost associated with development and delivery of the solution. In the traditional model, IT has control over the delivery assets, and has better insight into the cost/benefit associated with each solution, and of the relative cost/benefit merits of all solutions in the new development queue. However, the ability to procure applications and infrastructure "as a service" levels, at least to some extent, the discrepancy between IT and business management's technical understanding: the "how" (as in, "how could this IT/business system be developed, deployed and delivered") and the cost (which is now defined by the supplier) becomes less opaque when the discussion concerns a pre-packaged solution. In most cases, business leaders understand the business issues associated with and/or that need to be addressed by a new solution far better than IT does; IT understands broad technology issues associated with cloud (particularly with respect to integration, data management and security) better than business management will, but may not have a much deeper understanding of how a specific cloud solution functions than the tech-native executive would possess. As a result, in the cloud era, it is becoming common for business leaders to direct IT/business solution initiatives: in fact, a study from research firm Techaisle found that just within the US SMB market, business leaders currently control nearly $100 billion in IT budget authority, including both "authorized" systems and "shadow IT" investments that occur beyond the purview of the IT department.

The rapid spread of new systems enabled by cloud is having an impact on corporate perspectives regarding staff requirements and capabilities as well. An expanded reliance on IT systems means that employees need to be "double deep" – they are required to have both the domain knowledge that is essential to their roles, and an understanding of how to use the IT systems that are relevant to their jobs. Experts believe that there are "real shortages" of these employees today. In response, the working group has seen a trend towards IT-capable staff being engaged as specialized business consultants reporting into line-of-business operations. This helps the business unit to move quickly to adopt new systems, but does not address either the need for individual business staff to be technology-savvy or the broader requirement for the enterprise to take a coordinated approach to IT and IT skills development.

This combination of factors and interests defines a set of issues that provide an important perspective on cloud skills. Business leaders need to better understand the requirements around new automation, as – with their expanded formal and informal reliance on cloud-based solutions – they have effectively substituted their own imperatives for a managed position in the IT development queue, and have absorbed the responsibilities of the business analysts within their (non-IT) organizations. For its part, IT has at least partially lost the ability to exercise management control over new system adoption, and needs to expand its ability to understand and support the connections between new system functionality and user needs, while also building strategies to manage data, integration and security across an expanding and shifting IT perimeter. Progressive IT organizations are investing in these kinds of capabilities, but too many others are hunkering down with a 'no cloud' or 'cloud only as authorized by IT' policy, which is likely to exacerbate divisions between IT and business operations.

## Cloud as a means of addressing technical debt

At the same time that businesses are moving towards cloud as an enabling force, IT has its own reasons to embrace cloud. Most IT departments are faced with rapidly expanding requirements and static or shrinking budgets, in environments where responding to business-critical issues is non-optional. This combination of factors can lead to "technical debt" – systems that are outdated, or which are being stretched to cover requirements that they were not designed to address. And with cloud, this debt continues to compound, due to the increased demands associated with the need to extend data management, integration and security beyond internal data centers to new cloud-based systems.

But cloud isn't only a source of demand; cloud can offer an avenue for reducing this technical debt. Systems that address narrow functional issues can often be acquired more quickly and more cost-effectively than they can be developed. Platform (servers, storage, memory, networking) and related (security, DR/BC) technologies can also be leased on an as-needed basis, which reduces up-front CAPEX and helps associate expenditures with benefits. Taking a longer view, since infrastructure overall is migrating from in-house-only to hybrid-including-cloud, a proactive IT approach helps avoid future technical debt by developing skills that have value over time.

To capitalize on the potential of cloud to reduce technical debt, IT management needs to accomplish three tasks. It needs to plot a path from its current state to a future hybrid state, to identify where and when skills will be needed. It needs to persuade business management of the need to pay down technical debt in the pursuit of an agile IT/business platform that can respond to new business solution requirements. And it needs to ensure that current staff are able to see where and how traditional disciplines in the areas of security, data management and other issues can be applied to cloud and hybrid infrastructure, independent of a level of control that can no longer be applied to the overall IT architecture. Collectively, this combination of deep technical management skills and the capacity to support innovation with agile IT platforms is sometimes referred to as "bi-modal" IT operations, since it requires IT to provide both efficient infrastructure operations and planning and execution support for systems that extend the capabilities of line-of-business staff and processes – and in some cases, systems that affect the operating model of the business itself.

As Figure 8-1 illustrates, the competencies that mark both "double deep" business employees and "bi-modal" technologists define a challenging set of new capabilities for employees across the organization. From a skills perspective, the pressures driving cloud from above (business functionality) and below (technical debt) create an environment with many different requirements for different kinds of skills, developed at many different points within the enterprise. This isn't just a mandate for individual employees to get deeper in their domains – it also requires business staff to develop more and deeper technical skills, and IT staff to build a better understanding of business issues and requirements.

*Figure 8-1. Cloud responsibilities and their effect on skills requirements*

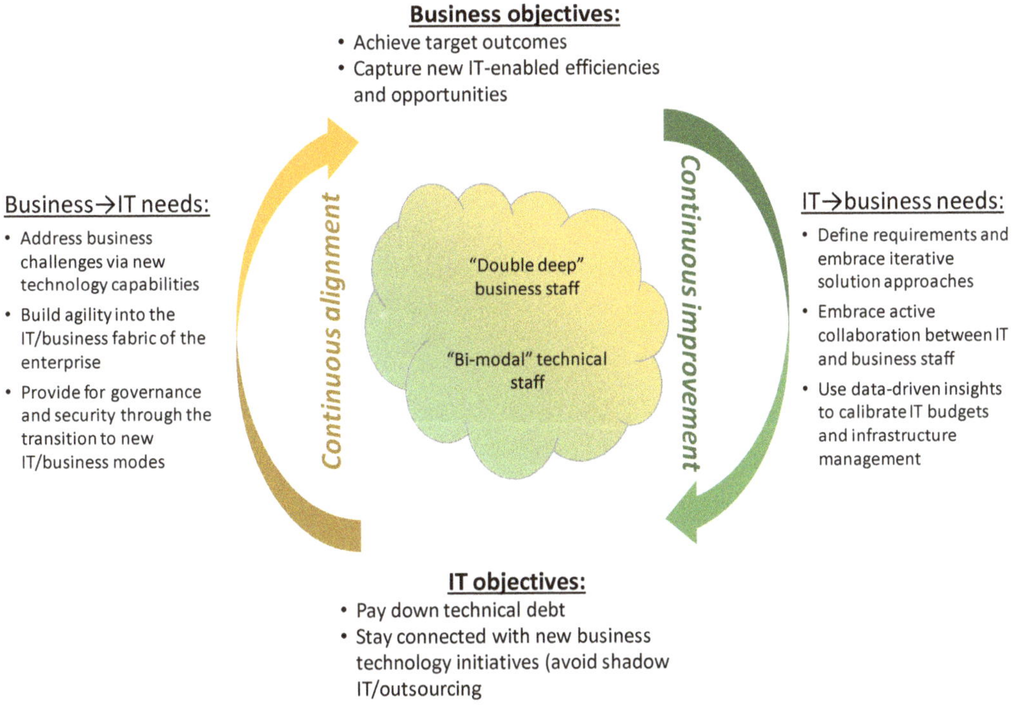

**Business objectives:**
- Achieve target outcomes
- Capture new IT-enabled efficiencies and opportunities

**Business→IT needs:**
- Address business challenges via new technology capabilities
- Build agility into the IT/business fabric of the enterprise
- Provide for governance and security through the transition to new IT/business modes

*Continuous alignment*

"Double deep" business staff

"Bi-modal" technical staff

*Continuous improvement*

**IT→business needs:**
- Define requirements and embrace iterative solution approaches
- Embrace active collaboration between IT and business staff
- Use data-driven insights to calibrate IT budgets and infrastructure management

**IT objectives:**
- Pay down technical debt
- Stay connected with new business technology initiatives (avoid shadow IT/outsourcing

*Source: TCBC/InsightaaS, 2016, with additional credit to NewPath Consulting*

There is a sense in which only half of Figure 8-1 represents 'new news'. The need for technologists to better understand business issues and imperatives, and to support the delivery of new capabilities (in preference to internal IT procedures, if necessary) is well understood. Less clearly articulated, though, is the need for business staff to develop an understanding of how IT functions. As the working group observed, with cloud, businesses have a much stronger bias towards use of technology to support workers, processes and outcomes. The managers and staff responsible for tasks that depend on technology are far better able to act as part of a 'team' with IT if they have an understanding of how IT delivers systems and why core procedures are important to the enterprise.

The importance of expanding the business professional's IT understanding is clear in the Agile concept of "product owner." Here, the business professional is responsible not just for a business deliverable but also for the systems that are important to creating, delivering and supporting that deliverable. In this role, the product owner is not simply a consumer of technology who requests changes where they might be beneficial: he/she has management oversight of the technology, with responsibility for directing and/or approving any changes that might be made to the solution or its underlying platform technologies. This position highlights two issues that are important to building the skills needed to capitalize on cloud's potential: it requires the businessperson to understand technology at a deeper level than might have previously been needed, and it demands effective teamwork involving business and IT staff – which in turn underscores the importance of developing "double deep" and "bi-modal" business and IT employees.

## Reference sources

Additional references that readers can use to better understand the key issues defining skills requirements and development issues include:

- Anurag Agrawal. SMB Shadow IT, BDM spending amount to nearly $100 billion in the US alone. Techaisle, December 2014. This blog discusses business management influence over IT spending.
- Gene Kim, Kevin Behr and George Spafford. The Phoenix Project: A Novel about IT, DevOps and Helping Your Business Win. IT Revolution Press, 2013. This novel provides a deep and engaging illustration of the connections between cloud, business objectives and system development methodologies.
- David Moschella. "Nobody Has a Monopoly on Digital Leadership." CSC Leading Edge forum, 2014. The article looks at the importance of "double-deep" employees, "individuals who know both their job – marketing, engineering, customer services, finance, etc. – and the IT that is relevant to that job." The author, David Moschella, goes on to say "While being double-deep will be expected of the employee of the future, there are real shortages in the marketplace today, creating important leadership and career opportunities."
- Michael O'Neil. "Three types of intelligence and their impact on cloud skills strategy." InsightaaS, August 2015. This article discusses the importance of intellect, domain knowledge and adaptability to cloud success.
- Carlota Perez. Technological revolutions and techno-economic paradigms. Tallinn University of Technology, 2009. This research paper discusses the economic shifts that have occurred over the past several centuries. Particularly

interesting is the notion of a time clock around these shifts, which are measured in roughly 50-60 year cycles. Currently we are right in the middle of the information age that started in the early 1970s with the invention of the semiconductor at Intel.

## Business objectives

Skills are essential to enabling businesses to achieve desired outcomes – and therefore, it's unsurprising that the business objectives associated with cloud skills are tightly tied to overall business goals.

With that alignment stipulated, the logic used by the working group follows broadly along these lines:

- The objective of any enterprise is to 'win' (customers, revenue, market share, profitability, efficiency, etc.).
- Cloud can help firms to 'win' by providing for accelerated and better automation of tasks – and the absence of effective automation (i.e., manual, paper-based systems that can't scale or be integrated with other systems) are not able to support winning business strategies
- One key problem that companies have in embracing winning approaches based on cloud technologies is a lack of people who have the skills needed to capitalize on the potential of cloud in their business context.

From this starting point, it is possible to identify several key skills development objectives relevant to the deployment and use of staff- or customer-facing systems. Some of these issues relate to developing business users' understanding of the potential of cloud technology, but the greater portion relate to aligning the perspectives and objectives of technical staff with desired business outcomes. Some of the important issues in this area include:

*Ensure that the technical professional understands the required business outcome(s).* The working group was clear on the need to align the definition of technical success with business success. Traditionally, business objectives have been translated into technical specifications, after which IT is gauged on the extent that it has meet this spec, but this approach is not well aligned with the business context for cloud, in which end-users (and often, customers) are directly exposed to systems as they are delivered. With cloud, it isn't sufficient to do a "great job" from a technical perspective – it's necessary to deliver technology that is directly supportive of clearly-defined business goals. This is a challenge for IT management, which needs to find ways of describing business targets in technology-relevant terms – but it is the working group's contention that this is the key to achieving "incredible innovation."

*Ensure that the technical professional understands the key business activities and processes.* The translation referenced in the previous point can only result in effective, relevant systems if the technical staff understands the underlying business tasks and processes well enough to provide support for improvements. This is more a balance than a single destination. On the one hand, a technical person who doesn't understand a specific process (for example, how a business measures cash flow) is unlikely to deliver a system that addresses unmet needs (to continue the example, within the accounting department). On the other hand, new features and functionalities need to be tuned to the needs and capabilities of the users. A system that is *too* different in its approach to process automation is likely to confuse users; however, a system that merely updates existing functionality won't unlock new value, making it more attuned to 'not losing' than to 'winning'. IT teams need to expand functionality without adversely affecting usability, and need to ensure that they are building capabilities in areas that deliver real benefit to the business. At the same time, both IT and business staff should recognize that 'new functionality' doesn't describe a static point: one set of improvements builds understanding and demand for additional capabilities. This process of continual evolution requires that the technical professional have an understanding of what users do, what they deliver and where improved accuracy, efficiency, integration, etc., would represent increased business success. It also argues for the iterative approach central to the Agile development methodology, rather than the requirements-driven approach used in traditional waterfall approaches.

*Consider Agile as an organizational model.* IT professionals understand that with Agile methodologies, there are product owners who have responsibility for deliverables who aren't necessarily technology experts, but who understand what the technology can do and what options are available to them. This approach emphasizes knowledge of the business potential of the technology, with support provided by technologists with knowledge of the solution's inner workings. It seems likely that over time, enterprises will focus on the ability to use cloud to address business requirements, and will view in-depth technical knowledge as an aspect of (rather than central to) the broader IT mission.

Professionals who understand Agile note that it has implications for business leaders as well as for software developers. One member of the working group observed that "Delivering software on a monthly basis is pretty easy to do once you rally the troops. Getting the rest of the business to think about sales, marketing, business model innovation on such a regular timeline is practically unheard of and requires a whole new discipline and leadership skills that are not that quickly developed." In today's world, the word "agile" has very different meanings within IT and the executive suite. Businesses that capitalize on the potential of cloud may need to include some of the structural elements associated with the 'IT Agile' in order to ensure continuous alignment between business opportunity and cloud options.

Another group member notes that with Agile (as a development methodology), there is an expectation that the business entrusts the technical staff to make technical decisions. Business process/product owners can be involved in scripting user stories, and are able to vet the outcome of technical decisions rapidly because new functionality is delivered on a regular basis, but they aren't expected to make a cloud/no cloud call – this is a matter of supporting the outcome (the technologist's domain) rather than defining the outcome (the responsibility of the product owner). Business leaders should trust technical leads to deploy systems on the best platform technologies, and they should also understand and expect that technical staff will increasingly focus on cloud as a means of delivering solutions to business requirements.

*Understand that 'cloud skills' is a multi-dimensional issue.* Firms looking to plot the optimal set of "double deep" skills will find a wide range of issues that need to be addressed. One is the list of functional domains that are important to organizational success, including sales, marketing, HR, accounting, and production. A second dimension covers the skills that are important to professionals using cloud in pursuit of business objectives: process design linking technology to task automation and integration, graphic design establishing intuitive interfaces that contribute to efficiency and productivity, the ability to test and adjust approaches based on test results so that systems can evolve over time, understanding and using analytics that capitalize on the data generated/captured by the new automation systems, and a host of similar technology-linked capabilities that connect cloud-enabled options with innovation in different business areas. A third dimension is rooted in the core role of the staff member – is he/she primarily responsible for delivering IT support or for delivering business outcomes? A full inventory of cloud skills connects these three perspectives into a roster of resources that support enterprise agility by capitalizing on the business potential of cloud-based systems.

This matrix of requirements, illustrated in Figure 8-2, is already apparent in training demand. One working group member whose company provides training states that the mix of courses is shifting away from "basic managing of equipment to creating an effective architecture" – demonstrating that IT professionals are aware of and moving to embrace the concept of aligning cloud, and IT generally, with broader organizational demands. Meanwhile, another group member observes that today's (non-IT) university students are comfortable with technical terms. Clearly, there is some convergence developing between IT and business domains – and equally clearly, this has changed the types of skills that are required, reducing the value of many traditional, certification-defined competencies and increasing the value of insight that connects IT systems and business processes.

*Figure 8-2. Cloud skills requirements form an IT/business matrix*

## Core technical competencies

| Business tasks | Process design | | Graphic design | | Test/modify | | Analytics | | Etc... | |
|---|---|---|---|---|---|---|---|---|---|---|
| **Sales** | IT | | IT | | IT | | IT | | IT | |
| | | Business | | Business | | Business | | Business | | Business |
| **Marketing** | IT | | IT | | IT | | IT | | IT | |
| | | Business | | Business | | Business | | Business | | Business |
| **HR** | IT | | IT | | IT | | IT | | IT | |
| | | Business | | Business | | Business | | Business | | Business |
| **Accounting** | IT | | IT | | IT | | IT | | IT | |
| | | Business | | Business | | Business | | Business | | Business |
| **Production** | IT | | IT | | IT | | IT | | IT | |
| | | Business | | Business | | Business | | Business | | Business |
| **Customer support** | IT | | IT | | IT | | IT | | IT | |
| | | Business | | Business | | Business | | Business | | Business |
| **Etc...** | IT | | IT | | IT | | IT | | IT | |
| | | Business | | Business | | Business | | Business | | Business |

## Departmental role

Source: TCBC/InsightaaS, 2016

## Best practices in cloud skills development

What can an enterprise do to successfully adapt to the skills-related requirements associated with the broader shift to cloud? The working group highlighted nine areas that collectively assist businesses in staying abreast of (or ahead of) the talent and training curve:

- *'Digital literacy' is a critical attribute.* Businesses that succeed with cloud need to establish and continue to develop a baseline of 'digital literacy' – comfort with technology, and the skills needed to use technology to be more efficient in performing work. IT is central to business success in companies of all sizes, in virtually every industry, and around the world. Cloud is a cost-efficient means of delivering advanced IT services across the enterprise and to connected staff, suppliers and customers around the world. Organizations need to build digital literacy to connect these dots across cloud potential and business success.

- *'Soft skills' respond to real demand.* There has been a tendency to treat 'soft' skills, such as communications and motivation, as being of less actual importance than the 'hard' skills associated with coding and system development. However, in the cloud (/Agile) world, soft skills are essential to business and IT success. As one working group member pointed out, historically, business has "thrown things over the wall" to IT; a request is submitted, requirements and specifications established, and then IT is left to deliver the new capabilities if/when/as it is able. This approach is at odds with best practices in Agile, and in cloud generally. As organizations realize the advantage obtained through rapid development and ongoing iteration to build and refine minimum viable products (MVPs), communications and other interpersonal skills are essential to progress.

- *Teamwork is a non-optional competency – and continuity is important to teamwork.* The point about soft skills highlights the importance of collaboration, which in turn, points to the importance of teamwork as a means of supporting ongoing development and refinement of cloud-based business solutions. Research shows that teams that are kept together over time go through a cycle. Immediately after a group is formed, there is often a period when members are apt to clash over assumptions and work modes. Teams that are kept together past this stage reach a "norming" level where members gain familiarity and trust with each other. The final stage in the cycle is "performing," where teams are most efficient in delivery. Attaining this "performing" state, though, requires continuity in the team's composition – and IT workers (and those with advanced cloud skills in particular) tend to have a high degree of mobility within and across employers. In environments where teamwork is important to success, it's important to address the needs not just of individual employees but also of the team as a unit. This can be especially challenging in cloud, where "the team" may include suppliers whose employees do not report to internal IT or business managers. Optimizing for the team is a management imperative that is uniquely important to long-term cloud success.

- *HR needs to remain current with workplace norms.* Building on the previous point, current and potential staff members who are comfortable with cloud are likely to reflect the ubiquitous, always-on nature of cloud in their own work habits. In particular, they are unlikely to be happy in a work environment that is rigidly defined in terms of location, and potentially, in terms of time and modes as well. "Cloud native" workers will probably see work as something that can be accomplished from anywhere that has an Internet connection, and may shift time to address a mix of business and personal objectives. HR professionals need to understand that rigid work environments are probably poorly suited to acquisition and retention of professionals who are attuned to cloud-based processes.
- *Open source is an indicator of cloud comfort.* Within the IT department, working group members have observed a link between comfort with cloud and adoption of open source technologies. Both cloud and open source represent advances in IT: new, faster, lower-cost, and often higher-quality ways of delivering IT capacity in support of business objectives. IT departments that aren't comfortable with open source will likely struggle with cloud, and may end up with "shadow IT" within the IT department as advanced users work with unauthorized open source resources. As an IT skills strategy, there is merit in trying to build familiarity in both open source and cloud.
- *Legacy IT is an inhibitor.* It's tempting to simply note that organizations that lack legacy systems have an easier time moving to the cloud than those with extensive traditional internal IT operations, but that would be unfair: any sizable enterprise with some history is likely to have legacy systems in place. The key issue here is the ability of the organization to transition to new tools where they help to accelerate productivity and business agility. This becomes a question of creativity, the ability to look for new ways to solve ongoing issues – such as tasking systems engineers to understand how to integrate capabilities sourced from multiple suppliers, rather than building a solution rooted in on-premise hardware. This may not be easy to define in skills development terms, but represents a crucial attribute for IT resources within enterprises that can take advantage of cloud capabilities.
- *Management FUD is a significant barrier.* Building on the prior point, the evolution of employee roles is challenging for staff members, but it at least promises an opportunity for developing new knowledge and competencies. The

impact at a management level (and uniquely, within IT management) is harder to anticipate. Oftentimes, managers grow into roles – and build credibility – by having successfully worked in the positions that they are now responsible for managing. What happens when staff members acquire new skills and perform new tasks? The manager's base of knowledge becomes less relevant, and it is entirely possible that these managers will react by trying to place limits on new activities, choking the creativity that is so important to ongoing success. HR needs to be cognizant of the need to work with management to create an environment that builds and prizes continuous evolution matched to staff members' fluid skills and assignments. Otherwise, the business risks losing a current generation of management that provides a valuable connection, via 'corporate memory', to the process needs of the business.

- *Continuous reinvention is an objective defined by a journey.* One working group member compared the current business and IT environment to the situation faced by factory workers in the 1970s, when automation and outsourcing fundamentally changed the work environment, right down to expectations of what constituted 'work' and where and how it was performed. This requires the staff member or manager to take stock of what they know about the overall business, rather than the performance of a specific task within the business. "It is about building your skills and understanding of where the business is going;" even if the requirement within the business is to manage outsourcer delivery rather than to perform delivery tasks, "that baseline of skills is not gone."

The final requirement – and most important issue – discussed in this context was *vision*. The working group agreed with the notion that "first and foremost and organization has to have a vision," adding that in the absence of a set of clear and common goals, "you get chaos." This led in turn to additional observations, including:

- Cloud is not a single entity; there are "a whole bunch of clouds" that are changing continuously, and which represent "the real technological landscape." Because enterprise cloud opportunity is defined by this range of evolving capabilities, it's important to stress agility and adaptability in training/skills (and workforce) design.
- In this context, the ability to focus on iterative planning that reflects immediate conditions is essential. Again, this is both a skills and a workforce design issue:

static plans used to organize traditional, hierarchical management structures fly in the face of what cloud requires and what it enables in terms of productivity and new capabilities.

- Staff direction can be, and should be, defined in terms of business outcomes. In the context of a business environment that is based on IT capacities that are in turn changing rapidly in response to both the expanding capabilities of cloud and the evolving IT management processes typified by Agile, it's counterproductive to manage and measure staff members in terms of completion of defined tasks. Successful enterprises will increasingly derive their success from individuals at all levels of the organization who have the freedom and creativity needed to innovate.
- Experimentation is critical to success. This is true on both a business level (and reflected in cloud's "fail fast" mantra) and with respect to corporate systems. Beyond training, in the cloud era, it's important to develop a culture that rewards experimentation.

Vision, agility, non-hierarchical management structures, a culture that rewards experimentation and is focused on outcomes...all of these are attributes that are derived from/delivered by leadership. And this was the final 'best practice' offered by the working group. The change in skills demanded by cloud isn't limited to IT or to staff members – it is enterprise-wide, and it both includes and starts with (and relies upon) the senior leaders within the organization.

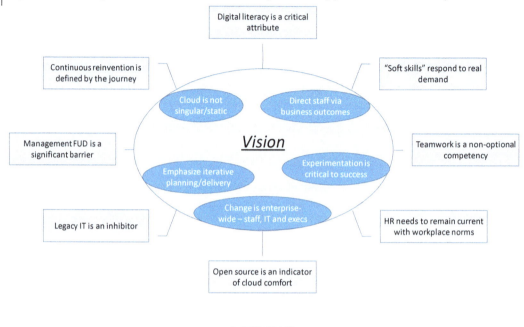

Figure 8-3. Best practices in cloud skill development: key focus areas and imperatives

*Source: TCBC/InsightaaS, 2016*

## Reference sources

Additional references that readers can use to better understand best practices in cloud skills development and related issues include:

- 2015 Continuing Certification Requirements (CCR) Program Updates, PMI, effective December 2015. The Project Management Institute (PMI) has changed its PMP certification guidelines to add emphasis on leadership and business and strategic expertise, reflecting increased requirements for 'soft skills'.

- Digital Talent: Road to 2020 and Beyond. Information and Communications Technology Council, March 2016. Report provides detailed analysis of Canadian IT labour supply and demand.

- Martin Reeves, Ming Zeng and Amin Venjara. "The Self-Tuning Enterprise." HBR, June 2015. This HBR article outlines key conditions for "dynamic management" and includes a discussion of Alibaba's approach, which is illustrative of some of the points made in the Best Practices section of this document.

## Metrics and milestones

Wherever possible, TCBC Best Practices reports conclude with a section on metrics and milestones that can be used by readers to calibrate their progress in the subject area. With skills, it is difficult to establish a rigid measurement framework that can be used across all environments, but there are milestones that can help mark the path to broad and relevant cloud-related competencies.

## Metrics

The working group asserted that there is no universally applicable, structured set of measurements that can/should be built into a corporate skills plan. There are certainly directions that are important to individuals looking (to borrow a phrase from gaming) to "level up:" for example, technical staff should be continuously improving both technical and leadership skills. But specific objectives vary by role, by experience/tenure, and by industry/business requirements. Similarly, there are organizational metrics that can be applied to cloud skills: Agile defines the primary measure of success as "working software," and there are metrics that can be applied to software – time to benefit, quality, and cost – that can be monitored for improvement. Again, though, specific objectives are defined in context rather than in absolute terms.

*Figure 8-4. Updating an old joke*

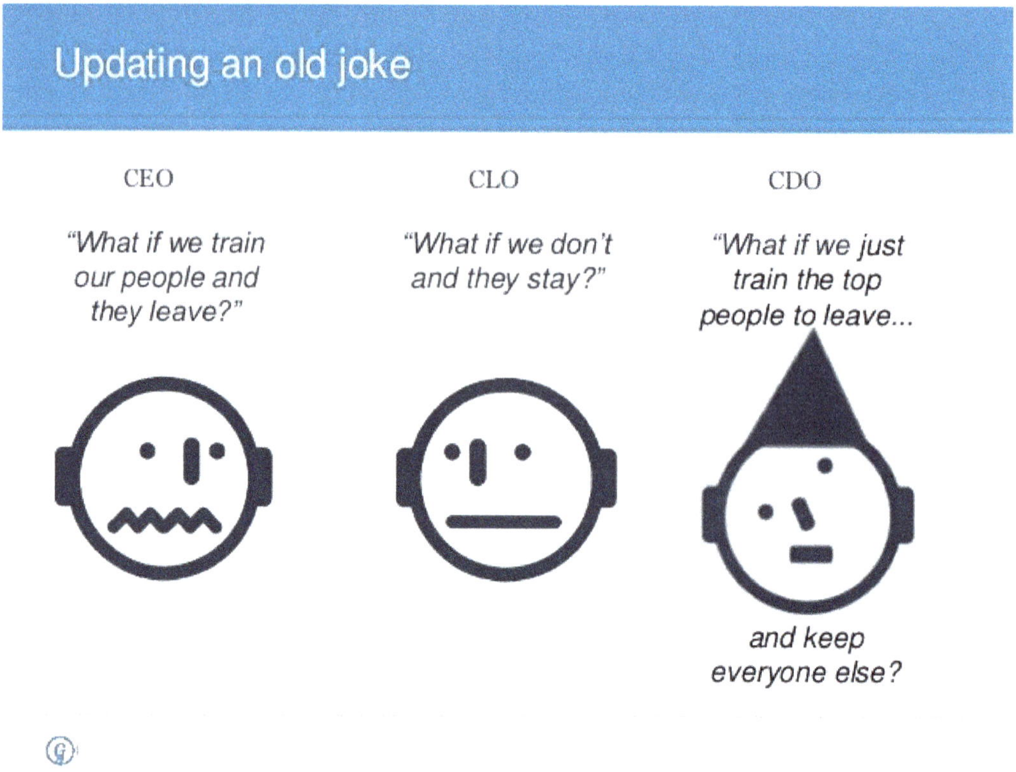

## Updating an old joke

| CEO | CLO | CDO |
|-----|-----|-----|
| *"What if we train our people and they leave?"* | *"What if we don't and they stay?"* | *"What if we just train the top people to leave...* |

*and keep everyone else?*

*Source: Grovo presentation "Teach Your Learners to Learn: How to Make Every Employee a Top Performer" (Slideshare.com)*

Most readers have likely seen the old joke in which one manager asks, "what if we train our people and they leave?" and another replies "What if we don't and they stay?" In this updated version, a third executive – the Chief Digital Officer – adds a third option: "what if we just train the top people to leave, and keep everyone else?" This sequence reflects a dilemma faced by enterprises adapting to a cloud-centric digital business environment: trained and experienced staff have many opportunities to leave for new employers, untrained staff inhibit effective use of ICT as a strategic attribute, and attempts to focus scarce training resources only on staff in specific leadership roles may well exacerbate the divide. The increasing pervasiveness of cloud and digital business requires broad skills improvement, and a strategy for effectively embracing multiple development strategies to optimize the connection between understanding and job/task effectiveness, and between investment and return.

Formal training is one important option for building skills. However, in an era of constrained training budgets, the working group notes that additional activities – reading relevant reports and other materials, job shadowing, etc. – should also be incorporated into the development plan. Regardless of available budget and other options, though, there is no pre-defined activity list that is associated with adequate (or best practice) cloud skills development/enhancement. There are sets of skills that are important to cloud success for different types of roles (for example, IT managers need to invest in understanding business architecture, business analysts should be capable in project management and vendor management, IT professionals will need detailed knowledge of virtualization and ITIL), but specific requirements change over time, since cloud and its uses change as businesses gain experience with cloud and as new product/service options become available.

## Milestones

If there are no firm frameworks identifying a development hierarchy for cloud skills, there are some clear signposts that indicate whether an enterprise is making progress in its journey to cloud competency. Aligning specific development activities with these broader outcomes and associated best practices is helpful in defining skills paths for staff and management across the organization.

The first step in this process is recognizing that the baseline metric for a business in the cloud era is *digital literacy*. Most enterprises today – certainly, most services businesses, and an increasing number of product businesses – employ technology as a critical component of task completion, process integration and end product/service delivery. Most customers of these businesses expect that their suppliers employ systems designed to improve accuracy and efficiency, which can be integrated where necessary as inputs to their own business infrastructure or consumer consumption patterns. Enterprises need to embrace and reflect a level of digital literacy appropriate to their environments. This level changes with industry, by region/geography and over time, so it isn't easy to establish as a fixed point – but it is important in most contexts, and should be monitored at an organizational level by the senior leadership team, and embedded in the strategies used within HR and across operating units.

As noted in the Best Practices section of this report, within the IT department, one indicator of a shift towards digital literacy is the use of open source software. In traditional IT shops, open source represents a form of "shadow IT" within the IT department; IT operations that embrace open source may well be more amenable to use of cloud as well. While cloud focus varies in relation to existing legacy systems, it's generally the case that use of cloud reflects a tight focus on core business outcomes rather than on platform technology management. In this aspect, cloud use itself is a milestone on the path to digital literacy and effective integration of technology and business operations.

*Cloud skills and organizational context*

There is an important connection between skills-related milestones and the broader corporate context. One working group member noted that business analysts, QA and development professionals, and line-of-business managers with project budget responsibility are often found in Agile development courses, but that other important constituencies – HR, finance, and senior executives – are rarely immersed in Agile training. At a task level, this discrepancy makes sense. Those steeped in Agile, though, view it as a cultural rather than tactical option for aligning the enterprise with the emerging options enabled by technology, and especially, cloud. In the "agile organization," one working group member observed, "you can't desynchronize" the process of evolving IT systems supporting business activities – which are updated on a regular, rapid basis – with evolution in the business activities themselves.

Corporate adoption of Agile aside, this linkage between IT and business evolution is a critical aspect of skills development in the cloud/digital economy. A business that continuously and rapidly enhances both the capabilities of its IT infrastructure and the agility of its business processes capitalizes on development of cloud skills, and rewards the individuals building those skills by connecting their effort and achievement to overall organizational progress. These businesses create an environment that attracts and retains IT and line-of-business staff who 'get' cloud and who build skills and understanding as they contribute to expanded digital capabilities within the enterprise. Firms that establish effective balance between corporate goals, management objectives and IT activities will ultimately be successful in establishing a context that encourages and nurtures the development of cloud competencies.

*Figure 8-5. Establishing organizational balance to support cloud skills development*

## Business

- Operations and IT evolve *rapidly* and *continuously*
- Emphasis on *digital literacy* across the organization

Changing mindsets

## IT

- Skills expand beyond *technical* to *leadership*
- Objective is *engagement* rather than *support*

## LOB Management

- IT approach changes from *passive* to *active*
- IT position changes from *user* to *owner*

*Source: TCBC/InsightaaS, 2016*

*Chapter 9.*

# Cloud Go-to-Market

Essential guidance for cloud suppliers on cloud marketing, cloud sales approaches and compensation, and cloud channel development

*Contributing community experts: Sylvia Bauer (CenturyLink), Anne De Aragon (GoDaddy), Craig McLellan (ThinkOn), Adi Morun (Microsoft), Matt Ambrose (PwC), Brian Ochab (Unity Connected Solutions), Norman Sung (Red Hat)*

*Initial publication date: January 2016*

# Cloud Go-to-Market

## Definition and context

The cloud go-to-market (GTM) group is one of two 2015 TCBC groups focused on supply-side development rather than buy-side insight and advice; it, like "financing cloud businesses," is intended for the Canadian cloud's chefs rather than the diners.

In its initial discussion, the working group members were clear on the need to focus on the key issues involved in marketing cloud, as (relative to traditional infrastructure) marketing takes on new meaning and expanded importance in a cloud context. The focus of the group also includes sales, and particularly, compensation models and the issues involved in building an effective cloud channel, defined broadly enough to include cloud brokers as well as traditional resale-oriented VARs. The focus also extends to consideration of the critical issues that suppliers of all types – vendors and channel members – should consider in building their cloud GTM plans.

## Defining the cloud 'marketing stack'

### *Above the stack – what sellers need from buyers*

It is possible to present (as in Figure 9-1) cloud GTM issues as components in a cloud 'marketing stack'. The highest level, which can be seen as beyond or above the stack, includes the contributions that suppliers need buyers to make to cloud evaluation. Two key items here include the ability to buy IT capability as a service rather than a product, and an openness to a portfolio rather than suite approach to software. The first of these issues is somewhat mechanical, and is largely a finance issue: is the finance staff able to evaluate and contract for OPEX-based, rather than CAPEX-based, suppliers and offerings? Will internal systems support matching of POs to capability be delivered as-a-service?

The second issue concerns the attitude of the buyer organization, and is at least to some extent an IT issue. For many years, companies have enhanced systems by adding on to a core suite of software. The software suite approach offers the benefit of tested integration, but has the drawbacks of high cost and very slow update cycles. With cloud, buyers are able to rapidly configure solutions to meet specific needs, and typically pay much less for new capabilities than is the case with on-premise suites. However, this requires the IT department to assert authority over both component selection and integration, which represents a new position for IT relative to software system capabilities.

*What buyers need from suppliers, and what sellers need to successfully serve buyers*
Once 'ready for cloud', buyers have a short list of requirements that all cloud vendors will need to address before they can be considered as service suppliers to the end user firm. The seller will need to connect with the buyer via means that are well-suited to buyer requirements; the buyer will require contracts and SLAs that help the finance department by providing clear and meaningful insight into the real costs and benefits of a service-based offering; and as per the above, the cloud supplier will need to communicate configuration and integration options so that IT can understand how a specific service fits into the broader IT/business infrastructure.

These buyer requirements in turn dictate some of the key aspects of supplier GTM portfolios. Cloud marketers need to develop compelling value propositions that link the business benefit of cloud to the business needs of a defined segment. Suppliers will need to develop online tools that marketing can use to engage and convert interested prospects – this is an essential attribute, part of the migration of new account acquisition responsibility from sales to marketing. Because commercial relationships in the cloud tend to expand from initial acquisition, successful vendors will build on their position by demonstrating value over time. And on another level, suppliers will need to develop and manage ecosystems that allow them to penetrate accounts that are outside their primary market focus, and to create stickiness within existing accounts.

*Working with the channel*
Cloud suppliers may choose to approach very small customers directly and without any third-party involvement, but most SMBs and enterprise accounts will have consultants, integrators, brokers or other channel members involved in their IT operations, and as a result, will need these firms to be involved in their cloud activities as well. The key to addressing the vendor/channel connection is to identify the components that are essential to the sustainability of channel businesses and channel/vendor relationships. One critical supplier issue is development of an ecosystem that is aligned with both the vendor's product(s) and the customer needs. Understanding which partners can best complete and/or deliver solutions to specific markets, how to stage out the introduction of partnerships so that they are timed to meet customer demand, and then working through the tactical issues of monitoring and managing partner relationships and

integrating partners into a coherent portfolio is complex with products, and even more so when the core of the relationship is formed around a set of services that may shift rapidly and unpredictably and which may have unique contracting and payment terms.

Some of the tactical considerations that impact vendor/channel relationships include: support from the vendor in understanding how to take cloud to market profitably, including how to structure sales compensation models that will motivate field staff without decimating operating reserves, how to price and package products in ways that are easy for the channel to communicate in turn to its customers, and how to recognize the ways in which different partners provide value by addressing different customer objectives.

The matter of how to go to market with cloud is even larger and more complex than the question of channel enablement. Cloud GTM spans multiple issues, including:

- Revenue recognition and sales compensation. Recurring revenue contributes to business stability (and high company valuations), but it can be problematic for firms used to living in a transactional world. Cash flow is impacted by contracts where a customer may pay $1/36^{th}$ of total value each month for three years. This strains management's ability to react to near-term pressures in the business. It also has an impact on sales metrics and sales compensation; it is harder to build easy-to-understand, easy-to-administer sales compensation models for recurring revenue than for transactions.
- Pricing and contracting. This is an issue in channel relationships, and it is also an issue in positioning cloud for end-users. Is the initial price clear? Is the cost of adding users and/or features well articulated? Are the SLAs clear, meaningful and appropriate?
- Roadmaps to the cloud. Cloud services don't, and shouldn't, be delivered in a vacuum. Cloud suppliers build trusted, profitable relationships with customers by helping them to see the 'big picture' – the ways in which cloud offerings can be combined to deliver increased value. Research has shown that this approach is a key characteristic separating successful/profitable suppliers from those that struggle to reach critical mass. It is also an essential element of channel success in the cloud. The vendor and channel roadmaps are likely to be different from each other, but should contain mutual elements that emphasize the value that all parties contribute to customer success.

- Appropriate marketing tactics. Cloud marketing is different from marketing traditional products; it includes opportunities for customers to try offerings before committing to them. This tactic emphasizes conversion – and while that can be antithetical to channel support, vendors need to react to common market expectations, and channels need to appreciate that this is a vendor requirement and adjust relationships and activities accordingly.

*At the base of the stack: what cloud suppliers need to consider to be successful in GTM*
Building a successful cloud GTM strategy requires that suppliers understand the connection between different layers of the marketing stack, and the tactics and investments needed for success within each layer. At root, though, there are a handful of truisms that can guide overall strategy. One is to limit complexity, which benefits the financial and IT functions within the buyer organization, and is also of high importance in channel relationships. The quality and depth of the ecosystem is important, because it supports customer roadmaps (as presented by vendors and/or their partners), and because it helps IT to understand how to configure components into systems/solutions. Specific to the partner relationships, suppliers need to find a way to reward proactive customer engagement without defaulting to the extensive training and certification used by product vendors: cloud is simply too fast moving, and has too many different permutations, to allow this approach to succeed. Finally, reliance on marketing disciplines – segmentation, development of well-articulated value propositions, and prospect/customer engagement – is essential to the success of the cloud GTM strategy.

The range of issues identified by the TCBC cloud GTM working group are reflected in Figure 9-1:

---

*Figure 9-1. Cloud go-to-market: key issues*

### What sellers need from buyers

The ability to understand and contract for OPEX-based
(rather than CAPEX-based) offerings (PO matching)

An openness to building agile, responsive solutions incrementally
by adding (and in some cases, unplugging) discrete components,
rather than adding onto a core platform over a period of years

### What buyers need from suppliers
- Appropriate supply options: direct for simple/transactional products, hands-on support
  for more complex solutions   • Clear contracts and pricing, meaningful SLAs
    • An understanding of ecosystem offerings/costs

### What sellers need to successfully serve buyers
- A compelling value proposition: what business issues does this cloud offering address, and why
  is it the best way to address them?
- A way to position the ecosystem rather than a point solution; a roadmap that highlights the
  incremental benefits of incremental cloud adoption/investment
- Effective online tools for demonstrating product features, and in some cases, converting tryers
  to buyers
- A demonstrated track record of providing viable products, reacting quickly to support requests
  and rolling out new features over time

### What the channel needs from vendors
- Managing recurring revenue: how to transition from product transactions
  • Clarity: what is cloud, why does it matter, how does it work for the partner?
    • An appreciation of the value that the channel supplies in helping
      end-users to absorb technology

### What vendors need to consider to be successful in GTM activities
- Simple core product portfolios: "every additional SKU doubles complexity"
- Extended ecosystems through which customers can source complementary services that are
  important to addressing business issues
- A management strategy that rewards meaningful activity without demanding proactive education
- Mapping of tactics to markets: direct to microbusinesses and narrowly-focused professionals,
  through integration channels to traditional SMBs, through brokers to firms establishing a roadmap,
  with high-end consultants for enterprises establishing a cloud-inclusive business strategy...

*Source: TCBC/InsightaaS, 2015*

## Reference sources

Additional references that readers can use to better understand the key issues defining SMB cloud GTM include:

- Louis Columbus. Key Take-Aways From The 2015 Pacific Crest SaaS Survey. A Passion for Research blog, November 2015. Survey results described by Columbus are useful in identifying appropriate targets (markets, growth rates, upsell) for 2016 campaigns.
- Joshua Shane. "How to Market the Cloud." MarketingProfs, January 2011. This article is a bit dated, but its central premise – that "Allaying the fear of new business disruptions is the overriding challenge of marketing the cloud" – is still relevant.
- Why Successful Cloud Strategies Start with a Solid Partner Strategy. Hostway. This PDF-format deck from cloud supplier Hostway articulates its pitch to prospective partners, shedding light on how and why cloud partner relationships work.

## Business objectives

### Marketing in the context of GTM strategy

Cloud affects GTM strategy in a fundamental way. In traditional product sales situations, the focus is on driving sales of licenses and hardware; in the cloud, the focus shifts to driving activation, usage and consumption. This has an enormous impact on GTM strategy: it changes compensation models, marketing activities and internal alignment between functions.

Cloud represents a unique proposition for sales and marketing, and for technical support. The "cloud sale" is rarely fully defined by the initial purchase: it tends to evolve over time. From an organizational standpoint, cloud demands a very high level of marketing activity and expertise, with marketing often effectively replacing sales as the key connection between interest and first engagement/customer acquisition. This has the effect of moving some of the requirements of pre-sales support to marketing – for example, by developing trial offerings that customers can use to evaluate a cloud service. Cloud suppliers, at least in some cases, have supplemented this marketing activity by investing in technical resources who can work with customers to help them to dig into cloud features, options and benefits.

## Pace and content

Cloud increases the speed at which marketing needs to operate. In part, this is a 'medium and message' issue. Cloud providers enable a wide variety of choices for marketing customers, with the ability to experiment and "fail fast" – but these options aren't limited to customers; the marketing functions within cloud organizations are themselves expected to capitalize on these new capabilities. One very important aspect of cloud marketing is building a process that leads to a customer trial: it is relatively easy for cloud suppliers (as compared with suppliers of conventional products) to offer trials to customers, and these trials have been proven to be an effective way of converting interest into business, but this has the effect of moving the challenge of getting prospects to commit to a first engagement from sales to marketing.

This shift has several important implications for go-to-market strategy. One that the GTM working group highlighted is the importance of simplifying the onboarding process so as not to lose potential customers after they've made the decision to engage with a service. Especially for small business customers, the ideal is described as "one [screen], two, and you are done" and ready to use the service.

Another key consideration is the frequency and content of messaging after initial activation. In traditional product sales, communications with customers tend to be sparse, focused on an upgrade or renewal one, two or three years after the initial commitment/purchase. With cloud, overall success depends, at least in part, on the ability to increase the number of users of an application, the number of features/options used by an account, and/or the overall number of applications used by a client. Cloud marketers have responded by digging deeper into the best ways to use regular communications to highlight options. Experience has shown that some proportion of users – perhaps one-third – are amenable to receiving regular, feature-based communications. Other users might react to a message containing step-by-step information needed to address a technical issue, but are less receptive to marketing messages. These users – and a third group, that doesn't require step-by-step technical instruction but also doesn't welcome continuous communications – needs to be approached with customized messaging tied to business challenges and cloud's ability to address them.

## Segmentation

At the same time that tactics and objectives are shifting, the audiences targeted by cloud marketers are also becoming more diffuse. Developers are an important segment for IaaS and PaaS providers, while business management (and in some cases, business users) represents the key market for SaaS providers, and an important part of the IaaS/PaaS customer constituency. CEOs aren't necessarily a direct target of cloud marketing activities, but other C-level executives are very important: CFOs need to understand the cost benefits of cloud (and how to purchase services rather than products), and line of business VPs, such as sales and marketing executives, need to understand the agility benefits associated with cloud. This has a tremendous impact on marketers for cloud organizations: they need to adjust both messages, to talk to business issues rather than the narrower concerns of technology professionals, and placement, to obtain access to non-IT buyers.

The working group has characterized the change in messaging as a shift from emphasizing new product information to a more business-oriented approach. At a technology level, this takes the form of helping customers to understand how and why a solution meets their needs, complemented by messaging that de-mystifies the implementation process; even if the implementation itself is complex (as it may well be in a large IaaS deployment), it's important for the vendor to make the steps and requirements clear at the outset, so that customers have an appropriate basis for comparing the cloud solution with conventional alternatives, and for budgeting and resourcing for cloud adoption. At a business level, the working group advises marketers to assume that customers are at least generally aware of how cloud address specific business issues, and to emphasize messages built around "you don't know what you don't know" – a way of expanding the parameters of the cloud discussion by drawing in examples of ways that cloud provides unique/additional benefits to organizations and/or professionals in positions that are similar to the one(s) occupied by the targeted prospects.

## The importance of the cloud ecosystem

The cloud ecosystem – the formal connections between different cloud vendors – provides an important way to build and expand relationships with customers. An ecosystem provides an "expanded portfolio," a more comprehensive suite of offerings that can be aligned with a customer's needs. An effective ecosystem management approach gives cloud vendors a way into accounts that have needs that are different from but complementary to their own offerings: for example, an IaaS or PaaS vendor may end up engaged with a new business user who isn't looking for infrastructure but who needs an application hosted on the IaaS platform, or a SaaS vendor may gain access to an account that is using a complementary and integrated application or platform service. These ecosystem offerings may also improve 'stickiness' within an account, as a multi-part solution drives can drive higher levels of use and make unplugging more difficult than a component-based approach.

Ecosystem success requires two different types of competency. One is in alliance management: to create a meaningful ecosystem and/or participate in meaningful ecosystems clustered around third party services, the cloud vendor needs to understand and invest appropriately in building alliances with relevant partner organizations. Translating this activity into revenue requires a second, marketing-based competency: vendors need to align targeting and messaging with key ecosystem members and attributes, ensuring that they are bringing a relevant value proposition to a specific type of customer, rather than simply promoting a broad menu of choices that are not directly connected to any particular set of needs. The point of connection between the two activities is often co-marketing/co-selling with ecosystem members: a cloud vendor works with a partner to identify a segment that is of common interest and messaging that highlights the unique advantages that the two parties bring when combined in a single offering, and then jointly invest in promoting this message to the target market. In some cases, this activity might include a third party – a cloud broker or other channel member – who can promote the advantages of the combined offering to a specific customer set, and add services that are important to customer success with the solution.

*The traditional channel in the context of cloud*
At a strategic level, it's also important for vendors to appreciate the value that partners bring to the purchase process. Many traditional vendors are used to seeing channels as a way of facilitating transactions with small customers, and believe that the channel's importance is diminished if the transactions themselves can be handled electronically at very low cost. But the channel also serves the buy side in IT solution deployment by providing the knowledge needed to successfully absorb new technologies into business processes. This need is not addressed through electronic transactions. Channels may not reduce deal friction from a seller's perspective, but they do assist with customer acceptance of cloud solutions.

## The importance of segmentation

The workgroup discussion of key cloud GTM issues raised important points concerning segmentation. In particular, it is clear that microbusinesses, SMBs and enterprise accounts have different characteristics that are important to determining appropriate marketing and sales options. Highlights from the working group discussion are captured in Figure 9-2. At each level of the market, we find important segmentation distinctions:

- The vast majority of all potential customers – between 55% (for 1-4 employees only) and 87% (for all businesses with 1-19 employees) are found in the microbusiness category. This group has low web penetration - less than 50%, according to credible estimates. They require a substantial amount of education. However, because the accounts are individually small, they must (for the most part) be managed programmatically via self-service options.
  - There is a particular issue in the microbusiness market with businesses owned by older, generally male, business principals. One working group discussion asked the question, "is it better to target a business owner who is approaching retirement age, or to wait for ownership/management transitions and focus instead on businesses that are already controlled by younger managers?" Neither approach is without risk: as noted above, microbusinesses represent an enormous part of the Canadian economy (employing a clear majority of Canadian workers), so they are an important target market, but communicating effectively about cloud benefits to owners who aren't inclined to view the web as a business resource is problematic on several levels.
- The SMB segment (small businesses with 20-99 employees, and midmarket firms with 100-499 employees) contains just less than 13% of all Canadian enterprises. These firms have existing IT operations, and require help in moving functions to the cloud and in integrating new cloud-based systems with existing on-premise systems. They are managed via segmentation strategies that emphasize commonality between 'like' firms; there are too many companies in this group to manage individually, and they aren't large enough to warrant discrete, account-level management. These accounts may well benefit from support via cloud brokers or the conventional channel.
- The enterprise segment accounts for less than one-quarter of one percent of all Canadian businesses, but is thought to drive about one-third of total Canadian

IT spending. These firms have extensive existing (online and on-premise) infrastructure, and will require integration between these systems. This market has traditionally been one that places a high value on business-focused consulting that leads to IT system deployment. Marketing to this group, and especially to its business leaders, warrants/demands account-level attention.

---

*Figure 9-2. Cloud GTM segmentation and characteristics*

Number of accounts; requirement for education

Size of accounts; requirement for custom configuration and integration

Microbusinesses (e.g., 1-5 or 1-20 employees): 55%-87% of all Canadian businesses; <50% web penetration

- Generally require point solutions; high requirement for basic info
- Can't be managed individually, require programmatic messaging
- Best engaged via self-service; small "web professionals" (SMB-focused cloud brokers) also an option

Small and mid-sized businesses (e.g., 20-99 employees, 100-499 employees): 11% (20-99), 1.7% (100-499) of all Canadian businesses; very high web penetration

- Require integration between point solutions and IT services
- Managed primarily with segmentation strategies; can't be managed individually or (effectively) programmatically
- Opportunity for cloud brokers and other channel firms

Enterprise accounts (e.g., >500 or >1000 employees): 0.2% of Canadian businesses; extensive web presence in all businesses

- Require integration between cloud and existing infrastructure and processes; high requirement for business-focused consulting
- Must be managed individually
- Opportunity for integrators and/or direct F2F sales

**Key**
- Market characteristics
- Marketing requirements
- Sales options

*Source: TCBC/InsightaaS, 2015*

## What to avoid

While there is clearly opportunity across the spectrum of Canadian accounts, it seems wise to add a word of caution to restrain marketers from pitching the full potential of cloud to all potential converts. It is true that the flexibility associated with configuring cloud-based infrastructure provides buyers with a tremendous range of options for aligning resources with requirements. However, there is a shadow associated with flexibility and configurability: *complexity*. In the words of the working group, it is possible to present cloud buyers with a dozen reasonable options, and for them to respond with something to the effect of "I don't have a 12-sided coin" with which to purchase IT. Cloud moves fast and opens new areas of opportunity on a continuous basis – and as a result, it is particularly important for marketers to take the steps needed to attach cloud potential to well-defined business needs.

## Best/proven practices in Cloud GTM

The discussion of segmentation and routes to market above points to the fact that there's no single 'silver bullet' that cloud suppliers can use to master GTM strategy. There are, though, some tactics that are well attuned to specific situations and requirements, which can be used to help formulate GTM approaches.

## Marketing issues

In general, the content that is presented to a prospective cloud customer, and the pace with which it is presented, varies with the complexity of the solution and the customers' business. Microbusinesses and enterprises have very different needs, and have to be approached in different ways. Across all cloud GTM strategies, though, there is a process (shown in Figure 9-3) that both represents a high-level best practice, and requires the application of actions based on specific best practice activities in order to deliver value to the supplier business.

The success of this high-level process, though, relies on best practices in developing the resources needed to support each of the steps. Closer analysis of market-specific issues finds that there are substantial differences in the approaches used to build presence within the microbusiness and enterprise segments. With microbusinesses, the best approach is to focus on very clear methods of engagement and persistent presence. Guidance from the working group is to keep sign-up screens clear and to a minimum – for example, two screens from initial interaction to transaction. Individuals who exit the process should be retargeted quickly and ubiquitously – for example, via video platforms and offers posted on/through other web destinations. One member noted, "Once the customers express interest you can do a lot to follow that customer in terms of their journey around the web and making sure that you stay top of mind…"

Offerings focused on enterprise customers and solutions also benefit from retargeting, but overall, both the pace and the content vary widely. An enterprise solution is used by many different people within the organization – and consequently, there are sound reasons for targeting information on enterprise solutions at different roles within the prospective customer's business. This calls for a range of content: the messages that resonate with an executive in the finance department, a manager in sales or marketing, or an IT development lead are likely to be very different.

This last sentence contains one observation made by the working group: that function appears to be more important than title in cloud marketing. Other observations made about this group include:

- Content syndication is very important – once the content is created, it's important to put it where it can be seen and consumed.
- Once initial contact is made via content downloads, prospects are assigned to nurture streams. Unlike with microbusinesses, follow up with enterprise contacts needs to be measured, with frequencies in the 2-4 week range.
- Lead scoring is used as a means of moving prospects from the nurture stream to the sales funnel. Only prospects shown to have a high propensity to buy are forwarded to sales; others are retained in the nurture stream until they progress.

*Figure 9-3. A macro-level view of cloud GTM best practices*

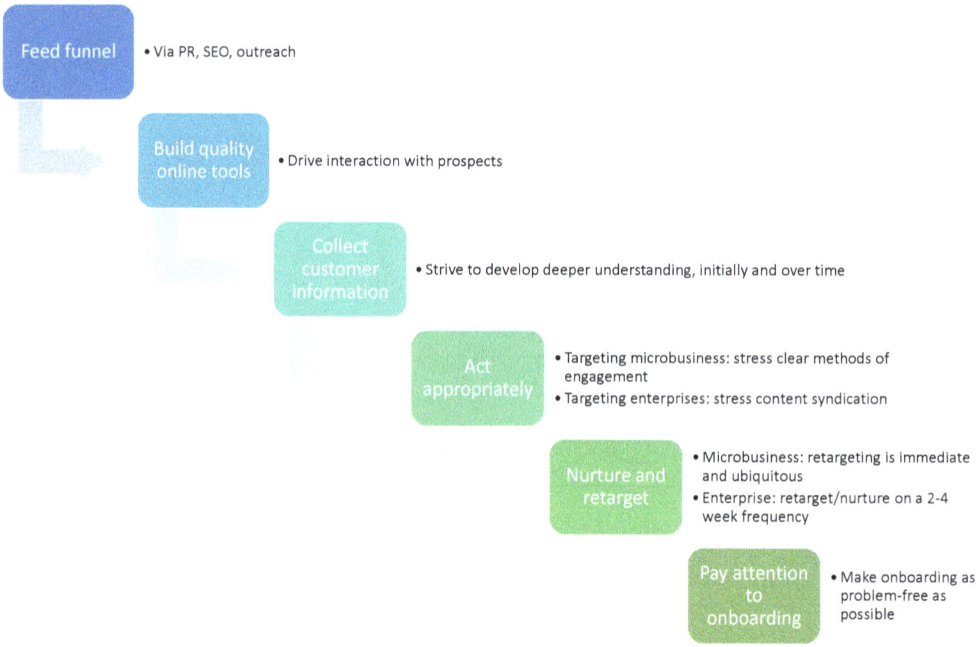

**Feed funnel**
- Via PR, SEO, outreach

**Build quality online tools**
- Drive interaction with prospects

**Collect customer information**
- Strive to develop deeper understanding, initially and over time

**Act appropriately**
- Targeting microbusiness: stress clear methods of engagement
- Targeting enterprises: stress content syndication

**Nurture and retarget**
- Microbusiness: retargeting is immediate and ubiquitous
- Enterprise: retarget/nurture on a 2-4 week frequency

**Pay attention to onboarding**
- Make onboarding as problem-free as possible

*Source: TCBC/InsightaaS, 2015*

One tactic that is common to both enterprises and microbusinesses is cross selling. Enterprise solution providers are generally looking to enter the customer organization in response to a specific buyer requirement. Typically, these suppliers have sophisticated portfolios – their task is to identify additional users and requirements that they can address, as a means of connecting the buyer with the entire product suite. Suppliers focused on microbusinesses will also look for cross/upsell opportunities. These may include adding features to existing packages, or sales of third party products that expand the cloud footprint – and the monthly bill.

Another issue that is common to marketers targeting all sizes of customers is the need to collect information from customers after they have engaged. One supplier that is part of the working group uses customer-supplied information to populate nine discrete segments, which in turn dictate the communications that they will target at the prospect/customer. Another noted that in an enterprise context, user-supplied information is used to fine-tune persona targeting. In both cases, the message is clear: it's critical to capture, aggregate and act on user-supplied information.

*Supporting key steps in the cloud marketing process*

Materials and activities that should be included in – or at least, considered for inclusion in – a cloud marketing portfolio include:

- *Internal sales tools.* Tools that help sales staff to offer consistent and convincing answers to questions and to stress key marketing messages are important in virtually all B2B contexts. They are especially important in cloud, where comparisons are likely to involve both competitive services and alternative delivery options (such as on-premise infrastructure). Marketing needs to ensure that the field staff has 'cheat sheets', how-to-sell guides and qualification questions to help them understand key offering elements and differentiators and to connect with prospects.
- *Online qualification questionnaires.* These online questionnaires can be simple (e.g., fewer than 10 yes/no questions) or relatively sophisticated (multiple entry points, multiple options and multiple scenarios), and they may have different objectives, with simpler systems designed to promote a single solution and more complex models designed to expand the scope of cloud within the user organization. In all cases, though, the primary goal is to gather relevant information on a prospective customer, and identify resources (whitepapers, reports, recommendations) that align with the customer's needs.
- *External education materials.* Both field staff and online visitors are likely to need some education before they take the 'next step' by committing to a meeting, launching a trial or placing an order. Depending on the sophistication of your solution and the customer set that is being targeted, external education materials may be as straightforward as an explanation on the vendor's own website, or as comprehensive as a library of whitepapers and third-party analyst reports. Simple resources can often be linked into an online customer acquisition process, while extensive sets of resources need to be mapped by customer need/scenario and/or buyer persona.
- *Demo tools.* Many buyers will want to gain a sense as to how a service works before committing to a trial or a purchase. These buyers require guided tours, which may take the form of a video or web-based, wizard-driven demo, in order to build comfort with a supplier's offering.

- *Well-structured and supported online trials.* As is noted earlier in this document, the cloud marketing process is often designed to lead to a customer trial; it follows that these trials themselves need to be structured in a way that makes them meaningful to prospects, and supported adequately, so that prospective clients aren't turned away by unexpected process complexity. There are two main approaches to these trials. One is the 'freemium' model, in which the customer gets access to a basic version of a service, and needs to pay to unlock desirable features or add-ons. The other involves time-limited access to a full version of the service, so that the customer can gain experience with the production environment. Generally speaking, firms with multi-faceted enterprise cloud offerings are most likely to use the second approach (and are well on the road to a sale once the customer takes the time to port data to the trial environment). Regardless of approach, though, the marketing objective is to ensure that customers who get as far as registering for a trial follow through with use, enhancing the opportunity for conversion.
- *Effective PR and AR.* Most cloud suppliers are challenged in building visibility for their brands and solutions. Using PR to place stories highlighting unique attributes and customer successes is important to feeding the top of the sales funnel and reinforcing brand throughout the consideration/evaluation/purchase process, and using AR to build visibility within leading analyst firms increases opportunities for consideration by customers research a particular service option.

## Channel issues

In cloud, "channel" can be defined in many ways – and as Figure 9-4 illustrates, partners don't just play a role in securing/facilitating transactions, but also in forming the "cloud product" and in shaping demand for cloud.

In many cases, traditional product vendors slot traditional B2B channels into a rigidly defined role. The vendor builds a product and creates demand through its own marketing activities, and relies on channel members – often, organized by geography, or perhaps industry and geography – to help intercept that demand. The ability of cloud providers to deal directly with customers regardless of where they are located has led some to view channels as extraneous to their GTM logic.

There are, however, many ways that business partners can contribute to a cloud vendor's ability to build a compelling value proposition, and to help customers to capitalize on the cloud vendor's offerings. Business partners can have a significant impact at all stages of the GTM process:

- *Product*. ISVs are important to cloud suppliers serving all types of customers. Cloud vendors looking to build an enterprise-level platform will need ISVs to provide capabilities that are essential to the core offering (e.g., security, development environments, user identification management, etc.). IaaS vendors attempting to penetrate target markets may work with a specific application vendor to demonstrate the relevance of their services; the ISV in turn may rely on the platform vendor to provide evidence of a trustworthy application delivery platform. And cloud platform suppliers – especially those targeted on microbusinesses – may position cloud applications as an extension of their core relationship with a customer, even as the ISV involved views the platform services vendor as a resale channel with excellent access to a high-value target community

- *Transaction*. Although the channel isn't generally essential to facilitating a transaction between cloud vendor and customer (most cloud transactions can be effected online), the traditional reseller channel does play a role in helping customers – especially SMBs with existing IT operations – to understand how to add new workloads on cloud, migrate existing workloads to the cloud, and integrate cloud and on-premise resources. Web professionals play an important role within microbusinesses, helping business owners to move onto the web, and to expand into other online applications. And as is noted above, IaaS providers and application vendors can act as complementary GTM partners.

- *Demand*. In addition to being important to the composition of the product and to the product transaction, partners are an important resource for buyers, shaping their understanding of how cloud can help them address business and technical challenges. In enterprise accounts, consultants work with business management to assess technology options – including cloud – in the context of business needs. At the same time, integrators are used to connect cloud systems with on-premise/legacy applications. And cloud brokers help microbusinesses to both identify a need for cloud-based solutions and to acquire these resources – meaning that they are fairly positioned as both "demand" and "transaction" partners.

- *Issues with market development funds.* It is typical for vendors and channel partners to collaborate on demand generation through vendor-supplied marketing funds, which can be allocated via programs classified as cooperative marketing (co-op), market development funds (MDF), business development funds (BDF), or similar headers. In most cases, the allocation of the funds is directly or obliquely tied to sales volumes, generally at about 1% of vendor revenues.

  This approach is problematic in the cloud. As one working group member said, a $100,000 product transaction delivers an immediate $1,000 co-op/MDF marketing credit. How does that same sale structured as a three-year XaaS contract - $3,000 per month for 36 months – work? Will the vendor credit $1,000 (actually, $1,080) to the channel partner's marketing account? Or will the credit be $30 per month for the next three years? Clearly, $30 won't pay for much marketing activity, but crediting the marketing funds in advance of the transaction is contrary to most channel SOPs. Vendor program terms will need to evolve if they are to keep pace with cloud channel demand generation.

  There is a second issue that should be considered in this context as well. Many co-op and MDF programs are targeted at transactional support – activities that build awareness of availability and/or pricing for products that are well understood by the target audience.  Because cloud is often at a relatively early stage of adoption, though, there is more need for education (both internally within the channel partner and externally to support marketing communications, especially for the SMB accounts that are typically managed by the channel) than is typical for hardware products like servers or PCs or printers. Internal users need resources like 'cheat sheets', information on how to sell cloud, and sales tools and guides, while external customers will need whitepapers and other materials that highlight cloud advantages. As is the case with vendor program terms, the list of activities included under the co-op/MDF banner may need to be modified to align with the unique requirements of cloud channel demand generation.

*Figure 9-4. Partners in a cloud GTM context*

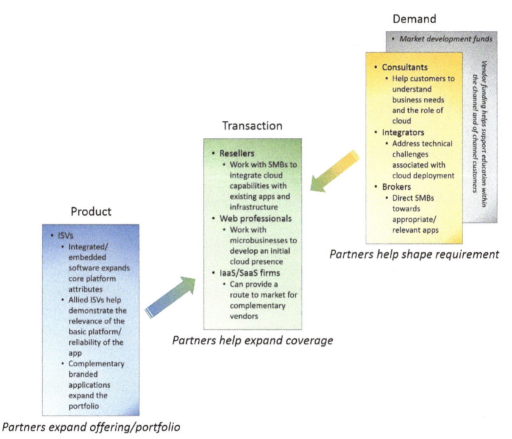

Source: TCBC/InsightaaS, 2016

## Sales issues

Executives building cloud sales initiatives face a combination of the sales challenges that accompany any complex technology solution and requirements that are unique to cloud. The working group identified three issues that a cloud sales executive needs to be aware of, including expectation management, the complexity of hybrid infrastructure, and disconnects between qualification processes for cloud and traditional product sales. The group also discussed different methods of structuring compensation models for cloud sales, which is an issue that all cloud sellers and resellers need to address.

### Expectation management

The term "cloud" is applied to many different types of offerings, which can be sourced and deployed in many different ways. The confusion that arises from this variety of offerings is viewed by the working group as a complicating factor in cloud sales: as one member noted, "the cloud experience has been painted for" customers, who want to adopt cloud as a platform for legacy applications – but "they can't get their heads around the challenges" of a 'brownfield' deployment requiring workload migrations. "They get frustrated" as large cloud vendors promote a vision of cloud promising ease of use that is mismatched with the real-world challenges associated with re-hosting legacy applications. Sales executives need to ensure that expectations are set correctly from the beginning of the customer interaction, since monthly recurring revenue is an important measurement of success, and churn associated with dissatisfaction has a negative impact on cloud business profitability.

### Hybrid complexity

Another issue – related to expectation management – is the complexity associated with managing dependencies within hybrid infrastructure. In this case, the expectations at issue start with corporate management insisting on use of cloud as a means of attaining new capabilities and/or reducing cost, but not grasping the difficulty of managing connections between on-premise and cloud-based systems. The IT department then needs to establish consistent user access and data integration across multiple production systems housed in multiple facilities and using multiple access/management technologies.  Here again, the sales executive needs to ensure that customers are entering into agreements with a solid grasp of the challenges ahead, or face the prospect that customers will withdraw from agreements when they realize how hard it is to connect production systems in a hybrid environment.

### Rigour in opportunity qualification

Qualifying opportunities isn't really a cloud sales issue – it is an issue that applies in all enterprise sales situations. However, the familiarity that experienced IT sales staff bring to qualification doesn't necessarily translate into success with complex cloud solutions.

For the most part, enterprise IT sales staff view the outcome of qualification as establishing whether there is budget available to fund an acquisition, what the timeframe is for the purchase, and the ability of the product(s) they represent to meet the customer's needs. In a cloud scenario, though, this logic changes in three important ways:

- The first issue in qualification is to understand if and how a hosted/cloud strategy fits within the customer's overall IT and business strategy – if the customer isn't ready to make a transition from current infrastructure to the cloud, there isn't a real opportunity to pursue. This is a change for sales reps experienced with traditional hardware or software products, as the business need and familiarity with the type of product that is being proposed is generally in place prior to the rep's engagement, meaning that there is less focus on high-level strategic issues.
- Similarly, the nature of cloud's consumption model means that the sales rep needs to evaluate both the near-term commitment and the longer-term opportunity to expand the presence of the cloud solution within the account. Again, this is a change from product sales scenarios, where the opportunity that is being qualified is generally defined by a single transaction.
- Lastly, the budget issue is different with cloud. Reps who are doing financial qualification for a product transaction opportunity are looking for dedicated capital budget; reps who are qualifying the financial aspect of a cloud opportunity need to be sure that the customer account is prepared to purchase capacity as an OPEX-based service rather than as a CAPEX-based product. The budget itself isn't as significant a hurdle as the experience and approach of the customer's purchasing and financial staff: are they able to acquire XaaS in place of physical products, using a process that is different from the procedures that they have used in the past?

## Compensation models

While each of the issues cited above is important to building a sales strategy, the most significant challenge faced by a cloud provider is creation of a compelling compensation model. Sales staff who have 'grown up' in traditional product environments are used to sales compensation structures in which they are measured and paid on the value of a discrete (and in the case of enterprise solutions, substantial) transaction. This model can't be applied directly to cloud sales, since there is no discrete transaction. The cloud customer generally signs a contract, but there is generally no single lump-sum payment: the customer pays a fee on an ongoing basis, potentially at different levels from month to month as consumption varies. The cloud provider doesn't have the benefit of all of the cash associated with the contract being paid up front, and therefore, will not typically be able to pay the sales representative for the full contract value – and even if the company *did* have an operating line that would cover such commissions, there is a risk of customer non-payment that most organizations would refuse to accept on behalf of the rep.

This discrepancy in the basis of payment for product transactions and cloud contracts has posed difficulties for firms attempting to add cloud to a product portfolio, or to migrate from traditional products to XaaS. Salespeople have a better understanding of how they are paid for traditional transactions, and generally, stand to make more money (certainly, more money in the near term) for a product sale vs. a cloud sale.

This change in mindset extends to sales management as well. In a product firm, reps and their territories are generally aligned against a quota, and sales managers look to retire some part of that quota with each transaction. This is not the typical mindset for cloud sales/territory management: instead, the emphasis is on building a book of business – a run rate that delivers sustainable cash flow to the rep. This is a common sales model in some industries (such as insurance), but requires sales managers steeped in enterprise product approaches to reconsider some of their core management assumptions.

How can a cloud company structure compensation in a way that motivates good sales reps, and is aligned with the realities of cloud business? Models that the working group has seen used, and the pros and cons associated with these approaches, include:

*Pay reps as a percentage of Gross Profit*

- Pros: well aligned with the underlying cloud business.
- Cons: It can be difficult to calculate GP for a service or customer; the cloud company may not want to expose its GP percentage to its reps.

*Pay reps as a percentage of total value – either for a fixed period of time (e.g., one year) or for the life of the contract*

- Pros: easy to calculate and explain; the typical approach of paying commissions on a trailing basis provides an incentive for the rep to stay active in the account.
- Cons: does not work well when contract values fluctuate; because payments tend to be on a trailing basis (e.g., paid on quarterly revenues at the end of each

quarter), there can be a long lag time between the act of the initial sale and the payment of the commission, which is viewed unfavourably by many reps; firms paying some or all of commissions on an accelerated (rather than trailing) basis need to have an effective claw back process to manage collections risk.

*Pay reps based on estimated consumption – at the beginning of a period (e.g., one quarter, one year), the rep provides an estimate of customer use of a service, and is paid what amounts to a draw based on that estimate; the cloud company 'trues up' payments with actual consumption at the end of each period*

- Pros: provides an opportunity for commission payment before the end of the measurement period; involves the rep in driving account usage/consumption on an ongoing basis; can be used in situations where actual consumption can vary within/across periods.
- Cons: can be complicated to measure and administrate; requires cloud company to pay commissions before all receivables are collected.

*Sell based on an assumed gross margin. This is really just a variation on volume-based payments. It is sometimes used in channel arrangements where the reseller is used to commanding a certain GP on managed services (e.g., 25%-35%) and requires each new service to fit into the overall corporate compensation structure.*

- Pros: allows cloud provider to work with managed service providers (MSPs), who have proven to be the channel best attuned to cloud offerings
- Cons: requires cloud provider to fit into a specific GP framework, which may or may not correspond meaningfully to actual costs and margins in the cloud business.

*Additional issues associated with cloud sales*

As part of the broader cloud sales discussion, the working group raised several points that don't fit neatly into the guidance offered above, but which reflect experience and understanding that can be helpful to the sales executive looking to build a framework that will pass internal and external review. Key points from this discussion include:

- *Professional services spending for migration associated with initial cloud adoption are more limited than has been thought.* This is important because many cloud providers who work with channels – and many channel members who add cloud services to their portfolios – expect that professional services associated with migration will help to provide margin that offsets, at least in part, the gap between the value of a cloud contract and the value of the product transaction it displaces. Limited professional services contracts have a negative impact on this calculation, and as a result, put additional pressure on the value and profitability of the cloud service itself.

- *When working with sales organizations that have both product and managed services portfolios, cloud should be positioned within the managed services portfolio.* Cloud may displace product opportunity, but it isn't a product – it is sold differently, and the compensation models are different, and often suffer by comparison with product transactions. Experience indicates that when a cloud firm's offerings are positioned as an alternative to a product sale, reps will default to promoting products rather than cloud. As long as overall margins are comparable, though, cloud services can be effectively positioned within a managed services portfolio. Cloud suppliers who are building channels are advised to look for partners with managed services practices and then to associate their cloud offerings with these services, and not with the products that are obviated by the cloud.

- *Be clear and firm on compensation policies.* There may be no perfect model for cloud compensation, but whatever model is adopted by the organization needs to be employed consistently. A policy that allows for exceptions will be too difficult to administer in the ever-changing world of cloud contracts. One suggestion from the group is to involve members of the sales team in putting together the compensation model, so that there is buy-in from across the organization.

- *Solutions that require extensive integration are difficult to sell.* This observation applies especially to the channel. There is an old maxim that holds, "products designed for direct sales are designed for elegance, products designed for channel sales are designed for relevance." The underlying notion is that a direct sales force might have the motivation and scope needed to work with a customer to establish a fit between a platform product and an organizational need, but the channel is more likely to succeed when it positions a well-structured product as an offering that meets a specific need within a well-defined target market. This dictum holds true for cloud services as well. It may be that you have a direct sales force that can work with customers and third parties to address a wide range of different requirements, and/or that you find a channel partner with inventive product managers who can align the attributes of your offering with a customer requirement...but these will be the exception rather than the rule, and sales managers should plan to scale by targeting well-articulated offerings at well-defined target accounts.

- *Roadmaps are essential – but they, too, need to be managed.* One of the primary goals of cloud intermediaries (integrators, brokers, VARs) is to establish a roadmap with a client, defining a migration path that leads to the book of business (and sustainable commission stream) discussed above. However, the working group cautions that reps should focus on successfully positioning and delivering one specific element of the roadmap at a time. Customers who experience success with a cloud offering often assume that 'with minor modifications', the cloud solution can extend to address other objectives (frequently, goals that were not specified in the initial project scope). This is a common approach in traditional software, but it isn't the way that cloud infrastructure is built: cloud is layered one service at a time, and modifications tend to be much more problematic/expensive in the cloud (where a provider will shy away from one-off modifications) than on premise. It's important to have reps establish a path and articulate the value of a specific service – for the firm to deliver the service – and for the rep to then move on to the next step in the path, without being drawn into difficult-to-deliver modifications that detract from cloud's real value as a defined, shared service.

- *Keep sales education and support materials lean.* It's a point that is so simple as to be self-evident, but a sales executive's task is to keep sales reps focused on selling. Suppliers who deliver extensive sales support materials are equipping the sales rep to deliver education to the customers, which is an important task in a still-evolving cloud market, but not one that the sales rep should be performing. Experience shows that reps who are given focused materials that define a specific offering (as per the 'relevance' point above), and who are provided leads resulting from marketing activities that uncover demand for that offering, experience high close rates and rapid time-to-close cycles; those who engage in education or configuration have much longer cycle times and much lower close rates. Reps who are positioning well-defined offerings that are aligned with other services already in use within the customer (as per the 'roadmap' observation) do better still, and can in the right circumstances achieve double-digit, first-call success rates. As noted above, this guidance isn't necessarily unique to cloud – but it is important to cloud sales success.

- *Stay focused on customer outcomes.* One working group member added this summary guidance to the list above: "The essence of a cloud-based business is about selling business outcomes, as opposed to the more traditional way of selling products + necessary installation / maintenance. This shift is what is driving the changes in role/relative importance that are mentioned: ecosystem/channel partners, online presence for full customer lifecycle including upsell and adaptation, sharpening value proposition and managing roadmap expectations."

## Reference sources

References commenting on best practices in cloud marketing, sales or channel development include:

- Examples of online qualification questionnaires. This questionnaire – a relatively simple set of questions used to qualify (primarily) smaller businesses for a single cloud service, drawn from the Unity website – and this "Hybrid IT Navigator," designed to address enterprise-level scenarios and drawn from the CenturyLink website, illustrates different approaches used to understand customer starting points and need for different types of cloud solutions.
- Todd Hewlin, J.B. Wood, Thomas Lah. Consumption Economics: The New Rules of Tech. TSIA, 2011. Considered the seminal book on cloud sales, Consumption Economics stresses models and approaches that identify the ways in which cloud providers should develop a go-to-market strategy.
- Alan Pelz-Sharpe, Owen Rogers and Matt Mullen. Zombie accounts and 'freemium' business models. 451 Research, via InsightaaS, 2015. This 451 Research report provides fascinating insight into the metrics associated with varying levels of success with the 'freemium' business model used by many cloud suppliers.

## Metrics and milestones

Given the vast variations in "cloud GTM" – including differences in product type (SaaS, PaaS, IaaS), target markets (even within our B2B focus, these range from one-person microbusinesses to the largest enterprise customers), target users (IT and line of business), price points, sales models, etc. – it's not possible to end this examination with a set of universal measurements that a cloud firm can use to assess its go to market activity. There are, however, some useful guidelines that may help inform strategy applied to a particular situation:

- Cycle length: Guidelines include:
    - When dealing with first-time microbusiness customers, the sales cycle can range from immediate (purchase as part of a visit to the website) to 3-4 weeks for offerings that require outbound sales support.
    - Cycles are clearly longer in midmarket businesses and smaller enterprise accounts (roughly, 100-1000 employees). One useful observation gathered from a working group member focused on midmarket and smaller enterprise customers is that accounts which have been in the sales cycle longer than 60 days should probably be returned to the nurture funnel until a new 'buy' signal is received.
    - Cycle times for enterprise accounts, including public sector, vary mostly with the complexity of the product. A 3-6 month cycle isn't unusual for opportunities involving a large enterprise, and RFP processes (such as those used in the public sector) can further extend cycle time, to 8 months or more.
- Close rates: In microbusinesses and even in midmarket accounts, cloud suppliers might expect a close rate of 10%-20%. Close rates for enterprises can be upwards of 20%, but as is shown throughout this document, the enterprise path from initial interest to final proposal can be long and demanding.
- IT suppliers focused on enterprise product sales tend to expect a 15:1-20:1 ratio of business closed per marketing dollar invested. Cloud firms are often investing at a similar rate, with 5%-6% of contract value allocated to the marketing activities described in this document.

As with IT product suppliers, cloud firms targeting solution sales to enterprise accounts are heavily invested in the creation and maintenance of nurturing funnels. There is no 'magic number' with respect to the proportion of firms in the nurture funnel who convert to sales leads, nor is there a specific timeframe over which these firms take to move from nurture to sales-ready. Working group members note that the key indicator of a firm's readiness to move from the nurture to the sales funnel isn't time, but rather, activities (such as downloading additional materials, using online tools or registering for a trial) that indicate that the firm is moving towards a purchase decision.

*Chapter 10.*

# Financing Cloud Businesses

Essential guidance for cloud service providers and intermediaries on financing their recurring-revenue operations through different growth stages

*Contributing community experts: Derek van der Plaat (Veracap), AJ Byers (JEDTech Group), Brandon Kolybaba (Cloud A), Oscar Jofre (KoreConX)*

*Initial publication date: February 2016*

# Financing Cloud Businesses

## Definition and context

The term "cloud" is applied to a wide variety of businesses. It is used to describe both capital-intensive businesses that supply on-demand infrastructure (IaaS or PaaS), and firms that supply cloud-based applications (SaaS), and it describes companies that are barely more than an idea, those that are launched and growing, and businesses (such as Salesforce or Amazon) that have revenues measured in billions.

From a financing perspective, there are some differences between IaaS/PaaS and SaaS providers, and many more differences between firms at different points in the growth cycle. In particular, there are many financing options available for firms that have $2 million per year in revenue and are cash flow positive; firms that are at earlier stages, with low cash flow and which are not yet past the break-even point, have far fewer alternatives for raising needed capital. The Financing Cloud Businesses working group is focused on defining capital availability issues and trends for firms at these different stages, with particular sensitivity to early-stage firms and their requirements.

## Early stage companies

The label "early stage" can be applied to start-ups that have not yet begun to build a customer base, and to those that have entered high-growth mode but have limited annual revenues – less than $1 million – and haven't (typically) achieved profitability. These firms often rely on personal contacts (friends and family) and angel investors; some may have access to specialized VCs, while others may be able to raise funds via crowdfunding, incubators, or accelerators as well. As Figure 10-1 illustrates, there are differences in the basis of valuation between start-ups and high-growth, yet-to-be-profitable early stage firms: the former are valued primarily on the strength of the underlying concept, or the strength of the relationship between the founders and potential funders, while the latter tend to be valued as a multiple of revenue, which could range anywhere from 1x-10x, depending on business model (somewhat higher multiples for SaaS vs. IaaS), growth rate and market potential. It's worth noting that supplier financing is often available to IaaS companies, and that this can help bridge the gap between investment in capacity and return from IaaS customers; supplier financing can be an important source of liquidity for early-stage IaaS companies.

## High growth/profitable firms

Companies that have achieved EBITDA of more than $1.5 million per year, which are profitable and which have sustained high growth rates are in a more enviable position than smaller firms that are growing rapidly but which haven't achieved profitability. These high growth/profitable firms have access to VC funding, mezzanine lenders and banks. Valuation may be based on a multiple of revenue or on EBITDA. EBITDA-based valuations have been increasing sharply; recently, public markets have assigned a multiple of over 14x EBITDA, up from 6x in 2009.

## Low/no growth, profitable firms

Companies with slow or flat growth and profitability based on recurring revenue from an established customer base may not be common in the cloud environment, but it is a normal stage in overall corporate maturation. Established firms can often tap into low-cost debt options, including bank debt and revenue financing. The valuations used to support financing are based on a multiple of EBITDA.

Figure 10-1 illustrates the options available to firms through these different stages.

Figure 10-1. Business lifecycle and financing options

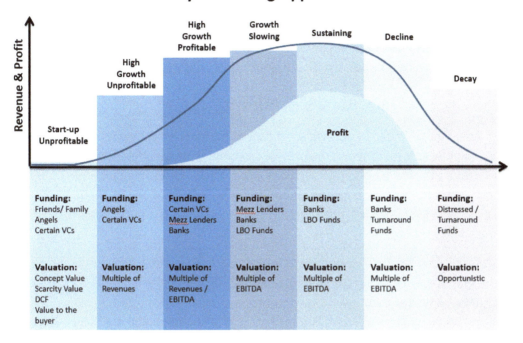

**Lifecycle Funding Opportunities**

*Source: Veracap M&A International Inc.*

## Reference sources

Additional references that readers can use to better understand the key issues defining cloud financing issues and options include:

- SaaS Capital resources and links. A collection of whitepapers and research briefs covering issues like the effect of churn, pre-payment discounting and growth on valuations available from the SaaS Capital website.
- Bessemer Venture Partners research. A collection of cloud research reports assembled by Bessemer, which has been investing in cloud companies since 1997.

- <u>Espresso Capital Recurring Revenue Financing.</u> A guide to recurring revenue financing posted by Espresso Capital. Includes an introductory video, guide to metrics and FAQ section.

## Business objectives

At a high level, it is easy to describe the business objectives that drive a requirement for funding. Typically, cloud businesses seek financing so that they can expand their operations (they may also seek cash injections to crystallize value for founders, but financers are often loath to take on future risk in this scenario).

At a more granular level, the connection between business objectives and financing is more complex. As is indicated in the previous section, firms at different stages of growth have different financing options available to them. Each of these funding sources in turn has its own set of requirements and objectives. Firms looking to secure financing need to align with funders' metrics and appreciate the scope business implications of different financing options.

A review of these options and requirements yields some interesting overall market factors that shape current and emerging options. The working group finds that "it is clear that new financing companies and products are providing more options to fund both traditional receivables as well as SaaS revenue companies, and are filling a void for yield-hungry institutional investors. For the time being, $1.5 million in EBITDA remains a threshold where, above this number, the availability of equity-type financing options improves substantially. The cost of these financing options remains high (typically more than 500 basis points above secured bank loans), however, as an alternative to equity investment, these solutions can create tremendous value for shareholders of companies that need capital to fund growth."

## Key business issues

Different investors will look at different issues within a cloud business, but there are a few constants that will be important in most situations. Companies that are able to demonstrate success in these areas are better positioned to attract the support of investors.

One key issue is growth. Firms that can demonstrate consistent period-over-period increases will attract more attention and higher multiples that those that can't. Generally speaking, firms that demonstrate growth rates above 20% are very interesting to potential funders. Those that post growth rates in the mid-20s are viewed as having positive but not exciting growth. Firms with growth rates below 20% a year are not especially interesting to funders.

Another important factor in investor evaluations is the total scope of opportunity for your offering. What is the total addressable market (TAM) that your business can capture? A market that will become saturated quickly is much less interesting than one that can sustain growth over a long period of time. In this regard, scope matters. Practically speaking, SaaS firms can address a global market. Firms offering hosting services or IaaS, on the other hand, may be more geographically limited in their appeal. This isn't entirely negative, since (as the next paragraph discusses) an IaaS firm may appeal to a niche market where it has an advantage over larger firms with greater economies of scale – but companies looking for funding need to carefully consider the balance between the shelter of a niche and the potential of a larger TAM.

As implied above, the nature of the addressable market is a third issue that can be impactful for potential investors. Some markets – especially, B2C markets – may offer vast potential but few 'sheltered harbours' where a firm can build a unique presence and value proposition. Niches within B2B markets might have less potential upside but provide an environment in which competition is limited and where longer-term relationships can be built without (excessive) fear of finding that an offering will be 'swapped out' for an alternative product, or simply ignored. SaaS firms focused within a niche have a second issue to consider: is their offering a platform or a feature? An offering that is seen by customers as a platform that supports multiple functions offers a sound basis for ongoing business, while a product that more closely resembles a feature can be obviated if the supplier of a central system introduces a competing product that is less expensive and/or better integrated within the platform.

There are of course other factors that affect investor interest and confidence, including profitability, the proportion of revenue derived from major customers, and recurring vs. project-based revenue. Taken together, these issues create a portrait of the business issues that affect interest and valuations. A company seeking investment needs to track these issues as key corporate (and management) objectives, in order to present a compelling case to prospective funders.

*Specific offerings tie to specific timeframes*

Another issue that is important in the context of business objectives is the timeframe associated with the investment. Does the cloud business require short-term capital to address immediate requirements and opportunities, or is it seeking longer-term financing to support a strategic expansion plan? Examples of options that may be available to cloud businesses seeking capital include:

*Short term working capital solutions*

Secured lending options, such as receivables financing, has long been a stronghold of the banks, but new entrants are encroaching on this territory by providing liquidity solutions that address a changing business model or by changing the way they go about the process. For example:

- Espresso Capital provides financing for a wide range of tax credits including SR&ED, various provincial digital media tax credits, OIDMTC, and Quebec`s Tax Credit for Development of E-Business.
- FundThrough is an online solution that touts it can approve a loan in 24 hours and fund within 48. FundThrough does not look at historical profitability or personal guarantees but strictly funds high-quality receivables.
- Canadian firms can also look beyond Canada to international options for liquidity or even growth funding. Online capital marketplaces are making it easier to tap into funders in the US and abroad.

*Longer term growth funding options*

In addition to traditional bank secured term loans – which might or might not meet the requirements of a growing cloud company – there are new revenue, mezzanine and royalty financing options available to cloud businesses:

- For recurring revenue SaaS businesses, Espresso Capital offers SaaS revenue loans of up to 6 times monthly recurring revenue (minimum $100,000 per month).
- Fraser MacKenzie Merchant Capital (FMMC) provides mezzanine loans from $2M to $10M for companies generating a minimum historical EBITDA of $1.5 million.
- Grenville Strategic Royalty Corp. starts at funding amounts of $1 million and Portola Royalty Corp. starts at $10 million. Royalties are calculated as

percentage of revenues so there are no covenants, no term, and payment varies with revenues.

Figure 10-2 presents a matrix of funding options for cloud businesses at different maturity stages.

*Figure 10-2. Overview of cloud funding sources (early stage to established businesses)*

| Funder | Examples | Type | Stage | Amount & Terms | Notes |
|---|---|---|---|---|---|
| Bootstrap, family, friends | n/a | Equity or loans | Seed, start-up | Typically $10K to $50K per individual | |
| Gov't investment, grants | MaRS, SR&ED, FedDev Ontario | Equity investment, grants, zero interest loans | Any | Up to $500K | More than 200 programs available to incent capital investment, support hiring and training, and research and development. MaRS Investment Accelerator Fund (IAF) invests up to $500,000 in early-stage companies. |
| Crowdfunding | Kickstarter, Indiegogo | Pre-sales, donations | Typically Seed, Start-up | Up to $10M | Has not been a vehicle for equity investment but rather a way to raise capital through pre-sales or other incentives. Ontario is proposing to cap equity investment at $2,500 per person per annum. |
| Angels, accredited investors | Maple Leaf Angels, Anges Quebec, Georgian Angel Network, Angel One | Equity, structured to provide priority in liquidation and tax efficiency | Seed, Start-up, Early-Stage | Typically $25K-$100K per person; up to $1M for a group. | Organized Angel groups have proliferated over the last 5 years. High net-worth investors are often looking for yield in the instrument. |
| Incubators/Accelerators | Highline, Execution Labs, INcubes, Bolidea, Founder Fuel, Ryerson DMZ | Equity, structured to provide priority in liquidation and tax efficiency | Seed, Start-up, Early-Stage | Typically $50K-$250K | Institutionalized Angel-type investment plus strategic advisory and relationships |
| Early VC | iNovia Capital, Real Ventures, Rho Ventures, Greensky Capital, Brightspark, Yaletown Venture Partners | Equity, structured to provide priority in liquidation and tax efficiency | Series A | Typically up to $5M | Series A means first institutional round. In Canada, that typically means generating revenue - not necessarily profitable but visibility to profits. |
| Growth VC | Klass Capital, OMERS Ventures, Georgian Partners, Kensington Capital | Equity | Series B and C | No limits | Institutional growth funding round. |
| Revenue financing | Espesso Capital, SaaS Capital | High-yield loans | Minimum monthly recurring revenue of $100,000 | Typically up to $5M | Specifically designed for SaaS and other sticky, high margin, subscription revenue companies. Structured as a credit facility, allowing borrowing of up to 6 times monthly recurring revenue. |
| Royalty financing | Grenville Strategic Royalty, Portola Royalty Corp., Alaris Royalty Corp. | Share of revenue or gross margin or TBD cashflow | Revenue generating but can be break-even | From $1M / target ROI in the mid-teens | Royalties are calculated as a percentage of revenues. There are no covenants, no term, and payment varies with revenues. |
| Mezzanine/Sub debt | BDC Capital, FMMC, Fulcrum Capital | Unsecured/under-secured high yield loans | Established, cashflow positive businesses; minimum historical EBITDA of $1.5M | Target ROI in the mid-teens | Fraser MacKenzie Merchant Capital (FMMC) provides mezzanine loans from $2M to $10M for companies with a minimum historical EBITDA of $1.5M |
| Venture debt | BEST Funds, Wellington Financial | Unsecured/under-secured high yield loans | Venture-funded companies | From $1M; target ROI in the mid-teens | |
| Specialized banks | RBC Knowledge Based Business Group, BDC, Silicon Valley Bank | Secured lender | Not early. Will look to cashflow if there is no security. | Secured operating lines. Cashflow loans up to 3-4 times EBITDA. | |
| Traditional banks | RBC, TD, CIBC, BMO, etc. | Secured lender | Need receivables or other tangible assets for security. | Secured operating lines. Cashflow loans up to 3 times EBITDA. | |

*Source: Veracap M&A International Inc.*

## Reference sources

Additional references that readers can use to better understand the business issues around cloud financing issues include:

- Victor Basta. "The rise (and coming fall) of $1B+ 'Icarus' businesses." Magister Advisors. This post looks at the difference between 'platform' and 'feature' companies and the long-term viability of the latter group.
- Evaluating Financing Options for SaaS Companies. SaaS Capital (no-cost registration required). A straightforward explanation of some common SaaS financing options and their real-world costs.
- Companies looking for examples of non-Canadian funding sources may wish to visit the websites of ValueStream (based in New York, focused on FinTech) or Arrowroot Group (based in California, focused on early stage SaaS/web companies) for examples of how these kinds of firms operate.

## Best practices in financing cloud businesses

The matrix presented in Figure 10-2 provides a clear, single-image illustration of the financing options that cloud businesses can and should explore as they progress through their growth cycle. The matrix in turn suggests some of the key issues that cloud businesses need to focus on as they pursue new capital. Cloud company founders and senior executives should be familiar with these options and the associated requirements as they look to obtain the capital needed to support start-up, growth and expansion.

## Options for early stage firms

### *Bootstrap, family and friends*

It's very likely that every entrepreneur has used a combination of "bootstrapping" (the entrepreneur's own money or personal loans) and investment from family and friends to provide initial liquidity for a new business. Depending on the personal situation of the founder, these types of investments can range up to $10,000, or as high as $50,000, per individual investor.

- Sources: Friends and family generally invest small amounts, and generally receive convertible notes that call for payback of the investment over time, but which give the investor the opportunity to convert the investment into shares in the company instead, providing the investor with a chance to participate in the success of the new company.

- Advice: Friends and family and principal investments are not just important to early-stage liquidity. Canadian VCs also look at these investments as a means of seeing whether the founder has 'skin in the game', and whether he/she is able to persuade others to back the company and its management.

### Government investment and grants

Canadian cloud businesses can pursue more than 200 different programs that are designed to support hiring and training and/or R&D, or to stimulate capital investment.

- Structure: Can take the form of equity investments, grants or zero-interest loans.
- Magnitude: Varies from small amounts to as high as $500,000 (MaRS Investment Accelerator Fund).
- Sources: Examples include MaRS, SR&ED, FedDev Ontario
- Advice: Many start-ups use accountants or other advisors to tap into SR&ED and other funding sources. These firms generally take 20%-25% of the grant as a success fee, making this a relatively high-cost method of raising funds (the practice is also sometimes thought to be viewed unfavourably within the government). However, it's worth noting that consultants can tap into less-well-known sources – and with changes pending to SR&ED and other funding sources (such as IRAP), consultants may be needed by many cloud businesses to help navigate the changing opportunities and requirements.

### Crowdfunding

Crowdfunding is in the midst of a transition. In its early form, it was not a source of equity investment; instead, "investors" tended to pre-buy new products, an approach that works better for entrepreneurs focused on discrete consumer goods than for providers of XaaS, especially B2B-focused XaaS services. However, the regulatory environment is changing, and businesses (especially, start-ups) will soon be able to tap into funds supplied by small, non-accredited investors.

- Structure: Has traditionally taken the form of product pre-orders, payments in exchange for prizes or straightforward donations, but is morphing into a source of equity investment, and is also expanding to include crowdfunded lending.
- Magnitude: While most crowdfunding campaigns target less than $100,000, equity crowdfunding can scale into the millions of dollars. Spacefy (Toronto)

raised $400,000, and Rentmoola (Vancouver) is thought to have raised $6.5 million via equity crowdfunding.

- Sources: Kickstarter and Indiegogo are two well-known crowdfunding platforms/communities, but these reward-based platforms are better suited to product firms (especially, with a consumer focus) than cloud businesses. Cloud businesses will want to dig into the rapidly evolving world of equity crowdfunding. The eBook "Equity Crowdfunding 101: The global guide to a financial revolution" (by TCBC member Oscar A. Jofre Jr.) has an extensive list of equity crowdfunding portals. Canadian portals focused on technology and/or SMEs include FrontFundr and SeedUps.

- Advice: The 'big two' equity crowdfunding options in Canada are the Accredited Investor exemption, which applies to high net worth individuals and families (1.4 million Canadians) and the Offering Memorandum exemption, which opens potential investments to a much wider community of individuals and families (20 million Canadians). These exemptions are provincially based and cannot be used nation-wide; they also have limits for the company and investor. Depending on location within Canada, other options may also be available: the Start-Up Crowdfunding exemption, which is currently in force in six provinces, provides early-stage companies with an additional means of raising limited amounts of capital, while the "45-108 integrated crowdfunding exemption," which allows for higher individual investments than does the start-up crowdfunding exemption, may also be an option for some early-stage cloud firms. Each of these options has a different set of eligibility requirements and funding provisions, and there are differences in regulations and availability across provinces.

### Angels, accredited investors

Accredited investors – basically, individuals or married couples with financial assets of more than $1 million, or those with more than $5 million in total assets, or those with sustained income in excess of $200,000-$300,000 per year, though there are other qualifying criteria as well – and angel investors, individuals or consortia who invest in start-up or early-stage companies – play a critical role in bridging the gap between friends and family/bootstrap funding and institutional funding. The two sources aren't identical – angels are generally looking for equity, while high net-worth investors may look instead for yield (assuming they believe that the firm can carry the payments) – but both provide funding to seed, start-up or early stage firms.

- Structure: As per Figure 10-2, "Equity, structured to provide priority in liquidation and tax efficiency." In practice, this means that angels and accredited investors will invest in preferred shares or convertible debentures (which convert into preferred shares) that have the highest priority in the event of liquidation, and which offer tax-deductible payback
- Magnitude: Typically $25,000-$100,000 per individual investor; consortium investments can reach up to $1 million.
- Sources: Maple Leaf Angels, Anges Quebec, Georgian Angel Network, Angel One Investor Network, Toronto Angel Investors. Wesley Clover, which describes itself as a "serial super-angel," is a different type of investor, active in different ways at different stages of growth.
- Advice: It isn't always easy for early-stage firms to identify investors willing to invest in their ideas – but then, there are challenges at each stage of business growth. Angels play a key role in bridging the gap between friends and family and early VCs.

### *Incubators/accelerators*
Like angels and accredited investors, incubators and accelerators are focused on start-ups and early stage companies. In addition to providing funding, though, incubators and accelerators help cloud founders to commercialize their offerings by providing strategic advisory services and by facilitating relationships with prospective partners and customers.

- Structure: Like angels and accredited investors, incubators and accelerators look for equity that is structured to provide priority in liquidation and tax efficiency.
- Magnitude: Investments typically are in the $50,000-$250,000 range.
- Sources: Highline, Execution Labs, INcubes, Bolidea, Founder Fuel, Ryerson DMZ
- Advice: Although incubators and accelerators are listed as part of the progression from idea to funded company, they aren't for everyone. Incubators/accelerators appeal to a particular type of company founder. They generally don't put a lot of money into companies, focusing instead on the development and use of a support ecosystem. Two additional observations bear notice here: one is that incubators/accelerators tend to prefer SaaS over IaaS

businesses, and the other is that involvement with these organizations tends to positively impact the perceptions of VCs when cloud businesses look for the next level of financing.

## Options for established cloud businesses

### *Revenue financing/royalty financing*

Revenue and royalty financing are two approaches that established cloud businesses can use to raise capital without selling equity or taking on debt with fixed repayment terms.

### Revenue financing

Revenue financing has developed around the specific requirements of SaaS firms which have 'sticky' recurring-revenue relationships with customers and which operate at high margins. Revenue financing is structured as a credit facility. It allows cloud businesses to borrow up to six times monthly recurring revenue.

- Structure: Revenue financing is a form of high-yield loan
- Magnitude: Revenue financing deals can involve as much as $5 million in credit.
- Sources: Espresso Capital, SaaS Capital
- Advice: See Royalty Financing, below.

### Royalty financing

Like revenue financing, royalty financing provides an alternative to equity-based investments. Royalties are calculated as a percentage of revenue (or margin or cash flow), meaning that payment varies with the success of the business. Royalty financing differs from other debt arrangements in that there is typically no fixed term for repayment, no firmly-defined interest rate (though overall rates are higher than bank rates), and no security against the loan.

- Structure: Royalty financing is a form of high-yield loan, with returns targeted at the mid-teens but with the potential to move higher if revenue is slow to materialize.
- Magnitude: Royalty financing loans can be up to (or more than) $1 million, and are generally for more than $250,000.
- Sources: Grenville Strategic Royalty, Portola Royalty Corp., Alaris Royalty Corp.

Advice re: revenue/royalty financing:

- Providers tend to be flexible in terms of participation via revenue or gross margin. Ultimately, the funding providers are looking to tie their income streams to something on the cloud company's income statement that is open to ups and downs, such as revenue or gross margin, with payments tied to a percentage of revenue or gross margin. This kind of funding arrangement is an ongoing revenue participation – it can be bought out, but ultimately, what the funding providers are looking for is an income stream based on forecasts that gets them a mid-teens ROI. In many cases, providers are public companies, funded by pension funders where the cost of capital is low and the spread (between capital cost and revenue financing) returns is relatively rich.
- This is not start-up financing. Espresso Capital requires revenues of $100,000 per month; Grenville's policies call for a minimum of five years' revenue history and $5 million in annual revenue. Firms like Grenville may deviate from these stated policies, but they are unlikely to deal with firms with less than $2 million in annual revenue.

## *Early VC*

Once a cloud business has built scale and a track record of growth, it can begin to consider working with venture capital firms. Figure 10-2 identifies two types of VCs, *early* and *growth*. Early VCs provide initial institutional investment – Series A – to cloud businesses that are (for the most part) generating revenues and which are either profitable or are on a clear track to profitability. As a general rule of thumb, these firms will look for companies with visibility to positive cash flow within 9-15 months, and will assume that the cloud business will look to raise another round within that period. Early VCs will also look for firms with at least some semblance of critical mass, but the overall revenue level varies with target market.

- Structure: Like incubators and accelerators, early VCs look for equity that is structured to provide priority in liquidation and tax efficiency.
- Magnitude: Series A investments typically range up to $5 million.
- Sources: iNovia Capital, Real Ventures, Rho Ventures, Greensky Capital, Brightspark, Yaletown Venture Partners
- Advice: Engaging with early VCs may require Canadian cloud businesses to do an international search for funding partners, as there is limited early stage capital

available in Canada. It's worth noting that VCs in different countries use different metrics to evaluate the investment-worthiness of a potential portfolio company. In general, though, growth metrics matter. Growth needs to be 'substantial' – certainly, in excess of 25% – in order to attract the notice of early VCs.

### Growth VC

After a business has raised and used its first round of institutional funding, and has built a demonstrably viable business, it can go to growth VCs for capital to fund further expansion. Growth VCs provide Series B and Series C financing – additional funding rounds that may be used for acquisitions or to support other growth strategies.

- Structure: Growth VCs invest in exchange for equity. These firms generally look for minority investments, not control.
- Magnitude: Series B and Series C rounds have no real limit. Desire2Learn ($80 million from New Enterprise Associates and OMERS Ventures in 2012), Shopify ($100 million in Series C funding from OMERS Ventures and Insight Venture Partners in 2013), HootSuite ($165 million in Series B funding from Insight Venture Partners, Accel Partners and OMERS Ventures in 2013) and FreshBooks ($30 million from Oak Investment Partners and Atlas Venture in 2014) are examples of Canadian SaaS firms that have received growth VC funding; there are no similarly prominent examples of Canadian IaaS firms receiving investments from growth VCs.
- Sources: Growth VCs based in Canada include Klass Capital, OMERS Ventures, Georgian Partners, Kensington Capital
- Advice: It's important to note that this group is very interested in scale – which in Canada, has translated into more interest in software than infrastructure.

### Mezzanine / sub-debt

Mezzanine financing, or "sub" (subordinated) debt, is a hybrid of debt and equity financing. Mezzanine financing generally has high interest rates, and while the mezzanine lender doesn't have the security or priority of a senior lender (such as a traditional bank), it does have the ability to convert money owed to it into equity in the cloud firm, and may have other types of equity attached to the deal as well. Mezzanine financing companies target cloud businesses that are established in their markets and cash flow positive.

- Structure: Mezzanine financing is a form of high-yield loan that builds in an option for the financing firm to obtain equity in the cloud business.
- Magnitude: Mezzanine financing deals can be up to $10 million.
- Sources: BDC Capital, Fraser MacKenzie Merchant Capital (FMMC), Fulcrum Capital
- Advice: These firms focus on repayment ability. Since mezzanine financing isn't secured, funding providers look for profitability – often, a minimum EBITDA of $1.5-$2 million.

## *Venture debt*

Similar to mezzanine financing, venture debt provides an alternative to equity financing by combining (relatively high interest) repayment terms with warrants that allow the financing firm to assume a limited equity position in the cloud company. It is generally used by venture-backed companies (with a minimum historical EBITDA of $1.5 million) in situations where they require capital to extend their runway, but where assets and/or cash flow don't allow for access to lower-cost financing from traditional banks.

- Structure: Venture debt is a form of high-yield loan in which the financing firm obtains both high interest rates and a small amount of equity.
- Magnitude: Venture debt deals typically involve sums greater than $1 million.
- Sources: BEST Funds, Wellington Financial
- Advice: Venture participation is very important to mezzanine debt providers – in fact, venture funding is a requirement for venture debt providers like Wellington.

## *Specialized banks*

"Specialized banks" can be somewhat of a misnomer – the phrase is applied to both specialists and to focused divisions of traditional banks that work with cloud (and other IT) companies. These firms typically provide financing to companies in their target markets at better rates than are available via revenue financing, royalty financing, mezzanine financing or venture debt. However, specialized banks are secured lenders, and require priority over other creditors.

- Structure: Specialized banks provide secured operating lines.
- Magnitude: Specialized banks will provide secured lines of up to 3-4 times EBITDA.

- Sources: RBC Knowledge Based Business Group, BDC, Silicon Valley Bank
- Advice: These firms provide cash management facilities. Firms using specialized banks need cash flow in order to take advantage of these services. Specialized firms like BDC and Silicon Valley Bank may be more open to providing funding to young companies.

## Traditional banks

Traditional banks are the primary source of loans to Canadian businesses and consumers. Relative to other sources, these firms provide financing at low rates. However, they require security against receivables or other tangible assets, and priority as a creditor.

- Structure: Traditional banks provide secured operating lines.
- Magnitude: Traditional banks will provide secured lines of up to 3 times EBITDA.
- Sources: RBC, TD, CIBC, BMO, etc.
- Advice: These firms provide operating lines. They can advance funds against receivables, limited to 60%-70% of qualified receivables (less than 90 days, creditworthy customers). Firms under $500,000 per year probably will not require personal guarantees.

## Figure 10-3. The Canadian cloud business financing landscape

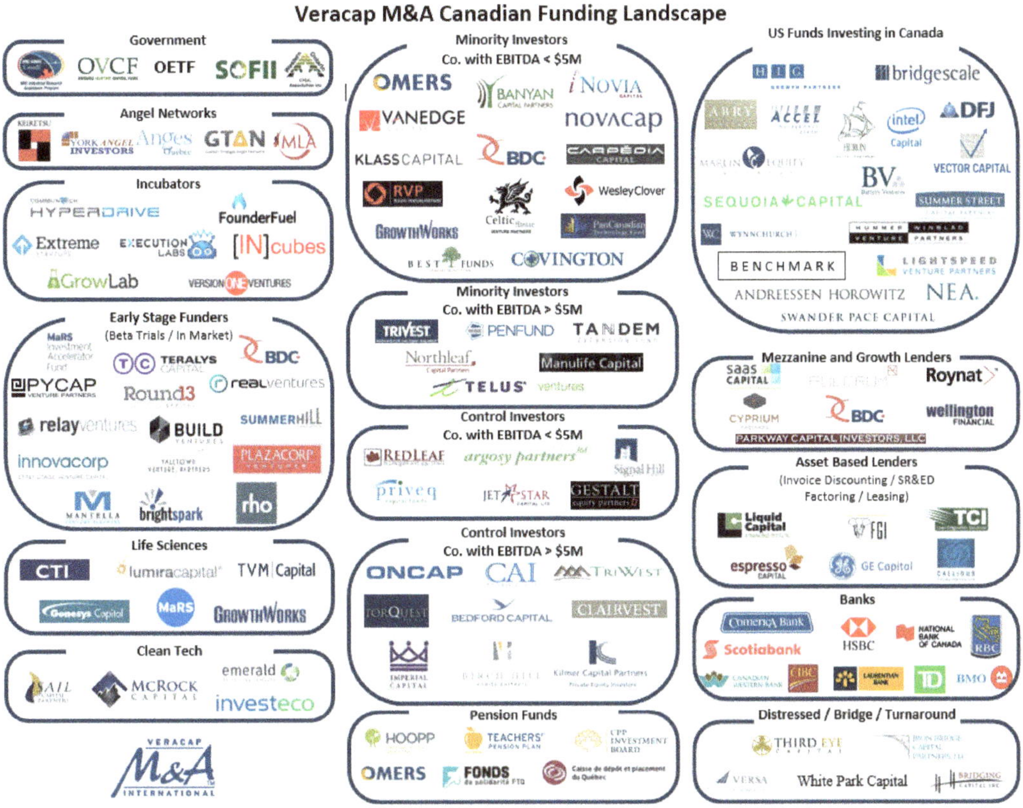

*Source: Veracap M&A International Inc.*

## Additional guidance

The first step in approaching the different types of investors on this list is to create a clear and compelling pitch deck that helps the investor to decide whether they have interest in evaluating your firm. Many cloud entrepreneurs struggle to build a pitch deck that will be persuasive to a potential investor. Key elements that should be presented clearly in a pitch deck include:

- Problem definition: The total addressable market for your cloud service and the customers' urgency around adoption are defined by the problem that your solution will address. Positioning statements rooted in problem definition are more compelling than those based on abstract market size estimates sourced from consulting reports.

- Solution definition/value proposition: A clear description of how your service addresses the target problem represents the core of your value proposition. This should be a business-level rather than technical explanation.
- Business model: Investors need to understand how you will generate revenue and profit, so that they can understand how they might benefit from investing in your business. This discussion needs to include a clear description of who will pay you, how they will pay, the types of third party organizations (if any) you will work with in market development and sales, and your margin expectations. Wherever possible, reference established firms that are currently making money with your business approach, and/or current customers and channel/market development partners.
- "Underlying magic": Guy Kawasaki recommends insertion of a slide describing the technology or "secret sauce" behind your product, adding that it is best to provide examples (diagrams, references to whitepapers and other objective proof sources) than text.
- Marketing and sales: What is your go-to-market strategy, and is it affordable in the context of your business and growth expectations? Are there other firms that have followed your approach, and if so, can you glean any guidance with respect to costs and results from their experience?
- Competition: who else is addressing the customer issues that you're targeting, and how and why do you stand out in this crowd? With respect to the question of who to include, Kawasaki adds "too much is better than too little."
- Management team: who is involved in your management team and advisory board? What investors have already committed to your business? List your strengths, and be candid about holes that you need to fill as you move forward.
- Financial projections and key metrics: This should include current revenue streams, growth rates and your TAM estimate. Guidance on key metrics and hurdle rates are included above, and should be reviewed at this stage. As was noted in another TCBC working group, what is included in the math is at least as important as the math itself – the credibility of the figures will rest on the underlying assumptions.

- Current status, accomplishments, timelines, use of funds: where is your business going, and how is a capital injection important to this trajectory? Kawasaki urges executives to "use this slide to close with a bias toward action."

## The elevator pitch

There are many guides to elevator pitches available on the web. One structure, which was promoted by software business development expert Jonathan Tice in classes that he taught in Toronto-area colleges, works like this:

- [Company name] provides [concise description of product/service]
- We help [target customers] to [business problem addressed by your product or service]
- Unlike [competitors with established market positions], [company name] [unique attribute of your product or service – the one that differentiates your company]
- [Target customers] rely on [company name] to [address the business issue that is the focus of your product or service] with/by [concise encapsulation of how/why your product addresses the customer business issue].

## Reference sources

Additional references that readers can use to better understand the business issues around cloud financing issues include:

- Chance Barnett. "The ultimate pitch deck to raise money for startups." Forbes, 2014. An article that reflects insights culled from review of thousands of early-stage company pitches, and which includes a linked investor pitch template.
- Brian Feinstein, Craig Netterfield, and Allen Miller. Ten Questions Every Founder Should Ask before Raising Venture Debt. Bessemer Venture Partners. This clear guide explains the 'whys', 'whens' and 'whats' of venture debt, and provides a description of the venture debt fundraising process.
- Financial Reports. Grenville Strategic Royalty Corp. These document offer interesting insight into royalty financing.
- Guy Kawasaki. "How to create a pitch deck for investors." MaRS, 2014. Guy Kawasaki's pitch deck template includes a slide-by-slide explanation of what's important in a pitch deck, and why.

- Investor pitch deck template. Crowdfunder. A template that can be modified for use by an early-stage firm, linked from the Forbes article.
- Oscar Jofre Jr. Equity Crowdfunding 101: The global guide to a financial revolution. KoreConX, 2015. This ebook, written by Financing Cloud Businesses working group member Oscar Jofre, provides insight into key equity crowdfunding issues: basics and process, as well as references that can help cloud businesses to find the resources needed to navigate crowdfunding investment.
- Oscar Jofre Jr. Equity Crowdfunding 101: Pre-Raise Handout. KoreConX, 2015. This document provides a consolidated view of the issues that cloud businesses need to address as part of the equity crowdfunding process. It covers pre-screening considerations, highlights key requirements for corporate information, financial information, and marketing/related information, presents a checklist for campaign content, preparation and marketing, and closes with the "golden rule" of securing commitments for 30% of your raise in advance of launching the campaign to the crowd.

Pitchenvy. A site dedicated to "showcasing only the best startup pitch decks."

- The Best Startup Pitch Decks. This website includes pitch decks from Airbnb, Facebook and Foursquare. Includes a random piano rendition of "video killed the radio star" as an accompaniment.
- Venture Debt Overview, Leader Ventures – PowerPoint-format deliverable provides an explanation of venture debt, including detailed examples of costs and uses and comparisons to other financing options.

## Metrics and milestones

While it is tempting to conclude this document with a set of metrics that cloud business owners and entrepreneurs could use to build a structured template to financing benchmarks and options, the reality is that this type of guidance can't be provided on an abstract basis. Each individual cloud business has its own mix of addressable market, business momentum and financing needs, and each individual funder has its own priorities and evaluation criteria.

There are clearly different funding options available to different types of firms: as this document shows, companies with revenues below $1 million per year, companies that have robust cash flow, companies that are profitable and companies that are stable with revenues in excess of $5 million have different options. Firms with revenues below $1 million attempt to justify investment on the basis of the expectation of market opportunity. Firms that are somewhat larger than that, and which are gaining traction, base their appeals on growth potential. Still-larger firms that can demonstrate profitability are looking for funds to support expansion or diversification.

The core metric indicating whether/when a firm is ready for investment is traction. In early stage firms, this might be gauged in terms of customer acceptance (e.g., downloads), but is most often measured in sales: Does your company have sales? What is the state of your funnel? What is your outlook for the next 12-24 months, and is this forecast believable? Valuations at an early stage are often based on multiples of revenues. This can be 3-4x for firms that have evident ability to scale (e.g., SaaS), and 1-2x for firms that will increase costs with volumes (e.g., firms offering cloud-related services, and IaaS to some extent).

Once companies have become established, EBITDA is the key factor in determining whether a firm is ready for a next stage of funding. It's worth noting that even if a firm has received one level of funding, there is no guarantee that they will get past the next hurdle; for example, only 10%-25% of firms that obtained angel funding succeed in getting Series A funding.

A possible progression for a young cloud company might follow a path along these lines:

- Young company with bright prospects attracts angel investment. The angels acquire 10%-20% of the company for $200,000 or so, valuing the company at about $2 million.
- First institutional financing involves a progression of value, and as a result, isn't a dilution for the angels. The VC might invest $1 million, with a valuation tied to growth: growth of 100% might attract a valuation of 5-10x revenue, growth of 15%-40% might attract 2-4x revenue.
- A cloud company that is established ($5-$50 million in annual revenue), profitable and growing might attract a valuation of 6x-10x EBITDA, or more if the company is very well established.

It's important to acknowledge, though, that this path won't apply to all businesses, and that there are choices to be made even if funding is available. For example, cloud business owners will need to assess dilution versus timeframe when evaluating the benefit of capital. If a business is offered $10 million in exchange for a 30% share of equity, the owner(s) needs to ask: how much of an infusion can we currently use? Could we work with $5 million in exchange for 15%, and then, after a year of growth, raise another $5 million later for 5%, or even 2%? Or should we pay attention to the old saying, "if someone offers you money, take it!"

Three points that relate more to general guidance than metrics and milestones include:

- It may be easier for firms seeking capital to go to the US than to find investors in Canada. There is more capital in the US, and Americans tend to be less risk-averse than Canadian funders. However, it can still be difficult for very early stage companies to raise small amounts in the US; as one working group member noted, "those types of raises are typically done locally," and it is rare that a Canadian firm would be successful in obtaining early stage funding in Silicon Valley.
- Investors are looking for unique and interesting businesses. If there are five other companies doing what you are doing, and they are ahead of you in the market, you probably will not find funding.
- Market feedback is important. It is very difficult to get meaningful feedback from a VC. However, seasoned advisors can be helpful in providing a 'reality check', especially to young executives.

# Contributing Experts

We gratefully acknowledge the contributions that these community experts have made to the insights contained in this book.

**Matt Ambrose**

PwC

Technology Advisory Leader, Private Company Services

For more than 18 years, Matt has been advising clients on effectively planning and managing their technology investments, ensuring their IT directions are aligned with strategic plans and current and projected operational realities. Matt has worked cross-industry with public, private, and not for profit organizations. He is currently focused on the middle-market where he is helping clients leverage technology to remain competitive by delivering technology strategy, governance, outsourcing, process improvement, service delivery, and project management services. Before joining PwC's Consulting Practice as a Technology Advisory Leader, Matt previously worked at another 'Big 4' in Technology Advisory, where he led the Canadian Cloud Community of Practice. His international experience includes living in Bermuda where he worked with the leading professional services/hosting/managed services suppliers servicing global clients.

**Brandon Kolybaba**

Cloud A

Co-Founder

Based in Halifax, Brandon is the co-founder of Cloud A, Canada's pioneering OpenStack-based IaaS provider. Cloud A addresses the needs of Canadian organizations seeking a combination of open standards, Canadian data residency, and advanced capabilities (such as automation, scalability and disaster recovery) that are built into the IaaS solution. The company's tremendous growth speaks to the importance of its core platform design.

Prior to launching Cloud A, Brandon was co-founder of Sheepdog, a pioneering ecosystem partner which helped customers to embrace industry-leading products like

Amazon Web Services and Google Cloud Platform, and which was at one point the only Premier Google Apps reseller in Canada. Brandon has also launched other cloud/web focused companies, including Norex (web application development) and Cloud Brewery (a new firm focused on OpenStack security and ecosystem development).

**Roy Hart**
Seneca College
CIO

Roy Hart is the Chief Information Officer for Seneca College with over 25 years of enterprise IT experience, including senior level leadership positions for more than 15 years.

Roy leads the delivery of IT services to one of the largest colleges in Canada, with some 26,500 full-time and 75,000 part-time students. Seneca College offers a diverse array of degree, diploma, and certificate programs from 9 campuses located in the GTA, and one in Peterborough.

Since joining Seneca in August 2011, Roy has led the modernization of IT and enabled a broad transformation of business processes across the College. Through the i3 ERP program, major core business systems underwent a complete upgrade, moving from an in-house developed solution to an Oracle PeopleSoft comprehensive platform. Simultaneously, Roy has implemented ITIL, enabled private cloud computing, moved email to Office 365, upgraded the network, implemented digital signage, and improved dozens of other information systems at Seneca. Roy is active in the technology community, in particular, the CIO Association of Canada, TechConnex, and now the Toronto Cloud Business Coalition.

**Stefano Tiranardi**
Symantec
Regional Manager, Technical Sales and Services

Stefano Tiranardi is the Technical Sales and Services leader for enterprise security in Canada and has been with Symantec for over 10 years. He started his career in technology over 25 years ago in systems programing and industrial automation. He holds several current professional certifications in information technology, security and audit. Having begun his career in programming and robotics, he soon after started heading down the path of information management and protection. Over the years, he has lead and participated in numerous projects in areas such as: SaaS security and controls, resilient infrastructure, information security governance, vulnerability and risk assessment, regulatory compliance and incident management. He`s had the opportunity to work with organizations of all sizes, both domestic and international within both the public and private sectors.

**Norman Sung**
Red Hat
Solutions Architect

Norman has joined Red Hat as a Solutions Architect, supporting sales and enablement with channel partners for Red Hat cloud products, including CloudForms, Openstack, Satellite, and Openshift.

Prior to joining Red Hat, Norman provided cloud strategy consulting to mid-sized customers focusing on Disaster Recovery and rapid application development, as well as market penetration strategies to emerging cloud vendors. Norman has over 20 years of experience in business development, technical solutioning and product management. Norman led the development and realization of cloud strategy at TELUS, launching Canada's first enterprise-class IaaS and PaaS cloud to provide a bridge between existing applications and new cloud applications and analytics. In that role, Norman helped more than 70 enterprises and mid-sized companies to adopting cloud.

**Sangameswaran Manikkayam**
Symantec
Principal Technical Specialist

Sangameswaran Manikkayam Iyer is a Principal Security Specialist with Symantec Canada. He brings with him over 17 years of industry experience in Information Security and Risk in large projects involving infrastructure software and emerging security technology solutions. He has designed IT solutions targeted in the arena of enterprise security, vulnerability assessment, end-point security enforcement & GRC. He has worked with customers across the globe in diverse verticals including: DoD, government, law enforcement agencies, telecom, banking & finance, transportation, energy and education.

Sangameswaran is a Symantec veteran for more than 15 years now and has experience in almost all Symantec security solutions, from programming to security architecture. He is a qualified security expert with leading industry certifications such as GSEC, CISSP, CISM, CRISC, CCSK and VTSP. He has also presented on diverse topics at various security forums like TASK and SecTor and was invited by Interpol to speak at the International Cyber security Conference held in New Delhi, India.

**Sylvia Bauer**
CenturyLink
Director, Marketing

Through a 13 year career as marketing director for CenturyLink, Savvis and Fusepoint Managed Services, Sylvia has established herself as a leader in cloud marketing as service demand has evolved from helping clients to embrace hosting to management of complex, interconnected systems. She has been part of the growth of both cloud suppliers and the customers who rely on cloud for an ever-wider range of business-critical workloads. In her current role, Sylvia works with the Canadian and Americas/headquarters teams to build and deliver programs advancing CenturyLink's presence in high-growth segments. Prior to joining Fusepoint, Sylvia was Canadian marketing manager for SAP.

**Tracey Hutchison**
Cisco
Director, Distribution Sales

Tracey is responsible for Cisco Canada's largest distribution relationship, generating more than $250 million in annual revenue. In this role, he is responsible for building a vision/strategy/execution/measurement plan to accelerate above-market growth, and for management of a 9 member product and services sales team and multi-million dollar marketing and incentive programs. In previous Cisco assignments, Tracey has had responsibility for driving data centre adoption of advanced products, equipping Canadian production data centres with server and networking technology.

Prior to joining Cisco, Tracey built the sales team at IDC Canada, and held sales positions with Bell.

**Craig McLellan**
ThinkOn
Founder

Craig is the founder of ThinkOn, which delivers secure, fast, scalable – and Canadian – Infrastructure as a Service to support business-critical workloads for applications such as enterprise applications, Big Data analytics, and disaster recovery-as-a-service (DRaaS). ThinkOn is unique in several respects: it delivers its virtual data centre services exclusively through ecosystem partners, and it has developed a set of "recipes" that enable these partners to work effectively with products from vendors such as Microsoft, CommVault and Veeam to deliver best practices to Canadian clients.

In addition to being an entrepreneur, Craig is a cloud-savvy CTO who has worked with Fortune 500 customers and as a technology executive on both sides of the border with Hosting.com and SunGard Canada.

**AJ Byers**
ROOT Data Center Inc.
CEO

AJ Byers is currently the President and CEO of ROOT Data Centers, who are deploying the next generation of data centres in Canada with ultra-efficient, high density cooling and a rapid deployment modular approach. Prior to this role, he was President of Rogers Data Centres, where he assembled one of Canada largest Data Centre services organizations, and President of BlackIron Data, Canada's most certified data centre company.

AJ spent 8 years as an executive at Primus where he assisted them in transitioning their business from a legacy telecom provider to a full solution technology services organization, and assisted in the sale of Primus' global assets across 5 continents. Prior to Primus, AJ ran one of Canada's largest independent Internet Services companies for business, Magma Communications.

**Jeff Cohen**
Yum! Brands Canada
IT Infrastructure Manager, KFC and Pizza Hut

Jeff Cohen is an IT professional with over fifteen years of broad and progressive management experience across a variety of industry sectors. His credibility in the industry, strong leadership skills and business experience has provided a high level of value to several high profile organizations in Canada and abroad.

**Brian Ochab**
Unity Connected Solutions
Practice Leader- Cloud Solutions

Brian is the responsible for development and leadership of Unity Connected Solutions' new Cloud and Managed Service business. This entails all aspects of solution development, partner relationships, go to market strategy, sales enablement, overall results generation and business unit profitability. Commencing with hosted voice telephony services, Unity is also developing managed services, network provision and hosting, to complement its existing premise based IP telephony portfolio.

Prior to joining Unity, Brian spent 15 years at Rogers Communications, in various Marketing and Sales Leadership positions, most recently leading the Business Solutions Enterprise and Commercial Sales teams in the GTA and Ontario Public Sector.

**Dave Collings**
Evolution-IT
Director

Dave is an experience mid-market IT Manager who has recently wrapped up a stint with Newmarket, Ontario-based Exco Engineering, a world leading builder of large high-pressure aluminum die casting dies and a major tooling supplier for tier-one OEMs such as GM, Ford, and Chrysler LLC in North America and Daimler AG in Europe.

While working in IT, Dave has deep understanding and background in manufacturing, including NC programming, post processing and, connecting CNC machines to the network for data communication, from RS232 to TCP/IP. This background skill is valuable to understand the storage requirements and graphic requirements of CAD workstations, enabling Dave and his team to organize and manage data logically such that it can be saved and utilized effectively and efficiently.

**Alex Sirota**
NewPath Consulting
Founder and Director

Alex is a pioneer in orchestrating cloud-based systems to meet the needs of small and medium sized business (SMBs). His company, NewPath Consulting, provides business-relevant technology advice and education to prepare SMBs for optimizing business activities through the cloud. NewPath Consulting delivers a curated and integrated suite of cloud-based products to help clients become more productive and profitable.

He gained small business experience while working at Apple Computer in the 1990s, at 2 tech startups in Toronto and in the Entrepreneurship Branch in the Ontario government. Alex is also an active participant in the small business web community including GoDaddy Pro, Wild Apricot, Toronto WordPress Meetup and Formstack.

**Chris Vernon**
Symantec
Technical Account Manager

Chris Vernon is a Security Specialist within Symantec's Technical Sales Organization, based out of Montreal. A Certified Information Systems Security Professional (CISSP) with over 12 years of experience, he has advised government and commercial organizations on information security practices globally. He regularly works with Canadian businesses to help solve the challenges of securing data in the cloud. Chris holds a B.Sc. in Computer Engineering from Queen's University.

**Shawn Rosemarin**
VMware
Chief-of-Staff for VMware's Systems Engineering Organization

Shawn Rosemarin is the Chief-of-Staff for VMware's Systems Engineering organization. As part of his current role Shawn is responsible for all Technical Pre-Sales Strategy and Operations as well as representing the Office of the CTO. Prior to this role, Shawn was the Executive Director of Architecture and Professional Services for all of VMware Canada. Shawn's passion is working closely with customers to help them navigate everything from the hybrid cloud to end-user computing transformation.

Dedication: Thanks to all who I have had the privilege to work with and learn from and to my wonderful wife and kids for their love

**Joe Belinsky**
Moneris Solutions
Vice President, Technology Infrastructure Services

Joe Belinsky is Vice President of Technology Infrastructure Services, for Moneris Solutions and has responsibility for all infrastructure and technology delivery for payment processing, employee collaboration and client solutions. Joe leads a dedicated team that supports Moneris in processing over 3 billion transactions a year for over 350,000 merchants – making Moneris one of the of North America's largest providers of payment processing solutions. Joe applies his passion for improving access to technology and applications with a focus on mobility and data centre evolution. Since joining Moneris he has run programs focused on improving IT Service Management, ERP implementation, and Customer Care call centre evolution. He has over 25 years distributed computing experience in entertainment, healthcare, and the financial service industries and has a Bachelor's degree in Management Information Systems from the University of Redlands, California and an MBA from the University of Wales. He currently resides in Toronto with his wife and three children.

**Anne De Aragon**
GoDaddy
Canadian Marketing Director

As the Marketing Director for GoDaddy Canada, Anne is helping
Canadian small businesses get online every day by adopting cloud-
based solutions to meet the unique needs of very small business.

Prior to GoDaddy, Anne was the Small & Midmarket Lead at Microsoft Canada where
she helped Channel Partners transition business models to the Cloud and was
responsible for marketing and selling Microsoft's Cloud-based solutions Office 365,
Intune and CRM Online to SMB customers.

**Adi Morun**
Microsoft
Microsoft Azure Product Lead – Canada

Adi is responsible for driving the growth of Microsoft's Public Cloud
Platform portfolio – Microsoft Azure. As the product lead, Adi
oversees the Canadian go-to-market strategy, ultimately driving Azure across all
channels from online to enterprise. Core areas of responsibility include: business
management, go-to-market strategy & investments, in-field marketing execution and
sales support & enablement. With the recent announcement of the locally-delivered
cloud services in Canada, the opportunity to drive cloud adoption in the Canadian
Marketplace is significant and provides challenges to be tackled every day! Prior to this
role, Adi was a Private Cloud Product Manager and Enterprise Inside Sales Manager.

**Andrew Nunes**
Fasken Martineau DuMoulin LLP
Partner, Vice Chair of Technology Group

Andrew has over 15 years of experience assisting companies with all
legal aspects of their business, with a particular focus on helping
companies navigate information technology issues. In addition to
buying and selling technology businesses and complex technology outsourcing
arrangements, he regularly advises clients on a wide range of issues and agreements
relating to the development, protection and exploitation of technology products and
services, such as development, implementation, consulting, acquisition, licensing,

distribution, maintenance and support, hosting, escrow, internet and e-commerce, open source, anti-spam, data protection, social media, cloud computing and cyber security. Andrew is a regular author and a frequent speaker on technology and commercial law topics. He is a past Chair of the Ontario Bar Association IT and E-Commerce Section. He has been recognized internationally and locally as a leading lawyer in Canada for Information Technology and Corporate Law.

**Derek van der Plaat**
Veracap M&A International
Managing Director

Derek started his career in Investment Banking with CIBC Mergers & Acquisitions where he specialized in technology growth company financing and M&A. In 2000, Derek co-founded a digital media company called Moontaxi Media Inc., which, by way of a partnership with Microsoft's Windows Media group, grew to become a leading internet broadcast network.

In 2003 Moontaxi launched the Puretracks music download service, the first in Canada to legally sell music online in association with the recording industry and leading distribution partners such as TELUS, MSN and AOL. Moontaxi secured financing from strategic investors such as Universal Music, Entertainment One and Standard Broadcasting.

Derek has over 20 years of corporate finance and M&A experience, both as an advisor and as an owner-entrepreneur and has guided start-ups and early stage digital media companies in the roles of CEO, CFO and Board Member.

**Paul Gragtmans**
ET Group
Principal

Paul is a principal with ET Group, which focuses on the design, sourcing, installation and service of all aspects of corporate video infrastructure. Working from a foundation rooted in a 30 year history as a corporate AV partner to corporations, ET Group has extended its capabilities to incorporate IT know-how into its collaboration system knowledge base. ET Group integrates total solutions for video conferencing, digital signage, control/operations centers, mobile corporate video, CCTV & IP TV.

Prior to joining ET Group, Paul had an extensive career with IBM Canada, including a role as General Manager for Education and Training and Chairman of PBSC Computer Training. He is currently a member of the board at TechConnex, the GTA IT association.

**Jeff Lamboy**
GoDaddy
Industry Strategy, Market Insights and Product Marketing

Jeff is a key member of the GoDaddy corporate team, responsible for expanding GoDaddy's relationships with SMB customers looking to increase productivity and streamline business processes by embracing hosted solutions. In this role, he works with a wide range of internal experts, business partners, customers and influencers to identify ways that GoDaddy can use its advanced capabilities, such as its managed WordPress hosting service and cloud-native applications to help small businesses drive better business results.

Prior to joining GoDaddy, Jeff was responsible for technology evangelism, industry strategy and analyst relations at PEER 1 Hosting. Jeff has also worked with Rackspace and with the Digett Interactive Agency.

**Matt Starkie**
Microsoft
Business Architect, World Wide Data Center Center of Excellence

As a certified IT architect within Microsoft's World Wide Data Center Center of Excellence, Matt employs a broad set of non-technical and technical skills to contribute to business and IT strategy development for multi-billion dollar enterprises in North and South America and around the world. Through the use of multiple architecture frameworks – along with the strategic thinking needed to support technology transformation initiatives – Matt helps large enterprises with executive-level business case development and justification. His work focuses on aiding and accelerating transformation to modern data centres and private, public and hybrid cloud solutions, optimizing time to value for strategic Microsoft clients.

**Joel Steacy**
VMware
Software Defined Enterprise Strategist

As the concept of Software Defined takes over the enterprise, Joel's role at VMware has evolved from focusing on automation, management and financial insight to taking a more holistic approach to helping clients become brokers of services. In his role as software-defined enterprise strategist, Joel helps customers understand, plan and execute on solutions like network visualization, hybrid clouds and hyper-converged infrastructures, positioning IT as a partner with the business rather than as a cost center.

Before joining VMware, Joel worked with Hitachi Data Systems, Metafore and IBM as a storage specialist, and with Calgary-based Pivot Data Centres, which was subsequently acquired by Rogers.

**Arturo Perez**
Solsteace Innovative Apps
President & CEO

Arturo is the founder of Solsteace, Inc. a software development company focused on developing innovative mobile and web solutions for business and consumer markets. Solsteace helps customers end-to-end, from ideation to the creation and launch of successful applications.

With an extensive background in networking, cloud and software development, Arturo brings great experience on the interdependence of transformative enterprise and SMB applications and cloud infrastructure. Prior to launching Solsteace, Arturo had a successful career at Cisco Systems where he had the opportunity to work with top enterprises and SMBs on the adoption of technology as well as leveraging technology to create innovative business services with telcos to reach their markets.

**Pam Maguire**
Global Knowledge Training
Business Development and Product Manager - IT Canada

Pam is responsible for IT product management and business development at Global Knowledge Canada, overseeing the IT training portfolio management for various technology areas including software development, virtualization, security, and cloud computing. Prior to Global Knowledge, Pam worked for several leading technology firms – including Juniper Networks, Redknee, QuickPlay Media and Nortel Networks – in a variety of engineering, manufacturing, product management and marketing roles.

Pam is an active member of Women in Technology (WIT) and IAMCP Canada, and is honored to be serving her community by working with Covenant House, developing IT and coding skills for homeless youth.

**Wil Stassen**
Equinix
National Account Director

**Jerrard Gaertner**
University of Toronto, Ryerson, CIPS Ontario
Adjunct Professor, Past Chair

Jerrard Gaertner is a chartered professional accountant (CPA) designated by the CICA as a specialist in information systems auditing and information technology. He is certified in the Governance of Enterprise IT (CGEIT), as an Information Systems Security Professional (CISSP), Information Privacy Professional *(CIPP/IT), Internal Auditor (CIA), Forensic Investigator (CFI), Information Systems Professional (I.S.P.) and Information Technology Certified Professional (ITCP).

Jerry is currently a Senior Vice President with Managed Analytic Services, a firm he co-founded. Prior to MAS, he held national responsibility for the systems assurance and computer audit activities of a Big 4 accounting firm. He is an Adjunct Professor of Computer Science at Ryerson University, and co-developed and teaches University of Toronto's Certificate Programme in Enterprise Analytics.

**David Sabine**
Berteig Consulting
Senior Consultant

David's professional career spans 22 years in software development and 8 years working with Agile teams, and highlights the intersections of business, technology, education & innovation.

David has significant "in-the-trenches" experience using Agile and Lean methods with design & development teams - including Scrum, Kanban, LeanUX, and OpenAgile. As an Agile Transformation consultant, he provides organizational expertise and practical recommendations at the senior leadership level. David is a regular guest lecturer at the Ivey School of Business, a TEDx speaker, and a seasoned Agile practitioner.

**Mathew Gancarz**
de Souza Institute
IT/Operations Manager

Mathew Gancarz leads the Information Technology (IT) team at de Souza Institute, where he manages all aspects of the technology platforms used to deliver online courses to health care professionals across Canada. Part of his responsibilities include managing the course development team composed of instructional designers and multimedia developers, that make de Souza Institute's courses an engaging experience for learners. Additionally, Mathew is also responsible for identifying, designing and implementing innovative technology and business solutions for the oncology and palliative care health professional learning community.

Prior to joining de Souza Institute, Mathew held system engineer and analyst roles with IT suppliers and with the University Health Network.

**Oscar Jofre**
KoreConX
Founder

A Chilean-born entrepreneur and technology innovator, Oscar brings a background of 25 years in senior management, marketing, investor relations and sales. He is currently Founder/President/CEO of KoreConX, a secure eco-system infrastructure platform (ESIP) provider that partners with equity crowdfunding portals to provide them a seamless solution.

Oscar is a member of the Crowdfunding Intermediary Regulatory Advocates in the USA (www.CFIRA.org) and the co-founder of the Equity Crowdfunding Alliance of Canada (ECFA Canada). He is the Regulated Crowdfunding Advisor to the world's first Equity Crowdfunding portal, Klondike Strike, and is Regulated Crowdfunding advisor to PetroPlata Oil & Gas Portal and the Spark.Exchange Technology Equity Crowdfunding portals.

**Don Sheppard**
ConCon Management Services
Senior Consultant

Don Sheppard is a senior IT consultant based in Toronto, Ontario. Don has worked to help de-mystify information and communications technology as an engineer, a manager, and a consultant for more than twenty-five years, currently as President/owner of ConCon Management Services. Don has previously been employed by CN Rail, CIBC, and The PSC Group.

Don is best known for his involvement in ISO standards for open systems interconnection and, more recently, for cloud computing. Don is a promoter of service-oriented approaches to IT and its management.

Don has managed technical groups in large corporations; chaired committees composed of world-class experts; developed and presented courses and seminars; co-written a book and authored numerous whitepapers; and has provided advice and guidance to numerous clients, especially in the public sector. Although RFP development has been a specialty, Don has also managed infrastructure projects, defined business requirements, promoted technology solutions and supported strategic planning processes.

**Marcus Cziesla**
Red Hat
Director, Cloud Solutions

Marcus is currently leading the team responsible for taking the Red Hat cloud portfolio to the North American market. His team works with organizations to develop and execute hybrid cloud strategies utilizing Red Hat and open source technologies to deliver business value through increased IT agility. His areas of solution expertise include Cloud, Virtualization, Systems Management, IT Operations, and App. Dev. Infrastructure software. Marcus came to Red Hat through the acquisition of ManageIQ, where he helped launch the ManageIQ product and built the team that implemented cloud and virtualization solutions at numerous enterprise customers. Prior to ManageIQ, Marcus held leadership roles at Network Associates, Sterling Commerce, Novadigm, and Hewlett Packard.

**Edmond Dengler**
CIPS Board Member

Edmund Dengler is a technology entrepreneur, software developer, and futurist. Formerly the CEO/CTO of eSentire Inc (a managed security company), Edmund is currently working with several startups in a variety of areas (big data analytics, commercial energy management, application security, and next generation software tools) helping them to develop and expand into new markets and opportunities, and continues to pursue advanced technologies in security.

Edmund teaches a Certificate Programme in Enterprise Analytics at the University of Toronto. and is a board member of the Canadian Information Processing Society of Ontario.

**Nima Honarmandan**
Berteig Consulting
Director of Training and Development

After completing his degree in Mechanical Engineering, Nima decided to work for an NGO abroad. He came to the conclusion that he liked helping people and would like to make a career doing that – embracing Agile for business was a perfect fit.

After a successful career in Pharmaceutical and Medical Device Sales; Nima has found his passion helping business people get the most out of their staff by empowering them with Agile processes. Nima is committed to helping businesses transform their people, process and culture.

**Stephen Symonds**
InsightaaS.com
Manager, Community Engagement

Steve is a Manager, Community Engagement with InsightaaS.com. In this role he is tasked with running the company's CRM system, operational logistics, assisting with research initiatives and the development of marketing material. InsightaaS is dedicated to exploring "the 'why' in enterprise technology." Operating under the InsightaaS umbrella are three peer based coalitions focused on accelerating the adoption and use of cloud in Canada (Toronto Cloud Business Coalition); facilitating a knowledge exchange on issues relating to IoT (IoT Coalition Canada), and Analytics and Big Data (Canadian Analytics Business Coalition.) With these communities, Steve operates on point with group members to keep the teams on track and on task with respect to their specific objectives.

Prior to joining InsightaaS.com, Steve has had a long and successful history working in marketing and research operations roles at IDC Canada and IT in Canada/IT Market Dynamics.

# Acknowledgements

The Toronto Cloud Business Coalition (TCBC) is a partnership focused on accelerating cloud adoption and use in Canada (and beyond). It includes individual and corporate members from many different cloud stakeholder communities: IT management from both enterprises and SMBs, global IT and cloud vendors, 'Born in the Cloud' suppliers, ecosystem/channel firms, academics, corporate finance experts, training providers, associations, executives at large with deep experience in the cloud industry, and other experts interested in developing best practices in key areas.

TCBC's activities are underwritten by our corporate members, including:

TCBC is operated by InsightaaS.